DEPARTMENT OF EDUCATION AND FAMILY RESOURCES
College of Home Economics
University of Nebraska
Lincoln, Nebraska 68503

HOME ECONOMICS
EVALUATION

HOME ECONOMICS EVALUATION

ALEENE CROSS
The University of Georgia

CHARLES E. MERRILL PUBLISHING COMPANY
A Bell & Howell Company
Columbus, Ohio

THE MERRILL SERIES IN
CAREER PROGRAMS

Published by
Charles E. Merrill Publishing Co.
A Bell & Howell Company
Columbus, Ohio 43216

International Standard Book Number: 0-675-08933-6

Library of Congress Catalog Card Number: 73-75679

2 3 4 5 6 7 8–77 76 75 74
Printed in the United States of America

THE MERRILL SERIES IN CAREER PROGRAMS

In recent years our nation has literally rediscovered education. Concurrently, many nations are considering educational programs in revolutionary terms. They now realize that education is the responsible link between social needs and social improvement. While traditionally Americans have been committed to the ideal of the optimal development of each individual, there is increased public appreciation and support of the values and benefits of education in general, and vocational and technical education in particular. With occupational education's demonstrated capacity to contribute to economic growth and national well being, it is only natural that it has been given increased prominence and importance in this educational climate.

With the increased recognition that the true resources of a nation are its human resources, occupational education programs are considered a form of investment in human capital—an investment which provides comparatively high returns to both the individual and society.

The Merrill Series in Career Programs is designed to provide a broad range of educational materials to assist members of the profession in providing effective and efficient programs of occupational education which contribute to an individual's becoming both a contributing economic producer and a responsible member of society.

The series and its sub-series do not have a singular position or philosophy concerning the problems and alternatives in providing the broad range of offerings needed to prepare the nation's work force. Rather, authors are encouraged to develop and support independent positions and alternative strategies. A wide range of educational and occupational experiences and perspectives have been brought to bear through the Merrill Series in Career Programs National Editorial Board. These experiences, coupled with those of the authors, assure useful publications. I believe that this title, along with others in the series, will provide major assistance in further developing and extending viable educational programs to assist youth and adults in preparing for and furthering their careers.

Robert E. Taylor
Editorial Director
Series in Career Programs

PREFACE

The major focus of this book is evaluating student progress toward or accomplishment of those objectives selected for any given module, unit, or course of study. A theme that runs throughout the book is the involvement of students not only in evaluating their progress but also in determining objectives and in selecting methods of evaluation. A companion theme is the integral relationship of evaluation to the teaching-learning process. Any teacher or prospective teacher should keep this focus and these themes constantly in mind as he uses this book.

The major concepts included in the book are highlighted as titles for the four parts. These are "Objectives-Teaching-Evaluation," "Paper and Pencil Tests," "Nontest Devices," and "Progress toward Objectives." Each chapter contains suggested individual and class activities and recommended readings. Whenever pertinent, sample questions and devices are included within the context of the chapter. Statistical procedures receive minor attention and only those measures which are easily computed are explained; such explanations are included to familarize the reader with frequently used terms and to provide usable methods to analyze tests and devices. Those wishing to know more should consult statistical texts and references.

The author has been influenced by many other authors and professors, although these persons may not always agree with the content of this book. Perhaps the greatest influence has come from those students and teachers with whom it has been my privilege to work. The intent of this book is to help home economics teachers to more effectively evaluate student achievement and to see evaluation as it relates to the teaching process.

Aleene Cross

CONTENTS

HOME ECONOMICS EVALUATION

Part I OBJECTIVES –
TEACHING –
EVALUATION

INTRODUCTION

No two people possess the same beliefs about evaluation, but there are probably more similarities than there are differences in the educational philosophies of home economics teachers. These similarities are probably a result of (1) the problem approach that has been the most widely used method of teaching home economics and of (2) the very nature of the content of home economics. Both students and teachers have beliefs and concerns about evaluation, but perhaps one of the truly great faults of our present school system is the gap that exists between what students feel they themselves have accomplished and what teachers feel the students have accomplished. One intent of this book is to indicate ways to narrow this gap.

There is also a discrepancy between stated beliefs or theories of evaluation and actual practices or methods. A teacher may say that he believes in student involvement but may rarely provide a means for students to evaluate themselves. A teacher may state that he believes evaluation should be in terms of behavioral objectives but fail to plan evaluation and state objectives concurrently. Another intent of this book is to help teachers effectively implement these principles in their teaching.

Stating objectives is the first and most important step in the evaluation process. The more precisely and clearly objectives are stated, the easier it is to select and implement evaluation procedures. Behavioral objectives should clearly identify the overt action expected of the student as a result of the learning experiences provided by the teacher. You, as a teacher, may feel that stating objectives is a time-consuming activity that is not worth the effort. If you try stating objectives in behavioral terms, you will discover that both teaching and evaluating have more direction and will recognize the relationship between objectives, teaching and learning experiences, and evaluation.

Objectives can be classified in several ways, for example, Bloom classifies types of learning or objectives as *cognitive, affective,* and *psychomotor* (Bloom, 1956). The advantage of this classification is that it encourages the teacher to consider values and skills as well as knowledge as he states objectives and evaluates in terms of these objectives. This is not to say that all course objectives must have all three types in order to be effective; it is simply to create an awareness of the three and how they all interrelate. If an objective concisely and clearly states the desired outcome in behavioral terms, selecting an appropriate evaluation procedure is relatively easy. The secret may be in identifying the major intent and in knowing which means of evaluation are appropriate for cognitive learning, for affective behavior, and for motor skills. It is possible and even desirable to develop a grid of objectives and techniques that shows the weight given each objective.

The five chapters in Part I attempt to relate teaching and evaluation to each other as well as to clearly defined behavioral objectives. The first chapter emphasizes the relationship of evaluation to teaching; the second explains how to state objectives in behavioral terms; and the third illustrates how to select evaluation procedures for a specific objective. Student participation in evaluation is the focus of the fourth chapter, and the fifth chapter enumerates the characteristics desired in an evaluation procedure. It is hoped that when you have completed the study of these five chapters, you will be able to state your own philosophy. The content of these five chapters states the beliefs of the author based on her own experiences and on selected authorities in the field of evaluation. You should question and analyze each belief before accepting, rejecting, or modifying it. A philosophy of evaluation changes with each new teaching experience. At a future time the author will no doubt expand and alter her own beliefs about evaluating students.

REFERENCE

1. Bloom, Benjamin S. (ed.), *Taxonomy of Educational Objectives.* New York: David McKay Co., Inc., 1956.

Chapter 1 THE RELATIONSHIP OF EVALUATION TO TEACHING

This chapter is concerned with five major concepts each of which forms a section of the chapter. These are (1) a definition of *evaluation*; (2) evaluation as teaching-learning; (3) principles of evaluation; (4) purposes of evaluation; and (5) methods of evaluation. Each of these concepts is discussed in the context of philosophy or beliefs and each section provides basic information for the chapters remaining in the book.

Evaluation

Evaluation has different meanings for different teachers. The following is the widely accepted definition around which this entire book is centered.

Evaluation: *A process which determines the extent to which objectives have been achieved.*

This definition implies the direct relationship of evaluation to objectives and suggests that rather than a single *event* which determines final completion or attainment of goals, evaluation is an ongoing *process* which measures the degree to which goals are being attained.

A concise and clearly stated outcome is the first essential in the evaluation process. This intended outcome usually implies or states a method of evaluation and may also suggest methods of instruction. In any case, without such a stated outcome the process of evaluation is likely to become indistinct and ineffective.

Evaluation procedures should be appropriate to the type of objectives. Objectives should be stated in behavioral terms, and since not all behaviors can be effectively or appropriately evaluated using the same devices and techniques, the evaluation process can be difficult and challenging. Some behaviors are primarily intellectual and deal mostly with knowledge; others are skills and result in products and actions; and still others reflect values and attitudes. Frequently all three types of behavior are included in a teaching-learning situation. It is then that the primary or most important behavior must be pinpointed in order to determine the type of objective and the evaluation procedure.

Evaluation should be a systematic and continual process. Too often evaluation is only done at the end of a unit or at the end of a grading period, but it should be done daily, on a planned schedule. Casual and unplanned procedures should be excluded except when a gap in the process becomes evident or when a modification of the process is appropriate and feasible. An important part of the process should be the involvement of students in periodic evaluation so that they recognize their own progress.

Evaluation involves interpreting data in light of particular situations. The varying abilities of students create situations which influence how evaluation data are interpreted. In addition, past experiences and environment create varying situations. A beginning teacher may find that he has created a situation by expecting too much of students or by using difficult tests and devices. Interpretation of data can take factors such as these into consideration. Chapters 3, 17, and 18 deal particularly with means for handling such situations.

Evaluation is a process of making an assessment of a student's growth. This definition is as acceptable as the one pinpointing objectives. In fact, a complete definition should include both statements; here they have been separated in order to emphasize objectives and thereby imply a group process and to place emphasis on individual evaluation.

Achievement in terms of individual progress should be measured as well as group progress. Most teachers are aware that students enter their classes with differing amounts of both knowledge and skills and with a variety of attitudes and values. The result is that some students have more distance to cover to reach excellency than do others. Teachers can evaluate a student's growth by knowing what he can do at the beginning and at the end of a series of learning experiences. Using data that indicate progress to determine a grade is difficult, but can be done if grading is compatible with the objective being evaluated. Suggestions for evaluating progress will be included in the two final chapters.

Achievement may be measured in terms of meeting certain established standards; the degree to which these standards are met may be classified on a continuum from minimum to maximum. Each student can decide whether or not he will meet minimum standards or work to achieve nearer the maximum. One of the most effective ways to teach standards is to evaluate a product by samples of varying standards, because products reflect skills and usually have accompanying standards. Another method is student utilization of a piece of equipment. Sometimes there can be no errors such as in the threading of a sewing machine, which implies a maximum standard, but there can be a minumum number of errors in the construction of a garment.

Achievement can be measured in terms of completed tasks. This kind of evaluation is often used with home projects and homework assignments. A progress chart showing completion of units of construction is one of many ways of evaluating progress. Again this may be difficult to include in a grade, but evaluation is a much larger process than assigning grades. Students can readily see their growth in this procedure, and the teacher can be aware of class progress and the need for help by individual students.

Achievement may be influenced by individual attitudes and values. The first step toward achievement of an objective may be the changing of an attitude or a reassessment of a student's personal values. Motivation comes before any great amount of achievement. An example is the overweight boy or girl whose attitude toward changing food habits is negative but whose desire to be accepted by his peers is high on his list of values. When he recognizes the relationship of food habits to acceptance by his peers, he will most likely work to achieve an objective of eating food that contributes to physical attractiveness.

Assessment of student growth must be on an individual basis; and because such individual assessment is so time-consuming, it is all too frequently deleted from the evaluation process. On the other hand, it pays the highest dividends of all methods, for the student recognizes his own achievement and his own worth.

Measurement involves obtaining quantitative, as opposed to qualitative evidence. On the other hand, *evaluation* includes both quantitative and qualitative descriptions of pupil behavior. Measurement is objective and includes data such as test scores; it does not include value judgments.

Measurement produces evidence as a basis for evaluation and becomes a part of the evaluative process when interpreted in light of a particular objective and a given situation. The quantitative data provided by measurement are used to determine progress and pupil growth. Only when measurement is used under these conditions does it provide a basis for evaluation.

Objective or quantitative measurement is not always appropriate, for example, when evaluating personal qualities such as values, attitudes, and appreciations. Quantitative measurement is rarely as appropriate for the less able student as qualitative descriptions or subjective judgments. Measurement is appropriate only when it can produce evidence that a particular objective has been achieved.

Qualitative evaluation is not always accurate because of the subjective value judgment that must be made. This judgment is likely to vary from time to time, from teacher to teacher, and from student to student. There are safeguards that increase the degree of accuracy when qualitative descriptions are the most appropriate and possibly the only means of evaluating a particular objective. These safeguards are included in Chapter 11 in the suggestions on developing and using observational devices.

Quantitative measurement is needed for assigning grades, but there are many objectives in home economics that are appropriately evaluated using qualitative descriptions rather than quantitative evidence. There are techniques that can be utilized to convert qualitative descriptions into a score even though the subjective judgment is not eliminated. When this is done, this evidence can be incorporated into the final grade along with the quantitative measurement.

EVALUATION AS TEACHING-LEARNING

Evaluation is a learning process and is inseparable from teaching. Those teachers who see evaluation separate from teaching and learning might well analyze the effect of their evaluation procedures on students. There is casual and unintentional learning in any evaluation. The following paragraphs discuss ways that evaluation is deliberately intended to be teaching and to result in learning. The four specific results discussed are identifying objectives, determining learning experiences, setting standards, and developing decision-making skill.

Identifying Objectives.   Objectives may be identified as a result of evaluation procedures and are the most significant aspect of the relationship of evaluation to teaching. The very nature of our accepted definition makes this true. Furthermore, defined objectives may be the major focus of selected evaluation procedures. As a teacher, you are no doubt concerned about motivation of students. Motivation usually occurs when together the students and the teacher determine objectives through an evaluation process.

Objectives can be developed from an evaluation of individual interests. Teenagers have interests that are very different from those of children or adults. Some of these interests may remain fairly constant from one group of teenagers to another, for example, interest in the opposite sex, clothes, and self-interest which may border on preoccupation. Such interests can vary in intensity from one group to another, and there are some interests that are peculiar to just one group of students. There are also individual differences within and among groups. The clever teacher can use evaluation procedures such as checklists and class discussions to arrive at these individual and group interests. Objectives can then be formulated on the basis of the summarized results.

Objectives can be developed from an evaluation of individual needs and although some teachers consider needs and interests together, it seems worthwhile to separate the two. For example, teenagers frequently need to change food habits but have little or no interest in doing so. The needs of students can be identified by comparing their actions with desirable practices. Needs can also be identified by determining personal values. Objectives are easier for students to determine when such data are identified.

Objectives can be developed from an evaluation of community needs. Teenagers frequently are anxious to serve and to make a contribution to adult life, and they can be made aware of needs at school and church, needs for recreation and community drives, and needs for child care services. Objectives in family and child development can be an outgrowth of community surveys and contacts with local agencies. These objectives can easily relate Future Homemaker activities and projects to in-class activities and home-degree projects.

Objectives can be developed from an evaluation of previous learnings. The use of a pretest is an obvious example of identifying previously gained skills, knowledge, etc. A checklist of what has been studied and what might be studied further and a comparison of last year's work with established criteria are still other ways for a teacher to help her students evaluate past learning experiences and to determine direction for another year.

Objectives can be developed from a job analysis in which each phase of the job is used to state an objective. This technique has become increasingly useful since the beginning of home economics related occupations, and it should be used in determining objectives in preparing girls and boys to be homemakers. The job of today's homemaker is constantly changing and emphasis is placed on skills different from those of the past. One study made by the author and three colleagues revealed that family relationships, child care, management of time and money, and food preparation were the most important jobs of today's homemaker. A study made by a teacher and her class might reveal specific tasks that were currently not included in a course. No doubt there would be some that were over emphasized.

Determining Learning Experiences.   Evaluation can offer suggestions for, and even help pinpoint, learning experiences, which usually become evident as objectives are identified. Evaluation of learning experiences can also help motivate students; for example, to help students see the need for planning of experiences and their evaluation, conduct a foods laboratory class without planning for it.

A desirable beginning experience can be pinpointed by evaluation. This may not be a logical beginning from the teacher's point of view but may be a means of getting to the heart of learning. For example, through an evaluation procedure the teacher may discover that students want to work with children in the nursery before doing any study. The greatest amount of learning may take place by beginning in "the middle" and eventually moving back to the factual information. Not many teachers are willing to permit students to sew until they have mastered the use of the machine. Yet student interest lies in the opposite direction, and a checklist may reveal this interest. Furthermore, there is ample evidence to support selecting the beginning experience by evaluating student interests and purposes.

The gaps in learning become evident through evaluation. Tests of knowledge, performance of skills, checklists of attitudes, and other means of evaluation frequently reveal that part, but not all, of what has been taught has been learned. This procedure indicates to the teacher what needs to be retaught and perhaps indicates a different learning experience for the same information. What is taught and how it is taught to the next class should also become evident as a result of all evaluation procedures used with the present class.

A change of direction may be indicated by results of evaluation procedures. The organized teacher makes a plan for a unit, and although this procedure has many advantages, he may become aware in the middle of the unit that student interest has shifted to other areas. This shift may become evident by student evaluation of the course, by analysis of tapes of class discussion, by recording of student participation in class discussion, or by studying of test results. When a change in interest occurs, the effective teacher, with the help of students, chooses different learning experiences.

Evaluation of student abilities dictates learning experiences and may include such methods as pretests and demonstrations to determine previously acquired knowledge and skills. In addition, study of student records may reveal much about abilities of students and make it possible for the teacher to gear learning experiences to desirable levels, to help some students catch up, to provide challenges for the more able students, and to determine the standards. Evaluation of abilities should be continuous throughout the year, since abilities are always changing.

Setting Standards.   One of the major goals of any home economics teacher should be the setting of desirable standards, but care must be taken to set them at a level that is both attainable and challenging. All too frequently standards have been set so high that they are unattainable by students or so low that students are unchallenged and bored. An alternative is to set minimum acceptable standards and to demonstrate maximum standards; then a student will learn to assess his own abilities and set standards that are compatible with them. When students leave a classroom, they no longer have a teacher to decide when a product or procedure is acceptable. Therefore the student needs to be able to recognize for himself what is a necessary (minimum) standard and what is a desirable (maximum) standard.

Standards can be taught through evaluation of illustrative materials and visual aids, most of which meet maximum standards. However, examples that are less than perfect are very effective in learning what is acceptable. Making such examples takes time but will save time when evaluation of products is necessary. Pictures of various products, particularly foods, can be used in lieu of actual objects.

Standards can be established through development and use of observational devices, which are frequently developed by individual teachers for their own use. When teachers involve students in the development of such observational devices, they are teaching acceptable standards for habits and behaviors as well as for products and procedures. In addition, students will more readily accept standards that they themselves establish. Thus, the teacher should provide various learning experiences so that the student arrives at his own decision about what is acceptable.

Developing Decision-Making Skill.   It should be the purpose of every home economics teacher not only to further the development of this skill but also to make students aware of the decision-making process.

Self-evaluation demands that students make decisions. Score cards, rating devices, checklists, diaries, logs, and summaries are some of the techniques that require a student to decide where he stands, what he has learned, how he might improve, and what he does next. The same device may be used by the teacher but then he makes the decision rather than the student. Comparing ratings can help the student to increase his accuracy in self-evaluation and his ability to make decisions.

Choosing and evaluating objectives is a decision-making skill. This fact reveals the very intertwining of objectives, evaluation, and decision making. Not all possible objectives can be accomplished in the allotted time. Someone must decide upon what basis objectives are chosen. The teacher who involves his students in this process insures an effective learning situation and provides an opportunity to develop decision-making skill.

Analyzing problem-solving questions increases decision-making skill. Problems require decisions whether real and personal or imaginary and impersonal. The use of problem questions and situations that are not personal helps the students to be more objective and provides the teacher with the opportunity to evaluate the students' decision-making skills. Problem-solving questions are discussed in detail in Chapter 7.

Assisting in the determination of a grade requires a decision. Not nearly enough teachers permit students to help decide upon their grade, perhaps because of historical precedence or teacher insecurity. However, both the teacher and the student can feel secure when there is ample quantitative evidence and a predetermined grading plan. The student gains skill when he decides his grade even though the evidence clearly points to what the grade will be. Students can help decide their score or grade from day to day as well as the final grade. Since homemakers make countless decisions each day, development of decision skills is a vital part of teaching-learning in every home economics classroom.

Principles of Evaluation

A principle is a statement that holds true in most, if not all, cases. It can be used as a guideline or accepted as a personal belief. There are numerous principles of evaluation but only five have been selected for discussion in this book. These five principles are based on the preeminent principle that evaluation is an integral part of the teaching-learning process.

Evaluation should be in terms of selected objectives. Perhaps the key word in this principle is *selected.* Objectives that are pertinent and attainable must be selected and stated by students and teacher, and evaluation techniques appropriate to the selected objectives must be chosen.

All too frequently teachers use one written test to evaluate all objectives of a unit or module. At least one specific technique should be identified for each objective and, if at all possible, this technique should result in a score that could contribute to a grade.

Evaluation techniques should be keyed to the *type* of objective. The identified behavior is the key to the type of objective. Some objectives have knowledge as the focus, others have manual skills, and still others have values, attitudes, or appreciations. Techniques such as written tests are most appropriate for cognitive or knowledge objectives. Observational devices are most suitable for evaluating skill objectives as well as personal qualities or affective behaviors.

An overall plan should be made to evaluate the objectives of a unit. This procedure insures that all objectives are evaluated at appropriate times and with appropriate techniques. Such a plan shared with students provides security for students since they know what is expected. It also provides security for the teacher because she will have accumulated the necessary evidence. One system of stating objectives includes the technique for evaluating. This system completes the plan with the stating of objectives. If the objective does not state the means of evaluation then this can be done below or in a column opposite the objective.

Evaluation should be comprehensive. This implies that all learning should be evaluated regardless of its nature; all objectives should be evaluated regardless of the difficulty. Comprehensive evaluation should be concerned with both means and ends and should occur throughout all of teaching and learning from the teacher's preplanning to the last class experience.

Because objectives vary according to type, and because both students and teacher tend to be more accurate when confronted with a variety of evaluation devices, comprehensive evaluation requires a number of different techniques. Since each objective has *at least* one technique that is very appropriate for evaluating student progress toward it, the decision of whether to use more than one and if so which ones must be made.

You are already aware that learning can be categorized as cognitive, affective, and psychomotor. Comprehensive evaluation must include all types of learning and there are objectives that reflect these three categories. Furthermore, there are appropriate techniques for evaluating each of these types. Usually one type of learning logically receives the most emphasis in a unit, and the other two types are secondary to it. It follows that appropriate emphasis should be placed on the evaluation devices.

The process of comprehensive evaluation is equally important as the end results. This permits a teacher to be experimental with the process of evaluation, to capitalize on student ideas, and to change the process when desirable.

Evaluation is a cooperative process. Cooperative evaluation is a dual process of insuring the simultaneous involvement of both teacher and students from the objective-stating outset to the final-grading end. Both the teacher and the students should express their concerns, their opinions as to whether or not objectives are being reached, and their satisfactions. This is a give and take process that pays high dividends.

But cooperative evaluation goes beyond the confines of the individual classroom. It extends to all interested parties—school administration, parents and certain concerned community members. The evaluation of a year's work can be greatly strengthened by involving parents, administrators, and lay people. Many teachers find an advisory board helpful in evaluating as well as planning programs and chapter parents serve a similar function for Future Homemakers of America.

Evaluation is a continuous process. It is not merely a unit-end activity. Neither is evaluation spasmodic; it is an ongoing, daily activity. The teacher and students who cannot identify their objectives and what they have learned during a class period have missed the most important element of the learning experience. Evaluation can and should occur at any time of the lesson, week, or unit.

A teacher may require each student to keep a daily account of what he intends to do that day and what he actually accomplishes. Once or twice a week this log is read by the teacher. This technique is particularly useful when individual work is being done. A teacher may also use a progress chart in a clothing construction class. If you, as a teacher, state a behavioral objective for each class day you will have built in a daily means of evaluation.

Continuous evaluation contains periodic checks on objectives. Some school days are set aside for the purpose of testing. These days may be indicated by the administration. They may occur at logical points such as at the end of a unit. Home economics teachers and students frequently evaluate a series of food experiences after a laboratory lesson. They also evaluate a unit of clothing construction such as the skirt or sleeve when it is completed rather than waiting to evaluate the entire garment. Although evaluation should center less on a grade than on what is being accomplished, measurement is necessary. This should be done at frequent periods so that students know how well or how poorly they are doing.

Continuous evaluation suggests ways for improvement. One of the major advantages of daily evaluation is motivating students to do better work. Success is a highly motivating factor, especially for the student who is not usually successful. To be able to accomplish and have recognized any small achievement provides a strong incentive. Evaluation that is continuous also prevents repetition of the same error. To help each student to achieve should be the aim of every teacher and means of evaluation ought to be selected so as to provide maximum opportunity for student success.

Evaluation is concerned with valuing. What is a value? Are your values really important in the teaching-learning process? Can values be evaluated? Should a specific set of values be taught? Every home economics teacher must find answers to these questions for values are important in the life of every individual and family.

Evaluation of values is personal and individualistic. Values are those things which a person cherishes. No two persons have the same values nor should they. The teacher who attempts to force his own value system on his students is being an intellectual snob. Values can be evaluated but not as to right or wrong. An individual student can be helped to identify his values and to see how these affect his personal goals and his decisions and he may rearrange his value system as a result of learning experiences, but values may not be evaluated in terms of right or wrong. If the student chooses to alter his value system, it should be because he did this personally and not to please the teacher or the other class members.

Value judgments must be made concerning evidence collected. This is true of both quantitative data and qualitative descriptions. The value judgment may be determined by the teacher but it is more effective when made cooperatively. This means that the controlling values would need to be identified. These then become group values more or less accepted by each class member as well as the teacher.

Purposes of Evaluation

There are many purposes for which evaluation is used other than the traditional one of providing a rating or grade. The definition of evaluation in its broadest sense implies the assessment of a situation, of abilities, of knowledge, of progress toward an objective. The six purposes listed below are within the context of the earlier definition of evaluation.

The major purpose of evaluation is to assess the attainment of an objective. A performance or overt action on the part of a student is most often the intent of an objective. However, objectives can be associated with programs, curriculum, and school plans among other things. As a home economics teacher, one is most concerned with the evaluation of students' performance.

The method of evaluating dictates the way in which learning takes place but the objective should dictate the method of evaluating. This then becomes a circle of activities as Figure 1-1 indicates. What this says to the teacher is that he must evaluate in the same manner as he teaches and as

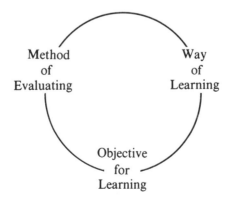

FIGURE 1-1

the objective implies. For example, if the objective is to thread a machine, the student should not merely be asked to identify the parts.

Students and the teacher do not always have the same objective and this causes concern and frustration when students are evaluated. For example, if the students' objective is to prepare meals and the teacher's objective is to identify principles of food preparation, inappropriate evaluation techniques will lead to unsatisfactory results on both sides. A teacher should set up objectives with her students, using their intent as much as possible. The two objectives given above are compatible and both performance and written tests could be used. The point is to be certain that both teacher and students agree on objectives and on the ways of evaluating each objective.

Measuring various aspects of learning is an equally important purpose of evaluation. Learning has been categorized as cognitive, affective, and psychomotor (Bloom, 1956). These terms may be defined briefly as knowledge, values, and manual skill. A home economics teacher may be equally interested in her students' learning principles of food selection, accepting desirable food habits as important, and choosing foods that meet daily requirements. If this is the situation, she has three objectives to accomplish and evaluate.

All types of learning should be evaluated in proportion to their significance. If the teacher mentioned above is equally concerned with all three, she and her students should give equal emphasis to the evaluation of each. Written tests will evaluate principles but not the other two. A three-day record will indicate food choices but not necessarily reflect attitudes or values. A diary or log could do this if the student recorded his reactions to food. An attitude scale or value scale could also be developed for use. Not all teachers will choose all three aspects of learning. More often than not, only one aspect will be emphasized.

One type of learning should not be evaluated when another type has been stressed. A written test on how to put in a sleeve does not test the skill of doing so. A listing of the basic four food groups does not evaluate planning meals. Knowing how long an average baby is at birth does not evaluate being able to dress a baby. Cognitive learning is more appropriately evaluated by most teachers than is affective learning or psychomotor skill. Perhaps this is the result of our long association with pencil and paper tests. The teacher will want to select the means of evaluation in terms of type of objective. This process becomes easier when you state objectives and plan evaluation concurrently.

Evaluation is a means of discovering what students already know. Every person who enters your classroom brings his past experiences with him. To begin with, that person is a member of a family and brings that learning with him. The student may also have had some home economics, been a member of a 4-H club, or had a mother who taught some homemaking skills to her children. It is important to assume that students already know some things and to try to discover what these are.

Past experiences and already developed skills can be a basis for instruction. For example, an excellent child development unit can be based on the experiences girls and boys have had while babysitting. A teacher who gave her students a questionnaire on home responsibilities found that many of the first-year students bought family groceries and prepared the night meal. She capitalized on these experiences and skills to develop an entirely new approach to a foods unit. Pretests, questionnaires, and checklists are three ways to evaluate what students already know.

Motivation to learn can result from evaluation. You as well as all other teachers realize that students must be motivated in order to learn. Many motivation techniques are utilized by you and your fellow teachers but most likely few of these techniques are concerned with evaluation. An impending test may motivate students to study but it is doubtful that much permanent or long-lasting learning takes place.

Results of evaluation can stimulate action. Surveys of recreation possibilities, of ways teenagers spend money, of food habits of teenagers, or of personal problems such as sex, alcohol, smoking, and drugs can form the basis for discussions, reading, and projects. A series of problem questions can spark interest in a subject such as family relationships where no interest has previously existed. A rating on a product can encourage a student to continue developing the skill. Almost every means of evaluation can be used to stimulate action if the teacher desires to do so.

Realistic objectives that motivate can result from evaluation. An interest index, a needs finder, a community survey, a job analysis are but a few of the techniques that can provide a basis for determining objectives. Pretests and skill demonstrations are also useful in motivating students to recognize what they need to learn as well as what they already know. Being aware of their needs and interests as well as their strengths and weaknesses is perhaps the most effective way to form a basis for students to state realistic objectives. Concurrently these students are motivated to learn simply because these objectives are their own and based on what they recognize they need.

Evaluation provides information for guidance and counseling. Information is needed if effective guidance and counseling is to occur whether the problem is personal or vocational. This information might include data relative to students' interests, vocational goals, work experiences, special abilities, personal qualities, social adjustment, reading abilities, and achievement scores. Many times such information is readily available but is not reviewed before a guidance session with a student.

Pertinent and accurate information is necessary for effective vocational guidance. An identification of student interests and job preferences is an excellent way to begin helping the student to make vocational choices. All too often I.Q. scores and grades are used to push a student into college when his vocational preference does not require a college degree. The opposite can also occur. Knowing the financial status of a student is information needed in order to counsel a student about acquiring financial assistance. Information about job opportunities is also vital in providing vocational guidance.

Frequently home economics teachers are asked by students to help them solve personal problems. The role of the teacher in such instances is usually to ask the questions needed for the student to make his own decision. However, personal data are needed to ask such questions. The teacher can also give a student a questionnaire, rating device, or test to obtain the information needed to make a decision. Helping students solve problems is more effective when pertinent personal information has ˪een collected and evaluated.

Evaluation results can be a basis for curriculum change. While many teachers alter their evaluation procedures as well as their teaching methods as a result of the analysis of tests and other means of evaluation, not nearly so many teachers use evaluation data as a basis for determining curricular change. Revision and updating of evaluation techniques, teaching methods and curriculum should be a continuous activity. Certainly home economics teachers need to constantly reorder their curricula to meet the changing socioeconomic conditions in which families live.

Follow-up studies of former students provide invaluable information for curricular revision. Two statewide studies have been done by the State Departments of Education in Virginia and North Carolina. Very simple ones can be done by one teacher in one school. Facts such as marital status, work experiences, education beyond high school, and how the graduates feel home economics has helped them are most helpful in reviewing and altering curriculum.[1] Changes should be based on evaluation data rather than on personal preference of the teacher.

A determination of interests, needs, and job requirements form an excellent base for curriculum content. Home economics teachers sometimes have found it difficult to design an occupational program. One reason seems to be the lack of experience with the occupation. Work experience or observation would help. Another reason has been the traditional technique of using present needs and interests of students as a basis for curriculum. Needs and interests should not be ignored but they do not give sufficient data for curriculum design. An analysis of the tasks performed in a given job or

---

[1]Twin instruments developed by a research team are available for use by home economics teachers and others. Aleene Cross, Anna Gorman, Helen Loftis, and Agnes Ridley, "Evaluation of Vocational Home Economics Programs in Terms of Effective Full-Time Homemakers and Homemakers Who Are Also Full-Time Employees," Department of Home Economics Education, University of Georgia, Athens, 1970.

cluster of related occupations would provide such data. This is as true of the homemaking occupation as those occupations that provide an income.

Methods of Evaluation

You have already discovered the difference in evaluation and measurement. You also know that both quantitative and qualitative evidence are used in evaluation. The methods described below are divided into two types categorized differently from those named above. However, these two types are more or less related to quantitative and qualitative evaluation. These two types are written tests and nontest devices.

Written tests include the objective types and the essay type. These tests are used to collect quantitative evidence of knowledge, comprehension, and application of facts. They can also be used to analyze and synthesize information.

Objective questions may be recall or recognition in nature. Recall questions are classified as free response, completion, and identification. Recognition questions are true-false, multiple choice, and matching. These are explained in full in Part II, Chapter 7.

Essay questions may have two different responses: restricted response and extended response. Essay questions are used to explain, contrast, point out relationships, present proof, analyze differences, draw conclusions, or state generalizations. Essay questions are discussed in more detail in Part II, Chapter 6.

Nontest devices are used to evaluate performance and the affective aspects of learning. These devices involve subjective judgment but can result in either quantitative or qualitative evaluation. Some of the nontest devices provide measurement data and some do not. The author has chosen to classify these as observation devices, reporting forms, audio-visual techniques and sociometric techniques. Part III describes and gives examples of each of these types of nontest devices.

Observational devices include checklists, rating scales, and some score cards. These can be used to observe performances such as laboratory work, habits, demonstrations, classroom behavior, and assumption of responsibility. They can also be used to evaluate products made at school and at home. Observational devices can be utilized to evaluate such affective behaviors as attitudes, appreciations, social interactions, and value decisions. Both the teacher and the student find these helpful in evaluating personal behaviors.

Reporting forms include reports, diaries, logs, questionnaires, and autobiographies. These are usually made out by students who do self-evaluation as they complete the forms. The teacher may use these for evaluating either performance or affective learning depending on the purpose of the reporting form. Questionnaires are frequently used to determine certain conditions and facts about students. These may be considered individually to profile each separate student or tabulated to learn about an entire group.

Audio-visual techniques include tape recordings, films, photographs, slides, and graphs. Tape recordings are very useful in identifying values and attitudes, in tabulating problems or issues, and in recording student participation. Films and video tapes may reflect either or both affective behavior and performance. Photographs and slides are frequently used to record change and progress as well as performance. Graphs are helpful in presenting tabulated data about groups of all kinds and can also be used to visually portray selected qualities of an individual. Audio-visual techniques are excellent teaching as well as evaluating devices.

Summary

This first chapter dealing with philosophy has focused upon the relationship of evaluation and teaching. Therefore, the author has chosen to write the summary as a list of some of her own beliefs about evaluation. I believe that:

- evaluation is a process that determines the extent to which objectives have been achieved;
- evaluation is a process of making a continous assessment of a student's growth;
- measurement is obtaining quantitative evidence;
- evaluation is an integral part of the teaching-learning process;
- evaluation can result in the identification of objectives, suggestions for learning experiences, and setting of standards;
- self-evaluation can help develop decision-making skills;
- comprehensive evaluation requires a variety of techniques;
- evaluation is a cooperative process;
- evaluation is a continuous process;
- evaluation is concerned with valuing;
- evaluation is a means of discovering what students already know;
- motivation to learn can result from evaluation;
- evaluation provides information for guidance and counseling;
- evaluation results can be a basis for determining curriculum change;
- methods of evaluation can include written objective and essay tests; nontest devices, and audio-visual techniques.

STUDENT ACTIVITIES

1. Rate each of the above statements of belief according to the way *you* believe with each, using a scale of (1) strongly agree, (2) partially agree, (3) do not agree.

2. List each of the statements with which you disagree and write two sentences giving your reasons; do the same for each statement with which you strongly agree.

3. Write a two page statement of your own philosophy of evaluation as it currently exists; do not consult this or any other text.

REFERENCES

Allen, Paul M. "The Student Evaluation Dilemma." *Today's Education* (February 1969), pp. 48-50.

Arny, Clara Brown. *Evaluation in Home Economics.* New York: Appleton-Century-Crofts, 1953.

Bloom, Benjamin S. (ed.). *Taxonomy of Educational Objectives.* New York: Longmans, Green, 1966.

Fleck, Henrietta. "The Process of Change." *Forecast* 15, no. 6 (February 1970), p. F-49.

Fleck, Henrietta. "What is Teaching?" *Forecast* 15, no. 5, (January 1970), p. F-21.

Gronlund, Norman E. *Measurement and Evaluation in Teaching.* New York: The Macmillan Company, 1971.

Hall, Olive A. and Paolucci, B. *Teaching Home Economics.* New York: John Wiley and Sons, Inc., 1970.

Horn, Gunnar. "Some Thought about Teaching and Teachers." *Today's Education* (February 1970).

Mager, Robert F. *Developing Attitude toward Learning.* California: Fearon Publishers, 1968.

Massialas, Byron. "Teaching and Learning through Inquiry." *Today's Education* (May 1969), pp. 40-44.

Williamson, Maude and Lyle, M. S. *Homemaking Education in the High School.* New York: Appleton-Century-Crofts, 1961.

_____. "Evaluation As Insurance." *Illinois Teacher* I, no. 9.

_____. "Learning-Teaching Efficiency." *Illinois Teacher* V, no. 4 (December 1961), pp. 188-92.

_____. "Basic Guides to Effective Evaluation." *Illinois Teacher* I, no. 9, pp. 22-25.

_____. *Penney's Fashions and Fabrics* (Fall-Winter 1965), "Evaluation."

_____. "Significance of Evaluation." *Tips and Topics in Home Economics,* VIII, no. 2 (December 1967).

_____. "Evaluation." *Tips and Topics in Home Economics* VII, no. 1 (October 1966) p. 5.

_____. "Evaluation, What Is It?" *Tips and Topics in Home Economics* IV, no. 3 (February 1964).

_____. "Learning Experiences." *Tips and Topics in Home Economics* X, no. 4 (April 1970).

_____. "Techniques for Teacher Development." *Tips and Topics in Home Economics* X, no. 1 (November 1969).

_____. "Plans for Teaching." *Tips and Topics in Home Economics* X, no. 1 (November 1969).

_____. "How Do Concepts Develop?" "Concepts—What Are They?" "Teachers Can Help," "Attitudes," and "Self-Direction." *Tips and Topics in Home Economics* VIII, no. 2 (December 1967).

_____. "Why Don't They Learn?" and "Feelings Are Important," *Tips and Topics in Home Economics* IV, no. 1 (October 1963).

Chapter 2 STATING OBJECTIVES IN BEHAVIORAL TERMS

You are already aware that evaluation should be in terms of objectives. This chapter will help you state objectives in such a way that each one is tied directly to an evaluation technique. The key to stating such objectives will be behavioral outcomes (performance objectives). This chapter includes a definition of behavioral objectives, including criteria for stating objectives, as well as objectives for various types of learning and how each type relates to another.

Definition of Behavioral Objectives

The term *objectives* will be used in this text almost exclusively although the author accepts *goals* and *outcomes* as having the same meaning in the educational process. Wherever the word *goals* is used, the term is meant to imply broad, overall course or program objectives.

An objective is a statement describing a proposed change as a result of learning. The change is designed to occur in the student's behavior and is the end toward which the teacher directs learning experiences. The behavior must be observable or no evaluative evidence will be provided. The behavioral intent of an objective can be stated as an overt action. This means that a teacher should be able to see the student perform a task, demonstrate a skill, take a test, work in a laboratory, and do many other activities. Overt action can also reflect various affective aspects of a person's behavior such as values, attitudes, and appreciations.

An objective should denote desirable behavior. This behavior can be a performance skill. Although home economics educators have in recent years placed much emphasis on concepts and generalizations, they are aware that homemaking skills are equally important. Performance skills are essential in home economics-related occupations as well as for the occupation of homemaking. Desirable behavior can exhibit knowledge and thinking skills. Knowledge includes terminology, facts, principles, and generalizations, as well as knowledge of methods, procedures, and techniques. Ability to apply knowledge, to interpret cause and effect relationships, to generalize from given data, and to recognize assumptions and limitations are all thinking skills. When thinking skills are related to homemaking and occupational tasks, they become essential behavioral objectives for home economics. Desirable behavior can reveal social skills and attitudes such as peer acceptance, social adjustment, and dating skills. Desirable behavior may be determined by the class as a whole and also by each individual student. This makes evaluation by the teacher complicated but less so for the student who is evaluating his own social skills and attitudes.

An objective should denote measurable outcomes. You have already learned that quantitative descriptions are measurable and that qualitative descriptions are not. However, behavior can be assigned a score even though subjective judgment may have to be used. An objective has little or no value unless it can be evaluated. A measurable outcome makes evaluation meaningful to the evaluator and to the person being evaluated. A specific amount and kind of knowledge is measurable and usable in revealing gaps in knowledge, lack of understanding, inability to relate information as well as in assigning a grade. Skills are measurable provided the necessary evidence has been identified. The product produced, the procedure used and the correct completion of a skill process are examples of measurable outcomes.

Appreciations are difficult to measure unless a type of reaction rather than an exact reaction can be identified such as critical judgment and expression of pleasure or enjoyment. Appreciations are individual and should be measured on this basis as should values and attitudes. Group values can be determined and personal values measured against these; a change in values as a result of learning experiences can be measured; values can also be weighted and a change in weight can be the criterion. Desirable attitudes can be ascertained by a class or an individual and evaluated in the same way as values. Knowledge and psychomotor skills are much more apt to be measurable than are values, attitudes, and appreciations. Nonetheless, a teacher is obligated to state objectives that denote a measurable outcome; otherwise, the teacher and the students cannot determine the degree of successful attainment of those objectives for affective learning.

Perhaps the greatest difficulty in stating behavioral objectives is determining what is desirable behavior. Perfection can not always be used as the criterion; in fact it can seldom be used. How then does a teacher make a decision? What are the bases upon which she might make such a decision? Does desirable behavior differ from student to student?

The desired behavior should be consistent with the ability level of students. Each teacher must determine the ability level of his own students and at the same time be aware that intelligence, socioeconomic background, and age all affect these ability levels. The intellectual level of students should affect the behavior desired. A teacher can not expect a group of slow learners to perform at the same level as a group of more able students. All too often these slow learners are expected to master the same information, construct the same garments, prepare the same meals, and analyze the same problems as other students. Perhaps eventually these students will reach the desired behavior if given additional instruction over a longer period of time. The secret is to key the first evidenced behavior to what is possible for the students.

The socioeconomic conditions of the community and of individual students affects the performance that can be expected. The student who has had many social and educational opportunities will most likely be able to perform at a higher level than the student who has not been so fortunate. Students who live in poverty areas may need to be taught those things that others have learned as a part of daily living. Girls and boys whose mothers work may have many homemaking skills that others who do not have home responsibilities do not possess. Desired behaviors need to be based on data collected about individual students.

More should be expected of older than of younger students. The older student is usually better coordinated physically, more self-directive, and better organized than the young student. A home economics teacher who had taught first-year home economics to fourteen-year-olds for many years decided to provide a course for seniors who had not taken home economics before. She found that the seniors' interest, ability to do quality work, and use of time were different from younger students'. The desired behaviors need to be greater and more exacting for seniors than for freshman.

The desired behavior should consider needed abilities. This is probably the most important and successful method of identifying the expected performances of students. The psychomotor skills, the cognitive skills, the social or relationship skills needed to perform in a given situation are identifiable by both the teacher and the student. Job requirements or skills form a basis for identifying behaviors. The level of acceptable performance for each task is evident as skills are identified. A careful job analysis will reveal the needed abilities and will make stating behavioral objectives more realistic. Already developed abilities affect the level of performance that can be expected. This should say to you as a teacher that objectives for a second course should be at a higher level than those of a first course and that additional skills should be expected. Many occupations have identified classifications, the first being at the entry level. The teacher of homemaking would do well to place emphasis in a first-year course on the essentials for being a homemaker and to leave the skills that enhance family living to another course. The same guidelines would hold true for the teacher of occupational home economics.

It is essential for the person who states an objective to communicate his intent not only to himself but to others who will be using the objective for purposes of learning and evaluation. Three clues for communicating intent are use of action verbs, providing a description of expected action, and defining the performance criteria. In the present judgment of the author the first two are the absolute necessities and the third adds strength to the objective.

An action verb increases communication of intent to others. Examples of verbs that indicate action are *list, apply, identify, determine, compare, analyze, select, contrast, solve.* Others are *construct, utilize, exhibit skill, perform.* These tell you what the action is but do not tell you the actual act. Although the verb in itself is not sufficient, it does provide an excellent beginning for stating behavioral objectives. An action verb identifies the type of behavior expected. Some of the above verbs tell you that the behavior will most likely be intellectual. The words in the first sentence, beginning with *list,* are more cognitive or intellectual in nature than most of the others. Those in the second sentence imply psychomotor skill as a general rule. Affective objectives stated in behavioral terms are the most difficult ones for which to find verbs. These may be *indicate awareness, recognize, express.*

A description of what the student will be doing increases the degree of communicating the intent. In other words the action verb needs an object upon which to act. It can provide a means of communication between student and teacher of what will be expected of a learner. The description should say exactly what the student will be doing to achieve the objective. Understanding how to plan menus does not indicate any kind of action. To be *able* to plan menus is an objective that can be evaluated using the student's behavorial performance. The description should identify instructional content. An objective such as "plan menus that meet the daily nutritional needs of individuals" should prevent the teacher from evaluating the form in which the menus are written rather than the nutritional content.

Communicating the intent includes defining the performance criteria. These criteria are really standards of acceptable performance; they tell how well the teacher wants the students to perform. The number of allowable errors may be one criterion. In some instances, it might not be possible to allow errors such as in threading a machine. On the other hand an objective in clothing might be "to construct a one-piece dress with not more than two seams with the incorrect width or broken threads." A time limit may be an acceptable criterion of performance: "To prepare a meal for four that requires no longer than twenty minutes," "to construct a blouse in class in two weeks time," "to make a bed using the hospital method in not more than five minutes." This is not to imply that all objectives need time limits; only those for which there is a reason.

Stating Objectives Based on Type of Learning

Home economics teachers are aware that several types of learning take place in their classrooms. The teaching-learning activity may result in obtaining and applying knowledge. It may focus on personal qualities such as appreciations, attitudes, relationships and values. The major purpose may be developing homemaking or occupational skills. Even though one of these three may be the primary objective, the other two types of learning usually occur simultaneously and may be secondary objectives.

Objectives have been classified by types of learning by Bloom and his associates and taxonomies have been developed for the cognitive and affective domains. The taxonomy for the psychomotor skills has not yet been developed by this particular group. The taxonomies were not designed to fragment learning into three categories but to focus upon objectives that involve various aspects of teaching-learning.

Cognitive objectives can include many levels of intellectual performance. Basic information consisting of terms and facts is needed before students can develop intellectual skills to any great degree. As you state objectives for this domain you should be aware of the difficulty level at which you want students to exhibit behavior. Those objectives explained in the following paragraphs include knowledge of terms and facts, application of knowledge, and problem solving.

Objectives for the knowledge classification are difficult to state in behavioral terms because little action is demanded. The objectives are based on recall and recognition of terms and facts. Since "to understand" and "to know" can not be observed, objectives need to be stated using words such as *recognize, identify, state,* or *write.* Following are a few sample objectives which may be helpful as you state objectives based on knowledge of terms:

(1) To define methods of cooking foods.

(2) To recall the name given to each stage of the family life cycle.

(3) To identify the parts of the sewing machine according to purpose.

(4) To define the various ways of meeting problems.

(5) To recognize insurance terms that are frequently used.

(6) To write definitions for values, attitudes, and goals.

Objectives aimed toward knowledge of facts are as difficult to state in behavioral terms as are those dealing with terminology. Words that are helpful in stating these objectives are *recall, state, list, name, recognize,* and *identify.* Examples of home economics objectives based on knowledge of facts are as follows:

(1) To state figures indicating marriage-divorce trends.

(2) To recall the criteria for evaluating a garment.

(3) To identify the methods for removing stains.

(4) To identify principles for guiding behavior of children.

(5) To recognize principles of food preparation.

(6) To state guidelines for arranging furniture.

Objectives based on application of knowledge are stated in terms of intellectual skills. These are easier to state behaviorally than are objectives based on terms and facts. Application is the use of knowledge in concrete situations; it is also transfer of learning from a book to a lifelike situation. Although application is considered an intellectual skill, the author believes it has relevance for the performance of various homemaking tasks. Words that are helpful in stating objectives for application of information include *recognize, choose, select, apply, present, explain, predict, distinguish,* and *analyze.* Examples of objectives that seem appropriate for application of home economics facts include the following:

(1) To interpret a blueprint of a house.

(2) To explain a cartoon in terms of parent-child relationships.

(3) To predict the outcome of a particular decision made by a young couple.

(4) To plan a personal budget.

(5) To explain the operation of a washing machine.

(6) To choose clothes that are appropriate for the person.

(7) To select foods that require a minimum amount of preparation time.

Problem-solving objectives have more validity for home economics than any other type of knowledge objective. Home economics teachers have been much more apt to teach by this method than they have been to evaluate by it. You may find that your students make much better scores on tests if you are consistent in the way you teach and the way you evaluate. Objectives in this category have key words the same as other types of knowledge objectives. Some of these words are *solve, construct, apply, exhibit skill, select, plan.* Examples of problem-solving objectives are:

(1) To coordinate fabric, pattern, and notions for a new garment.

(2) To analyze why a person reacts in a particular way in a particular situation.

(3) To identify a technique that may promote self-control on the part of a particular child.

(4) To solve a parent-child conflict by suggesting action.

(5) To plan to prepare and serve a meal in an hour.

(6) To apply food preparation principles in altering recipes.

(7) To alter a budget to meet an emergency.

Objectives focusing on personal qualities are essential in home economics and include those traits or characteristics that are uniquely one's own. Personal qualities are affected by study in other subject areas, but perhaps not as much as in home economics since these are an integral part of child and family development. A teacher can do much to help students identify and evaluate their personal characteristics. Among these qualities are values, attitudes, interpersonal relationships, interests, and appreciations.

Values are what a person cherishes and are determinants of goals and decisions. The most important aspects of evaluating values are first, to determine one's own values and, second, to recognize the effect of values on decisions that one makes. Objectives in this area are very difficult to state in behavioral terms but have little use unless they are so stated. Some of the words you may find helpful in stating value objectives are *identify, determine, differentiate, compare, analyze, become aware.* Examples of home economics objectives that are value focused are:

(1) To identify one's own values and their place in one's value system.

(2) To analyze how values affect family decisions.

(3) To relate one's values to one's decisions.

(4) To differentiate between personal values and family values.

(5) To explain why a particular value becomes more or less important at a certain stage of life.

(6) To analyze how personal values affect decisions about spending money.

Attitudes are observable in behavior, they reflect values, and are a reaction to something or someone. Once a desirable attitude for a given situation has been determined, it is possible for a student to fake the attitude. The teacher can only record the behavior that indicates an attitude and in this way evaluate it. The student can identify his own attitudes and can make efforts to modify, eliminate, or develop a particular attitude. Frequently students are unaware of their attitudes and the objective may be to identify an attitude that does exist and to evaluate its effect on others. Stating objectives for attitudes is not easy since they are personal and apt to change. Perhaps these words will help you to state such objectives: *identify, analyze, determine, differentiate, compare.* Examples of home economics objectives concerned with attitudes include:

(1) To identify own attitude toward persons who are of a different race, creed, nationality.

(2) To analyze sources of own food preferences and prejudices.

(3) To determine the effect of one's own attitude on someone else's attitude.

(4) To differentiate between own attitudes and those of one's family.

(5) To compare own attitudes with those of selected peer group members.

(6) To exhibit a "wholesome" attitude toward self.

Interpersonal relationships inside and outside the classroom are important enough to warrant stated objectives. The ability to get along with fellow class members, one's peer group, and one's family is and has always been a focus of home economics. Evidences can be observed in the behavior of students that indicate the kinds of relationships they have with others. Objectives for interpersonal relationships are somewhat difficult to state in behavioral terms but are easier to evaluate when so stated. Words that may be of help are *exhibit, analyze, cooperate, show awareness, indicate, react.* Some examples of objectives that you might use are:

(1) To become aware of the various ways in which members of one's own family interact with one another.

(2) To indicate an acceptance of qualities that contribute to the uniqueness of a particular individual.

(3) To establish communication with one's own family members.

(4) To recognize self as a unique individual participating in varied social situations.

(5) To analyze the effect of various child-adult relationships on behavior.

(6) To exhibit ability to cooperate with others.

(7) To assist another in solving a problem or doing a task.

(8) To indicate empathy with a fellow classmate.

The development of appreciations has been and continues to be a major objective of home economics. Ways of creating beauty have probably been of more concern than the appreciation of beauty that exists; both should be important objectives. Ways of creating beauty are more related to knowledge or cognitive processes than to personal qualities or affective behavior. How can you state objectives dealing with the personal appreciations of students? Perhaps the first step is to decide what kinds of behavior you wish students to exhibit. These could include *express pleasure or satisfaction, choose something beautiful, ask for more information, duplicate, imitate, create, appraise, respond.* The objectives given below have been selected to aid you in stating your own appreciation objectives:

(1) To express reactions to each picture on display.

(2) To choose the room that has the most appeal and state why you think it is beautiful.

(3) To create a flower arrangement you consider beautiful.

(4) To indicate an awareness of aesthetic factors in a dress.

(5) To write a personal response to three pieces of furniture.

(6) To react to three plates of food as to whether or not appealing.

The determining of interests and needs is vital to students as well as to the teacher of home economics. Many other kinds of objectives are based on the identified interests and needs of students. Home-degree projects are usually chosen on this basis. Evaluating interests and relating these to personal values should be a meaningful experience for most students. Objectives designed to determine interests are relatively easy to state because interests are more recognizable than are values, attitudes, and appreciations. Words that are useful in stating such objectives include *identify, list, recognize, select, determine.* Examples of objectives related to interests are:

(1) To identify recreational and leisure time interests.

(2) To list homemaking skills interested in developing.

(3) To determine which activities hold the most interest for weekends.

(4) To select those topics about children interested in studying.

(5) To identify personal financial needs.

(6) To determine occupational interests.

Objectives for skills are the action parts of home economics for they are the essentials needed for the occupations whether inside or outside the home. There is much evidence that more emphasis has been given to skill development than to knowledge, principles or personal qualities. This evidence indicates that the development of skills needs to be balanced with other aspects of home economics. Objectives for skills are categorized in the following paragraphs as management of resources, ability to operate equipment, and creation of products.

Management objectives include effective use of resources such as time, energy, and money. The development of work habits is an essential objective included in this category. This objective, closely tied to the principles of management, must be coupled with knowledge objectives for management. While management is not a psychomotor skill, the use of energy does frequently require manual skills. Terms you will find useful in stating these objectives are *decide, select, manage, spend, utilize, arrange, plan,* and *analyze.* Examples of management objectives include:

(1) To utilize safety practices when preparing food.

(2) To utilize effective work habits when cleaning a room.

(3) To plan a food budget for a week.

(4) To utilize management techniques to conserve time and energy.

(5) To develop a plan for accomplishing tasks.

(6) To utilize techniques for maintaining orderliness.

Objectives concerned with operation of equipment will always be related to skills. New pieces of equipment appear on the market every year. The operating procedures differ slightly from old to new models. These factors only make it more imperative for home economics teachers to assist their students in developing skill in operating equipment. Students must learn to read and follow directions; they need to understand the basic principles of operation of various pieces of household equipment and to feel secure in using the equipment necessary to do household tasks. These objectives indicate how you might state your own:

(1) To use pressing equipment to care properly for clothing.

(2) To operate a washer and dryer in care of clothing.

(3) To use small appliances skillfully in preparing food.

(4) To operate a dishwasher.

(5) To operate a food disposal.

(6) To utilize a vacuum cleaner when cleaning a room.

The creation of products is still an important objective in developing homemaking skills. Products are easy to evaluate because behavior is observable and objectives involving products are quickly arrived at by a class. Objectives involving products usually begin with *construct, alter, develop,* or *prepare.* The following are a few examples most of which you are already using:

(1) To construct a garment.

(2) To alter a garment to fit a particular person.

(3) To alter a pattern according to body measurements.

(4) To make a stuffed toy for a child.

(5) To prepare the night meal.

(6) To bake a cake.

(7) To arrange a tea table.

The three types of objectives—affective, cognitive, and psychomotor— have a relationship to each other. Frequently, at least two if not all three types of learning occur simultaneously. What you, as a home economics teacher, choose to do about this relationship is your own decision. You may decide to concentrate on one objective at a time and permit the others to be incidental. You may decide to correlate two or more objectives. Providing a scheme for doing this correlation is the intent of this section.

Secondary objectives can be related to the primary objective. First, the major objective should be identified. This could be a knowledge or a skill objective or even a personal quality objective. Whichever it is, the objective must be the major focus. The second step would be to select one or more secondary objectives. It is not always necessary or appropriate to have secondary objectives but the possibility needs to be considered. Whenever secondary objectives are selected they should be obtainable through the same series of learning activities as the primary objective. It is possible to incorporate all three types of objectives as components of one behavior or action. A student may be developing a skill and at the same time be acquiring an attitude or value as well as a knowledge of principles related to the skill. Very frequently the acquiring of knowledge results in performing a skill or task. The success or lack of it affects an attitude or value. Figure 2-1 is an illustration of this global relationship.

FIGURE 2-1

A primary objective can lead to a secondary objective in a series of activities; this occurs very often in home economics courses. Knowledge is gained before a task is undertaken; a task or series of activities is summarized in stating generalizations and principles; attitudes or values result from either of these processes; interests that have been identified point to needed knowledge and skills. The following diagrams illustrate this system of relating objectives.

Knowledge——►Skill——►Personal Quality

Skill——►Knowledge——►Personal Quality

Personal Quality——►Knowledge——►Skill

Skill——►Personal Quality——►Knowledge

Personal Quality——►Skill——►Knowledge

Knowledge——►Personal Quality——►Skill

Examples of related objectives may help you to state your own objectives in this fashion.

Primary Objectives	Secondary Objectives (a)	Secondary Objectives (b)
To identify principles of food preparation.	To prepare a night meal.	To exhibit interest in learning to prepare food.
To construct a dress for self.	To display an appreciation for sewing skills.	To recognize principles of clothing construction.
To direct the play activities of small children.	To list guidelines for directing children's activities.	To express an interest in young children.
To utilize effective work habits in cleaning a room.	To show a willingness to develop effective habits.	To state management principles related to cleaning a room.

An advantage to this system can be illustrated by analyzing what could happen to each of the above objectives. In the first example the skill could have been developed without highlighting the preparation principles which was the major intent. In the last example management principles could have been taught without the experiences of using the principles in cleaning a room.

Summary

The stating of and adherence to responsible objectives is a foundation of effective teaching-learning. The following are guidelines for construction of such objectives. It is necessary to:

- state objectives in behavioral terms;
- determine outcomes that are measurable;
- identify behaviors that are consistent with established goals of home economics;
- identify behaviors that are consistent with the age, socioeconomic, and intellectual levels of the students;
- identify behaviors based on job requirements;
- use action verbs in order to communicate the intent of the objective;
- describe what the student will be expected to do;
- define the performance criteria whenever feasible;
- state objectives according to type of learning as well as in behavioral terms;

- include in knowledge objectives those that focus upon intellectual skills as well as basic facts;

- place emphasis on application of knowledge and problem solving objectives;

- utilize objectives in teaching that focus upon values, attitudes, interpersonal relationships, appreciations, interest and needs;

- focus upon objectives for skills based on management of resources, operation of equipment, and creation of a product;

- recognize that all three types of objectives have a global relationship to each other;

- correlate types of objects by identifying a primary objective and relating one or more secondary objectives to it.

STUDENT ACTIVITIES

1. View and discuss the filmstrip-tape "Educational Objectives," Vincet Associates, P.O. Box 24714, Los Angeles, California, 90024.

2. Evaluate several objectives found in curriculum guides or other such material as to whether:
   a. stated in behavioral terms
   b. described desired behavior
   c. defined the necessary criteria

3. Restate several faulty objectives that you have found so that they meet the above requirements.

4. View and discuss the filmstrip-tape "Selecting Appropriate Educational Objectives," Vincet Associates, P.O. Box 24714, Los Angeles, California 90024.

5. State five objectives focused upon each of the following:
   a. knowledge of terms and definitions
   b. scientific facts and principles
   c. application of knowledge
   d. problem solving

6. State three objectives focused upon each of the following personal qualities:
   a. values
   b. attitudes
   c. interpersonal relationships
   d. appreciations
   e. interests and needs

7. State five objectives focused upon each of the following homemaking skills:
   a. management of resources
   b. operation of equipment
   c. creation of a product

8. State a primary objective for:
   a. knowledge and secondary objectives for a skill and for a personal quality
   b. a personal quality and secondary objectives for a skill and for knowledge
   c. a skill and secondary objectives for knowledge and for a personal quality

9. Write your own decisions about using and relating objectives for knowledge, for personal qualities and for skills.

REFERENCES

Ahmann, J. Stanley and Glock, M. D. *Evaluating Pupil Growth.* New York: Allyn and Bacon, Inc., 1959.

Bloom, Benjamin S. *Taxonomy of Educational Objectives; The Classification of Educational Goals, Handbook I: Cognitive Domain.* New York: David McKay Company, Inc., 1956.

Bloom, Benjamin S., Krathwohl, David R., and Masia, Bertram B. *Taxonomy of Educational Objectives, The Classification of Educational Goals, Handbook II: Affective Domain.* New York: David McKay Company, Inc., 1956.

Gronlund, Norman E. *Stating Behavioral Objectives for Classroom Instruction.* New York: The Macmillan Company, 1971.

Grolund, Norman E. *Measurement and Evaluation in Teaching.* New York: The Macmillan Company, 1971.

Hall, Olive A. and Paolucci, B. *Teaching Home Economics.* New York: John Wiley and Sons, Inc., 1970.

Hoover, Helen M. "Levels of Conceptual Understanding." *Journal of Home Economics* 59, no. 2 (February 1967), pp. 89-92.

Mager, Robert F. *Preparing Instructional Objectives.* California: Fearon Publishers, 1962.

Moorison, Edward J. "The Use of Behavioral Objectives in Instructional Materials Development." *American Vocational Journal* (February 1970).

Simpson, Elizabeth Jane. "The Classification of Educational Objectives, Psychomotor Domain." *Illinois Teacher* X, no. 4 (Winter 1966–67), pp. 110-45.

———. "Cognitive and Affective Learning." *Tips and Topics in Home Economics* VIII, no. 2 (December 1967), p. 3.

_____. "Guidelines for Stating Objectives." *Tips and Topics in Home Economics* X, no. 1 (November 1969).

_____. "Conceptual Teaching-Learning." *Tips and Topics in Home Economics* 3, no. 2 (December 1967).

_____. "Considerations in Developing Educational Objectives." *Illinois Teacher,* IX, no. 5 (1965–66), pp. 235-55.

_____. "Schema for Educational Objectives." *Illinois Teacher* X, no. 3 (Winter 1966–67), pp. 99-102.

_____. *Illinois Teacher* I, no. 9; II, no. 3; III, no. 5; and IV, no. 9.

Chapter 3 SELECTING EVALUATION PROCEDURES FOR OBJECTIVES

The preceding chapter has explained how to state objectives in behavioral terms and described the three major types of objectives. This chapter will focus upon the selection of evaluation techniques or methods that are appropriate for a particular objective and will capitalize on the material presented in the previous chapter. This chapter is concerned with your responsibilities as a home economics teacher and will attempt to help you see the relationship between the intent of an objective and the methods and techniques chosen to evaluate it. The grids or tables of specifications provided are not only a tool to facilitate planning for evaluation but also a safeguard against overemphasis on one type of objective. The last section explains the stating of objectives for a course, a unit, and a lesson.

Identifying Appropriate Methods

Appropriateness of method is directly related to the intent of the objective: intellectual skills, personal qualities, or psychomotor skills. You will recall that intellectual skills include knowledge of terms and facts, judgment and problem solving; that personal qualities are values, attitudes, appreciations, and interpersonal relationships; and that psychomotor skills are performance of occupational and homemaking tasks. Methods can be classified as paper and pencil tests which are objective and essay, sociometric techniques, observational devices, reporting forms, and audio-visual techniques. Each of these is more appropriate for one type of objective than for the other two types.

Intellectual skill objectives are most appropriately evaluated by written tests. These may be either the objective type or the essay type. Both types are useful for evaluating knowledge, judgments, or problem solving. Part II explains these two types in considerable detail.

Methods for evaluating knowledge include both pretests and posttests. Objective questions such as matching, multiple choice, and true-false are very successfully used. Other objective forms include completion and short answer. Restricted essay questions are also appropriate for evaluating knowledge objectives. These questions may be asked orally and are an excellent method of evaluating as a group.

Methods for judgment objectives are very similar to those for evaluating knowledge. The major difference is the type of answer requested; a decision must be reached rather than knowledge identified. The objective questions would need to be based on a situation which eliminates matching and completion. Essay questions would also indicate the situation about which a judgment must be made. Judgment also involves evaluating products and processes. Diagnostic charts, criteria lists, and rating devices are used in such evaluative judgments.

Problem-solving objectives are evaluated by methods that describe the problem. These descriptions may be followed by essay questions asking what should be done and why, or by cluster true-false or matching questions that provide alternative solutions from which to choose. Problem-solving objectives may be met by carrying out a project which would involve evaluating knowledge gained and the product produced.

Methods that are most appropriate for personal qualities objectives in-clude observational devices and reporting forms. Audio-visual techniques are also very useful. All of these methods are subjective in nature and for that reason rarely result in scores that can be used for grading purposes. These methods are explained in detail in Part III. Essay questions are also successfully used in evaluating personal qualities. Values may be determined through the use of essay questions which are projective and structured to point up values. The open-ended question is another excellent paper-and-pencil method. Questionnaires, opinionnaires, diaries, and auto-biographies are reporting forms which may be designed to determine a person's values. Tape recorders and pictures can be used to reveal values.

Interests and needs are personal qualities that are often used as a basis for planning instruction. These also need to be evaluated for the information of the student as well as the teacher. Interest inventories, questionnaires, criteria, and listings are appropriate for objectives aimed at identifying interests and needs.

Appreciations are as difficult to evaluate as to include in behavioral objectives. The reason is that there is no right or wrong answer although teachers frequently want students to appreciate the same things that they do. Analysis of pictures or objects is perhaps the most appropriate method. Essay questions and daily logs can be used if they are structured to point out appreciations.

Relationships can be evaluated by a variety of observational devices, reporting forms, sociometric techniques, and personal contacts. The observational devices include checklists and rating scales frequently answered by the students as well as the teacher. A personality inventory is an example of a checklist. Reporting forms may be anecdotal records, logs, diaries, and autobiographies. Sociometric techniques are sociograms, who's who, social distance scale, and role playing. Conferences, home visits, and observation are methods that can be used to evaluate interpersonal relationships objectives.

Homemaking skills are most frequently exhibited by performance at school and at home. The methods that are most appropriate for recording quality of performance are observational devices. The same types of devices can also be used to evaluate products and conditions that result from performance.

Products are appropriately evaluated by rating scales and score cards. These may be used in laboratory situations at the end of a demonstration or at home. These devices may be used to evaluate products produced by the teacher and thereby establish standards for a product.

Performance objectives may also be evaluated by rating scales and score cards. The checklist is the simplest of the observational devices to use for performance. A progress chart is another method that reveals progress toward a completed project.

Conditions may be considered products and may be evaluated by the same devices: a checklist for cleanliness and order; a rating scale for attractiveness and comfort of a room.

The methods selected for each objective should meet the criteria for effectiveness. These criteria include the following:

(1) The method should be keyed to the major intent of the objective.

(2) The difficulty level of the method should be matched to the intellectual level of the student.

(3) Students' skill at evaluating as well as that of the teacher should dictate the difficulty level of the method.

(4) Time should be available to use the chosen method.

(5) Reproduction of the device or test should not be costly.

(6) The method chosen should provide a learning situation.

(7) There should be an awareness of which methods produce scores for grading purpose.

(8) Variety should be maintained in order to prevent boredom.

The following chart is a summary of methods that are appropriate for various types of objectives.

Objectives for:	Written Test	Observational Devices	Reporting Forms	Audio-Visual Methods	Sociometric Techniques
Intellectual skills	X		X		
Personal qualities		X	X	X	X
Homemaking skills		X		X	

Development of a Grid

A grid is a table of specifications designed to reflect both the objectives and the amount of emphasis placed on each concept. A grid can be developed for an objective test, an essay test, or a unit as a whole. The grid for a test serves as a guide during the construction of a test and insures a desirable balance of items. The grid for a unit or course is a guide for planning methods to evaluate each objective. It also insures that an appropriate balance is kept between emphasis on each concept and proportion of grade provided for each score.

A grid may be developed by following general rules. The rules for a test include the following:

(1) List the concepts that are to be covered by the test in the first column.

(2) Decide which intellectual skills are to be covered such as knowledge, application, judgment, problem solving.

(3) Provide a column for each chosen intellectual skill.

(4) Decide on the total percentage of items to be devoted to each concept and record in a column on the far left.

(5) Decide the proportion of each total percentage that will be allotted to each of the designated intellectual skills.

(6) Total all percentages so as to arrive at 100 percent.

EXAMPLE 1

GRID FOR AN OBJECTIVE TEST
FOOD AND NUTRITION: FIRST YEAR

Concepts	Knowledge	Application	Total
Personal food needs	5	5	10
Daily food requirements	5	5	10
Food preferences and prejudices	0	5	5
Nutritional contribution of snacks	0	5	5
Food away from home	3	5	8
Selection and storage of foods	5	10	15
Arrangement of small equipment	4	5	9
Use of equipment	3	5	8
Principles of preparation	5	15	20
Table service	5	5	10
	35	65	100

Note: Percents in columns are based on emphasis placed on each concept.

EXAMPLE 2

GRID FOR AN ESSAY TEST
FOOD AND NUTRITION: FIRST YEAR

Concepts	Knowledge	Judgment	Percent of Grade
Personal food needs	3	5	8
Daily food requirements	6	6	12
Food preferences and prejudices	4	6	10
Nutritional contribution of snacks	5	5	10
Food away from home	3	7	10
Selection and storage of foods	7	5	12
Arrangement of small equipment	2	6	8
Use of equipment	5	5	10
Principles of preparation	3	2	15
Table service	2	3	5
	40	60	100

Note: Percents in columns are based on emphasis placed on each concept.

(7) Review percentages to ascertain whether they are appropriate for emphasis given and time used for teaching each concept.

The same rules are applicable for developing a grid for a unit. Objectives rather than concepts are listed in the first column. The selected methods are recorded in the second column with percent of contribution for each method recorded in the third column. Examples 1, 2, and 3 provide a visual explanation of grids for an objective test, an essay test, and a unit in food and nutrition.

EXAMPLE 3
GRID FOR EVALUATING A UNIT IN FOOD AND NUTRITION

Objectives	Methods	Percent of Grade
To determine the food needs of teenagers.	Objective and essay questions. Summary of how food affects health.	3 3 (6)
To acquire knowledge of the food required daily for optimum growth.	Objective and essay questions. Report of home-degree project.	4 5 (9)
To analyze sources of food preferences and prejudices and how these affect own diet.	Objective questions. Analysis of personal tastes and prejudices. Report on home project.	3 5 5 (13)
To recognize the contributions of snacks to daily food needs.	Analysis of own meals and snacks.	5 (5)
To exhibit skill in selecting food away from home.	List of guidelines. Objective questions.	3 3 (6)
To establish criteria for selecting and storing foods.	Objective and essay questions. Checklist for various forms of food. Home project report.	6 5 5 (16)
To arrange utensils and small equipment in a convenient manner.	Checklist on arrangement. Objective and essay questions.	5 3 (8)
To skillfully use appropriate equipment in food preparation.	Checklist on use. Objective and essay questions.	5 3 (8)
To utilize principles in preparing food.	Rating Scale. Objective and essay questions. Report of home project.	5 6 5 (16)
To exhibit skill in serving food.	Objective and essay questions. Checklist for practical test. Home project.	3 5 5 (13)
		100

Stating Course, Unit, and
Lesson Goals and Objectives

Goals for a course, a program, or a curriculum have a relationship to the more specific outcomes of a unit of instruction and to the behavioral objectives for a particular day. Out of course goals grow unit objectives and from these the daily objectives are derived. Each step makes the final student behavior clearer and the objective more precise. The following diagram explains this relationship.

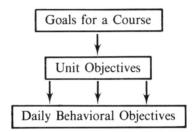

Course objectives are broad overall goals. Earlier in this book a distinction between objectives and goals was made. This difference is utilized in this section for the obvious reason of making distinct the difference in course, unit, and lesson objectives. A goal is a long-term aim and encompasses several short-term objectives. Therefore, it needs to be stated in such a way that it implies action without naming the specific action.

The identification of course goals is the first step in stating more specific behavioral outcomes. Sometimes these are already defined in the total curriculum plan. An example would be "relating to peer group" for a beginning home economics course and "knowledge of marriage preparation" for a more advanced course. You might identify course goals by listing the main reasons for teaching the course. Another identification method would be to list what you want students to know and to be able to do when the course has been completed. Such lists would not be long or detailed but would be inclusive of all major purposes.

Goals for a course are stated in general terms. You will note the examples given above are general and only imply the behaviors that will be expected of students. You may do this by identifying the major subject matter concepts of home economics that you want to include in the course. This would need to be related to the particular level to be taught. Level is sometimes based on age and sometimes on the year such as first- or second-year home economics. Remember that goals are behavior directives and not merely statements of subject matter to be covered.

Goals for a course can be stated in types of learning. You already know that the three domains of objectives provide a very workable system of classifying learning. In stating goals you could ask these three questions: "What do I want students to know?" "What do I want the student to be able to do?" "How do I want students to act?" List concepts you expect students to know, values and attitudes you expect them to exhibit, and skills you expect them to perform. Such lists become the goals for the course you are planning.

Goals for a course point to more specific behavioral objectives. The lists suggested above are not specifically detailed. They simply provide a framework for determining specific behavioral objectives. Each goal needs to be broken down into more detail. Goals for a course may be no more than two or three for each unit of instruction. Sometimes it is possible to have one major goal for each unit. This goal may highlight only the most important outcome of a unit. Goals for a first-year course might be:

(1) Meeting own clothing needs

(2) Managing personal resources

(3) Meeting family food needs

(4) Caring for small children

(5) Relating to family and others

Obviously more specific objectives need to be stated but these goals clearly imply both content and expected behaviors. One advantage of stating goals for a course is that advanced courses can build on the first course. Another advantage is relating the learning experience to the needs and interests of the age level being taught.

Unit objectives are stated as specific desired outcomes. Unit of instruction is a term widely used by many teachers but not always accepted by educators. This author has discovered no other usable term. It is a term very adaptable for dividing a year into various areas of home economics. The five areas that were identified in the national curriculum project are frequently used as a basis for five units in a course of study.[1] This does not mean to imply that all five units are used in every course but they do give direction for dividing a course into subject matter units.

Unit objectives are more specific than course goals and less so than lesson objectives. Unit objectives are a refinement of course goals and give further direction to the ultimate behavioral outcomes. The course goal of meeting own clothing needs could have these unit objectives:

---

[1] *Concepts and Generalizations: Their Place in High School Home Economics Curriculum Development* (Washington: American Home Economics Association, 1967).

(1) To select own clothes.

(2) To launder own clothing.

(3) To make necessary repairs on own clothing.

(4) To construct a simple garment for self.

No doubt you recognize more clearly what the goal means and what the unit will contain. Not all these objectives would be included by every teacher and some teachers would add other objectives.

Concepts can be related to unit objectives. Some authorities suggest stating objectives before identifying the concepts and others recommend the opposite approach. If the objective is clearly determined, it does not matter which approach is chosen. The assumption of the lead sentence is that knowledge is a part of every objective. Knowledge may not be the primary purpose but it does accompany every skill or behavior. What are several concepts that a teacher might emphasize for the unit objective to be able to select own clothes? The major concept is "selection of clothing." This needs breaking down into subconcepts. The following is a list of possible subconcepts.

(1) Social aspects of clothing

(2) Psychological effects of clothing

(3) Clothing needs of individual

(4) Compatibility of clothing and personality

(5) Money available for clothing

(6) Fashions and fads

These subconcepts make it clearer how this unit objective will be met but there is still a lack of identification of expected student behaviors.

Supporting objectives for each major objective provide clearer direction for planning learning experiences and evaluation. One approach is to key these supporting objectives to subconcepts. Another approach is to ask what you expect students to do in the unit. The list of objectives given below is keyed to the above named concepts but could have as easily been determined by the second method:

(1 To identify effects of social activities and clothing on each other.

(2) To use the knowledge of the psychological effects of clothing on individuals in making clothing choices.

(3) To determine ways of identifying clothing needs of different individuals.

(4) To select styles of clothing and colors in harmony with own personality.

(5) To determine ways that clothing choices are influenced by availability of financial resources.

(6) To identify current fads and fashions affecting teenage clothing.

Although these objectives are not as detailed as possible, they are stated in behavioral terms and give direction to the stating of lesson objectives.

Lesson objectives are stated in terms of precise behaviors. A daily lesson may have one or more than one objective. Sometimes the same objective extends over several days. In this case there may be several supporting objectives. Lesson objectives are the most important of all for they determine the learning experiences, the expected behavior, and the means of evaluation.

A lesson may have concurrent objectives. Frequently there is a cognitive objective, an affective objective, and a psychomotor skill objective. Usually one of these is primary. The objective toward which students know they are working may be to exhibit skill in food preparation and this is the primary objective. The secondary cognitive objective would be to identify principles of food preparation. The secondary affective objective might be to exhibit pride in preparing a meal.

A lesson may have two or more sequential or related objectives. This would result from two or more activities occurring in a day and each would require an objective. For example "to analyze the behaviors observed in children at the nursery school by relating to age, sex, and personal qualities" and "to determine criteria for selecting toys from those in the department for a child of a given ability and age." The first objective would be tied to a previous nursery school visit and the second to the next visit when the students would be playing with the children.

Individual students may have different daily objectives when individual instruction is being given, such as in a clothing construction class. All of the objectives will eventually be reached by each student but not on the same day. An individualized progress chart helps students as well as the teacher to know which objective each student is to accomplish that day. Objectives for a day may be set up for two or more groups. This occurs in large foods classes when one group is preparing food, one evaluating their performances, and the third group planning their next laboratory lesson. Again all objectives are eventually accomplished by all students.

A daily lesson objective should meet all the requirements described in the other sections of this chapter. It should state the expected behavior and define the performance criteria wherever applicable. Each teacher must decide for himself exactly how much he wishes to state in his objectives. Somewhere and somehow he has to decide the level of expected behavior that is acceptable and which method or technique will be used for evaluating the behavior. If he does not include this in the statement of objectives, he should state it somewhere else and in a way that indicates the relationship. It takes time to state daily objectives but it saves time in getting the class under way and in evaluating the progress of students. Daily objectives are worth all the time and effort they take to state in behavioral terms.

Summary

This chapter will be summarized as guidelines for teacher action. In establishing proper modes and devices of evaluation, the teacher should do the following.

- use key words to point up the major purpose of an objective;
- select verbs for objectives that denote action upon the part of students;
- pair appropriate receiving nouns with action verbs;
- use key verbs that denote knowledge, judgment, or problem solving in intellectual skill objectives;
- use key nouns that denote values, attitudes, appreciations, and relationships in objectives for personal qualities;
- focus upon products, performances, and conditions in objectives for homemaking skills;
- relate chosen evaluation method to intent of objective;
- use written tests to evaluate intellectual skills rather than personal qualities and homemaking skills;
- use descriptions of situations as a basis for evaluating problem-solving ability;
- evaluate personal qualities with observational devices and reporting forms;
- evaluate performance of homemaking tasks by using observational devices;
- use appropriate criteria for selecting each method of evaluation;
- develop a grid for each unit or course of instruction and use as a preplan for evaluation;
- develop a grid for each written test that is consistent with the time spent on each concept.

STUDENT ACTIVITIES

1. Write objectives and underline the verb that reveals the major intent for each
    of the following:
    a. knowledge
    b. judgment
    c. problem solving
2. Write objectives and underline the noun that reveals the major intent for each
    of the following:
    a. values
    b. attitudes
    c. appreciations
    d. relationships
3. Write objectives and underline the verb and the noun that reveal the major
    intent of each of the following:
    a. products that result from a homemaking skill
    b. performance of a homemaking skill
    c. conditions created by a homemaking skill
4. Name one appropriate technique for each of the ten objectives in the preceding
    three questions.
5. Develop a grid for:
    a. an objective test
    b. an essay test
    c. a course of study
6. Select an area of home economics which you are teaching, have taught, or may
    teach and state:
    a. course goals
    b. unit objectives
    c. concepts that accompany the unit objectives
    d. objectives for five consecutive lessons

REFERENCES

Arny, Clara Brown. *Evaluation in Home Economics.* New York: Appleton-Century-Crofts, 1953.

Ahmann, J. Stanley and Glock, M. D. *Evaluating Pupil Growth.* New York: Allyn
and Bacon, Inc., 1959.

Gronlund, Norman E. *Measurement and Evaluation in Teaching.* New York: The
Macmillan Company, 1971.

Gronlund, Norman E. *Stating Behavioral Objectives for Classroom Instruction.* New York: The Macmillan Company, 1970.

Hall, Olive A. and Paolucci, B. *Teaching Home Economics.* New York: John Wiley and Sons, Inc., 1970.

_____. "The Challenge in Evaluative Procedures *"Illinois Teacher* VII, no. 4, pp. 176-85.

_____. "How Do You Evaluate?" *Tips and Topics in Home Economics* III, no. 2 (Spring 1963), p. 8.

Chapter 4 STUDENT PARTICIPATION IN EVALUATION

The students of today are more interested in determining their own worth and direction than any previous generation of students. They want to select and even insist upon selecting their own goals, values, and modes of behavior. Perhaps the greatest educational service we can provide the homemakers of tomorrow is skill in setting and evaluating their own goals. This chapter will discuss various reasons for student participation in evaluation as well as how to involve students in determining objectives, selecting means of evaluation, and evaluating their own progress.

Reasons for Participation

The greater the extent of participation by the student, the more valuable the evaluation is likely to be—valuable in terms of psychological security, recognition, personal satisfaction, and increased learning.

A student develops a feeling of psychological security when he participates in his own evaluation. Knowing what to expect helps prepare all human beings to participate and to accept the results of a new experience. The students are more at ease with themselves in knowing for what they are accountable, and the possibility of having disappointed students and irate parents is greatly lessened.

Student participation lessens fear of failure. The student will most likely make a greater effort to improve when he recognizes his own failures. There is no way for a student to be unaware and also afraid of failing if he is participating in his own evaluation. A student feels more secure when giving reports to his parents if he has assisted in his own evaluation. He has had time to prepare his parents for the kind of report he will bring home. The very fact that his reports will probably be better because of his participation gives him a psychological advantage.

Evaluation becomes a more pleasant experience when a student possesses a sense of security. It would be foolish to say that all students enjoy evaluating themselves for no one likes to admit inadequacies, but most persons do experience pleasure as well as security when they decide how far they have progressed toward obtaining their goals. No doubt you have enjoyed taking some tests or using some devices but have felt very insecure in answering others. However, you would be the first to admit that evaluation is more pleasant and satisfactory when the student is participating than when the evaluation is done only by the teacher.

Student evaluation makes learning more significant. Whenever students are involved in determining their own progress toward objectives, they recognize the importance of what they have learned. Frequently they also become aware of what they have not accomplished and what else they need to do. Self-evaluation by students as well as their involvement in cooperative evaluation promotes an awareness of the relevance of what the class has been studying.

Students are frequently motivated by the process of evaluation. One home economics teacher found a progress chart an excellent means of motivation in a clothing construction class. Each student made a concerted effort to keep pace with his classmates. Another teacher used a similar technique in a senior family relations class except that each week each student compared his participation with that of the previous weeks. Periodic evaluation of progress toward an objective tends to spur a student to greater effort.

Evaluation promotes classification and acceptance of instructional objectives. Techniques such as pretests, questionnaires, checklists, and interest inventories are invaluable in evaluating the current status. This information can be used with students in determining objectives and establishing "benchmarks." An awareness of needs and interests becomes apparent with students involved in evaluating what they do and do not know and what they can do.

Involvement of students in the entire process of learning can be stimulated by the process of evaluation. This involvement can begin with the establishment of objectives based on evaluation data and can progress through the final evaluation of the accomplishment of objectives. A teacher must be sincere about the involvement of students in the evaluation process.

If he is not, he will probably discover that his students have lost both interest and faith.

Evaluation can become a successful teaching-learning technique. A student teacher once commented to this author that she would not have much time to teach if she spent as much time evaluating as was recommended. If you had been in my place, what would have been your answer?

A vital part of the teaching-learning process is the setting of personal goals. Much has already been said about evaluative data being the basis for instructional objectives. Even more could be said about the personal goals of each individual student. Evaluation of the student's status at the beginning as well as at the end must involve what has been learned. The skill in determining personal goals must be developed through the various learning experiences directed by the teacher.

The understanding and acceptance of desirable standards is a teaching-learning process to which evaluation can make a tremendous contribution. No doubt you have used rating devices, illustrative materials, and pictures of products to help students recognize characteristics that are considered top quality. By the same process you can help students decide what their own personal standards for a product or a performance are. It is doubtful that any other kinds of experiences would be as effective in teaching and learning about acceptable standards.

Evaluation is frequently a relearning process. Students can be guided to see the gaps in their own learning and to take the necessary steps to learn what they do not know. A test that is not used as a teaching technique has lost much of its potential value. This would mean the student should not only see the results of the test but also be given an opportunity to be retaught the information covered by the test. A teacher who does not share the results of an evaluation device or test with students has denied them involvement in evaluation as well as the opportunity to learn.

Decision-making skill and ability to make judgments should be two very important results of instruction in home economics. Evaluation involves both of these to such a degree that it would seem almost impossible to develop these skills without student participation. These two skills will be sufficient reasons to have student participation not only in their own evaluation but also in the evaluation of others.

Students can receive personal satisfaction from participating in the evaluation process. Perhaps this is the most important reason of all for involving students in their own evaluation. A feeling of worthiness can encourage persons of any age and ability to do more and try harder. This should say to you that evaluation techniques should be selected with student satisfaction as a criterion.

Evaluation results can provide recognition for student accomplishments. The more able students almost always experience recognition in the evaluation process. It is up to you as the teacher to select some evaluation techniques that will provide recognition for students of lesser ability. An idea for you to ponder is selecting evaluation techniques that parallel the abilities of your students. An example would be an attitude rating device that parallels the ability of the slow learner who makes a maximum effort. Another device for participating or work habits could also match with this student's best quality. All too often the recognition is given only to those who do well on tests.

A feeling of independence can result from student participation in the evaluation process. The student who has identified an objective and a means for evaluating it can proceed independently. Since students will not always have the guidance of a teacher, it is important for them to be self-directive. Evaluating one's self can promote independent action now and in the future.

The evaluation process is designed to reveal the degree of goal attainment. A student experiences satisfaction as he determines how well he has met his objective and the teacher shares this satisfaction with his students. He also experiences a feeling of personal satisfaction for his own teaching success. Personal satisfaction may not be the most important aim of a teacher but it does compensate for whatever failures and frustrations he may experience.

Determining Objectives

A teacher's philosophy of teaching and of evaluation determines the degree to which he involves students in the process of determining objectives. If you believe that students learn more when they assist in the setting of course objectives, you will involve them to the maximum degree. If you believe that students should evaluate their own progress and achievement, you will provide the means for them to evaluate their selected objectives.

Preplanning by the teacher insures appropriateness of objectives. One of the reasons that many teachers do not involve students in determining objectives is that they feel that inappropriate objectives will be selected. Another reason is that they do not have the knowledge and skill needed to guide students in determining the correct objectives.

The first step in preplanning is determining one's own objectives for the class. The danger that exists in this procedure in the inclination to consider these objectives as final and to steer students to accept them. This may be appropriate for certain courses at advanced levels but it eliminates student participation which is very essential for their growth. High school courses that are comprehensive and units of courses in the areas of relationships and management should almost without exception be based on student-determined objectives. Your own objectives may be formulated by you, selected from curriculum guides and textbooks, or adapted from these sources.

The second step in preplanning is deciding how to involve students. When I teach a college course I frequently give to the students the objectives and ask them to delete, add, and modify. When I taught in high school I went to class with a plan for involving students and for determining objectives. Without a plan it is possible to arrive at objectives that are not educationally sound. One young teacher who was beginning a foods unit asked her students what they wanted to learn and the answer was to cook hamburgers and french fries. If she had planned her procedure the students would have probably arrived at a wider scope but one which included their current food fads.

Flexibility must be provided in the preplan. Even if you are a very young teacher, you may discover that your students have interests and needs that you have not recognized. Each group of students is different from every other group and therefore has different ideas and objectives. One teacher found that jotting down ideas rather than formulating objectives helped her to be flexible in accepting student ideas. Flexibility is an *attitude* more than anything else. It is being willing to listen to students, to accept their ideas as worthy, and to give up those ideas that are vital to you but not to your students.

Setting the stage for determining objectives provides a direction for students. This is as important as preplanning. If objectives selected by the students are not realistic in their approach, you may be guilty of not setting the stage for determining objectives. Below are a few ideas for preparing students to decide what they want to achieve in a course or unit.

The scope of the course or unit needs explaining and is an important phase of setting the stage. Every course or unit at any level has limited content and may also have physical limitations. If you teach in a middle school or junior high, you are obligated not to encroach on home economics offerings at the senior high school level. If you teach in a department shared by two or more teachers, the use of the laboratory space may be a limitation. State, county, or city curricula may more or less dictate the scope of a unit or a course. Any and all limitations as well as the possible scope need to be outlined to students before deciding upon the objectives.

Collected data should be presented to students as a part of setting the stage. These data can include student interests, needs, abilities, and prior experiences. Knowledge and skills held are also a part of the data you can use in setting the stage for determining objectives. A pretest can be used which may be either objective or essay in form. Observational devices, reporting forms and audio-visual techniques can help you collect data about interests, needs, abilities, and previous experiences. These data can be collected before school convenes or on the first day and should certainly be available before objectives are identified.

The collected data can be used for stating objectives. For example, one teacher gave a pretest on food preparation and meal planning on the first day of class. She also asked students to indicate on a checklist those responsibilities for food preparation they assumed at home. The next day she presented the tabulated data from both the pretest and checklist to the class. It was obvious where the gaps existed and thus made stating of objectives much easier.

Objectives should be stated in terms understandable to students. All too often teachers are inclined to change student ideas into educational jargon or pedagogy. This is the way these teachers have stated objectives for their college instructors and even their supervising teachers. As acceptable as these terms may be, they do not communicate as effectively to students as does their own language.

Frequently the students' words are more meaningful than those of the teacher. A student might suggest learning why some children grow faster than others. The teacher would probably have the urge to state the objective as "to identify the factors that influence the growth rate of children." Both statements have the same intent but the one in student language communicates better to the class members. You will want to *control* the urge to restate the student objectives.

Objectives communicate effectively when stated in terms of behavior that is observable. Students do understand when the objective is to construct a dress, prepare a meal, plan a budget, solve a relationship problem, or guide the play of a small child. They may understand to a lesser degree when the objective is to develop skill in clothing construction or to understand why people cannot get along together.

Objectives should be concise and precise if students are to understand their intent. This really means to cut out all unnecessary words and to say exactly what is meant. Objectives that are vague, long, or involved tend to confuse and frustrate students. Double objectives are also confusing and may cause half of the objective to be ignored. An example would be "to construct a garment and evaluate its quality and worth." Although concise and related, two processes are involved. Using two separate objectives would be less confusing for students.

Selecting Evaluation Techniques

The step in student participation that follows the determining of objectives is the selecting of evaluation techniques. These should be selected to meet certain identified criteria.

The chosen evaluation techniques should be appropriate for the objective. The first step in keying techniques to an objective is to point out to students the major intent. Words such as *perform, construct,* and *prepare* indicate a product. Knowledge can be revealed through terms such as *identify, recall, name,* and *recognize.* These are verbs but the nouns that follow them also indicate the intent of the objective: *Identify the problem, prepare a meal, construct a blouse, set a table, thread a machine,* and *select the equipment.* These words not only identify the intent but also provide clues for technique selection.

The second step is to identify all possible appropriate techniques. For example, "to prepare a meal" can be evaluated by a checklist of work habits, rating scales for the various foods, an objective test for principles, and a summary of satisfactions and dissatisfactions. Not all objectives have this many choices and some have even more. Students need to be made aware of all the possible alternatives.

The third step is discussing each technique before making a final choice. It is important for students to know the advantages of one over another and also to become aware that they can choose more than one technique for an objective. The key to selection must be the appropriateness of the technique for the purpose or intent of the objective.

The chosen evaluation techniques should provide for self-evaluation. This criterion is vital if student participation is to be an inherent part of evaluation. The next section gives more specific suggestions for guiding students to do self-evaluation.

A technique should be understandable if students are to use it. This means that the directions should be simple as should the wording of the characteristics that are to be evaluated. A complicated device makes self-evaluation a difficult process for even the most able students. You may find the time well spent in demonstrating the use of each device before using it.

A technique should demand no more skill than students possess. Self-evaluation is a skill that must be developed. Observational devices are the techniques that best lend themselves to self-evaluation. These are described and illustrated in Chapter 11. The simplest of these devices is the checklist, then the rating scale, and finally the scorecard. It is best to use checklists with beginning students and slow-learners. Once a student has gained skill in evaluating himself using a checklist, he is ready to use a rating scale or a scorecard.

The chosen techniques should increase decision-making and judgment skills. The major purpose of self-evaluation is to increase decision-making and judgment skills and any teacher would be remiss if he did not choose devices that would accomplish this end. The difficulty of the device as indicated in the previous paragraph is one clue to increasing these skills. Another clue is discussing with the student his decisions. Needless to say, skill is increased by continuous experiences. In other words, provide devices for students to do self-evaluation as frequently as possible.

Variety should be considered when selecting evaluation techniques. This criterion is easy for the teacher to consider but more difficult to guide students to consider. Sometimes all that is needed is a casual comment such as "We have used that device so many times, let's find another and more interesting one." It is important to have variety in order to provide for different abilities, obtain scores for grading purposes, and prevent boredom.

A variety of techniques can be an effective means of providing for students with different abilities within the same class. Observational devices usually result in higher scores than do written tests. If both are included in the evaluation procedure, both students who are very able and those who are not have somewhat the same opportunity to excell.

A variety of techniques is needed in order to obtain scores that contribute to a grade. You will most certainly use evaluation techniques that cannot be used for grading purposes. Most of these are more useful for self-evaluation than are techniques that contribute to a grade. If you are fortunate and are not required to give grades, this is not a necessary criterion. However, most teachers are expected to assign grades at the end of a specified period of time. Grades are more representative if they are based on a number and variety of scores.

A variety of evaluation techniques prevents boredom. Self-evaluation as well as teacher evaluation tends to become routine unless there is a variety. Using the same device over and over is not only tiresome but also tends to become automatic. A variety provides for development of evaluation skills since each technique requires a somewhat different process of decision making.

SELF-EVALUATION

A realistic appraisal of one's own worth is probably the greatest benefit of self-evaluation. A twin benefit is that a person can determine his own direction and chart his own actions as a result of realistic appraisal. Self-evaluation should have cooperative evaluation as a partner. Cooperative evaluation may involve the teacher, peers, parents, or school officials. In terms of self-evaluation, it is more often than not a joint process between a student and the teacher. Self-evaluation by pupils involves, besides cooperative evaluation, development of instruments, scoring of devices and tests, and determination of a grade.

Students can participate in the development of instruments for self-evaluation. This process can be built into a series of learning experiences without any difficulty. Perhaps you are concerned about the quality of such instruments since you may be unsure of those that you develop. Truthfully, you can develop rating devices with your students as effectively as those developed, validated, and tested for reliability by a group of experts. As you follow the steps outlined in the next paragraphs, you must remember that your major purpose is student participation.

The first step in student-teacher development of a rating device is listing the criteria or characteristics. This may be done by the class and placed on the chalkboard in the order named. Arranging in a logical order is relatively simple and can be done by numbering the list on the board. These characteristics may be for a particular behavior such as work habits, classroom behavior, dating behavior, lab habits, or food preparation activities. This kind of list may easily be developed into a checklist. If students are skilled in this process, you may guide them to write two or more descriptions for each characteristic with the results being a rating scale. The third type of device is a score card which would necessitate deciding on a total value for each characteristic. Chapter 11 describes the development of these three observational devices in more detail.

The second step is writing directions and providing space for recording answers. You may decide to do these without the assistance of students although it is to their advantage to participate. In order to save time and to demonstrate to students how to write directions, you can do this on the chalk board after the characteristics have been named. Once skill has been developed, you can ask students to rework the directions and to suggest how to record the answers. A copy of this can be made for you by the "secretary for the day." You are now ready to reproduce the device in sufficient quantity for class use.

The third step is trying out the device to see if it works. One way is to ask two or three of your students to use and criticize the device. These students might be in the class that developed the device or in another but similar class. Teachers who have student aides can use them for this purpose. Another possibility is to ask other home economics teachers to review the device and make suggestions. Reviewing it yourself after it is "cold" is also an excellent procedure for improving the wording.

Students can participate in the scoring of devices and tests. This is in truth the very essence of self-evaluation. Most observational devices, like those described in the previous section, are designed for rating one's own performance. It is much easier to permit students to use these devices than it is to score their own test papers.

Scoring of own devices and tests by students has both advantages and hazards. The major advantage is the learning that takes place. Another important advantage is the self-understanding that can result. A hazard, the possibility of inaccurate rating, can be remedied through cooperative evaluation. Cheating is frequently considered a hazard in scoring one's own test paper. The advantages far outweigh this particular hazard which can be eliminated through properly setting the stage.

Guidance of the self-evaluation process is essential if the maximum is to be achieved. One of the deterrents to this process is the stress frequently placed on grades. Your first job may be to relieve students of any anxiety they may have about passing. If objectives are realistic and evaluation techniques appropriately chosen, all students should be reasonably successful. This philosophy can permeate class activities to the degree that students lose their feeling of possible failure. Students can be motivated to be honest. A class code is a possibility but many home economics teachers find this unnecessary. They simply let their students know that they expect honesty and they receive it.

Scoring by peers is a process similar to self-scoring, and is very appropriate in group work such as food labs, oral reports, clothing labs, and class discussions. Teachers frequently ask two girls to evaluate the food preparation procedures carried out by two other girls. Since the process is reversed the next day, the two evaluators are apt to be honest as well as generous. You may feel as I do that a test paper should not be scored by another member of the class. The only advantage is to the teacher who gets the papers scored more quickly than if she did the scoring. The decision to have peers do the evaluating should be based on whether or not the evaluator is learning by the experience.

Students can participate in the determination of a grade. They can participate in determining a grade for a paper or a unit, for a day, week, semester, or year. The proper guidance and preparation can make the process of grade determination one of the most satisfying for both the student and the teacher. There are at least three steps that you might follow as you direct students in determining their own grades.

The first step is deciding which scores will contribute to a grade. This could have been done when you and your students were determining how to evaluate each objective. A guideline which you may wish to use is to have at least one grade for each objective. One teacher who has to assign quarterly grades attempts to have an average of two per week. You should involve students in deciding your guidelines whatever they happen to be. If this step has been taken earlier all that is now needed is a review to see if any scores need to be deleted or added.

Sometimes it is necessary to decide whether to weight a score or not. Experts frequently say that if there is a large number of scores weighting is not worth the effort. You might take the hint from your students as to whether or not to let one score count more than others. If they feel that this should be done, you would be wise to follow their suggestion. There is no need to lose their faith in this procedure by overriding their suggestions unless absolutely necessary.

The second step is for students to total their own scores. A prepared sheet may be very helpful. A similar procedure is to write on the chalkboard the names of those evaluation instruments whose scores are to be used. Students can make their personal copies and record their own scores. Once this is done they need to total their scores. This may require a conversion of scores so that they are in the same form. Both summary sheets and methods of recording scores are explained and illustrated in Chapter 16.

The third step is making a decision about a final grade. This step can be very simple unless the grade hits a borderline. An example is a student who had five As and six Bs on her summary sheet for a quarter grade. She felt that her improvement and effort deserved an A rather than a B. She wrote her justification with which the teacher agreed. The teacher could have made this decision but you must agree that it was more beneficial for the student to make the decision herself. This step may call for a conference to reach a final decision.

COOPERATIVE EVALUATION

Cooperative evaluation is a logical concurrent process to self-evaluation. *Cooperative* means two or more persons working toward the same goal in a concerted joint effort. If evaluation is to be a teaching-learning process, it has to be by nature a cooperative enterprise. This cooperativeness must begin with determining objectives and proceed through all evaluation processes to determining the final grade.

There are several techniques which are helpful in doing cooperative evaluation. One is providing columns for both student and teacher scores on observational devices. This provides a means of reconciling differences and of helping students to do realistic self-appraisal. Student-teacher conferences are almost an essential for effective self-evaluation. You may use observational devices, tests scores, reports, home-degree projects as well as other evidences as a basis for the conferences. Students summary sheets are also more effective when cooperatively used. Both summary sheets and student conferences are discussed in the final chapter. The individual student folders is another aid to cooperative evaluation and this is explained in Chapter 15.

There must be an accepting attitude on the part of both the student and the teacher if cooperative evaluation is to be effective. The student who feels rejected, disliked, or unsuccessful will be defensive and unwilling to talk freely about achievements and failures. Although this attitude must exist on the part of both, it is up to the teacher to set the mood. There is a procedure called the "sandwich method" which is first to be complimentary, second to be critical, and finally to be encouraging. This method provides a means of building confidence, denoting shortcomings, and pointing to future successes. An accepting attitude may well be the secret to student participation in both self-evaluation and cooperative evaluation.

Summary

Student participation in all phases of the teaching-learning process is vital. The following are principles which the effective teacher must accept and practice in the pursuit of satisfactory student participation in evaluation:

- the greater the extent of participation by the student, the more valuable the evaluation is likely to be;
- a student develops a sense of psychological security when he participates in his own evaluation;
- student participation in evaluation makes learning more significant;
- students are often motivated by the process of evaluation;
- student participation in evaluation can be a successful teaching-learning technique;
- acceptance of desirable standards can be furthered by student evaluation;
- students gain decision-making skill when participating in evaluation;
- preplanning by the teacher insures appropriateness of objectives;
- collected data provide a base for determining objectives;
- student language should be used in stating objectives;
- the chosen evaluation techniques should be appropriate for the objective;
- the chosen evaluation techniques should provide for self-evaluation;
- a technique should demand no more evaluation skill than the student possesses;
- a variety of techniques can provide for different student abilities;
- a realistic appraisal of one's worth is probably the greatest benefit of self-evaluation;
- students can participate in the development of instruments for self-evaluation;
- students can participate in the scoring of their own devices and tests;
- teacher guidance of the self-evaluation process is essential if the maximum is to be achieved;
- students can participate in the determining of a grade;
- cooperative evaluation is a logical concurrent process to self-evaluation;

– an accepting attitude on the part of both teacher and student is essential if cooperative evaluation is to be effective.

STUDENT ACTIVITIES

1. Select five of the above statements with which you strongly agree and write a paragraph for each explaining the intent of the belief.

2. Select five of the above statements about which you have some doubt and explain why you do.

3. Select five of the above beliefs and explain how you would implement them.

REFERENCES

Arny, Clara Brown. *Evaluation in Home Economics.* New York: Appleton-Century-Crofts, Inc., 1953.

Ahmann, J. Stanley and Glock, M. D. *Evaluating Pupil Growth.* New York: Allyn and Bacon, Inc., 1959.

Jarrett, James L. "The Self-Evaluating College Teacher." *Today's Education* (January 1969), pp. 40-41.

Hall, Olive A. and Paolucci, B. *Teaching Home Economics.* New York: John Wiley and Sons, Inc., 1970.

Williamson, Maude and Lyle, M. S. *Homemaking Education in the High School.* New York: Appleton-Century-Crofts, Inc., 1961.

Chapter 5 CHARACTERISTICS DESIRED IN EVALUATION PROCEDURES

Five concepts comprise the basis for the characteristics considered to be desirable in evaluation procedures: usability, objectivity, discrimination, reliability, and validity. Each of these will be defined, discussed, and related to a philosophy of evaluation. These five concepts will be referred to in many of the other chapters and in a context that will become most applicable to you and your evaluation procedures.

Usability

To the home economics teacher, the least sophisticated but probably the most important of these five concepts is usability. Usability implies convenience, availability, serviceability, advantage, and practicality. It involves administration, scoring, cost, and application of data.

Usability is increased by ease of administering a test or other evaluation devices. As a teacher you are naturally concerned with administering a test or a rating device with a minimum amount of frustration. You want your students easily to grasp what they are to do and to leave the class with a feeling of satisfaction. An easily administered test satisfies all three of these concerns.

A test that can be given by persons with limited training in administering tests possesses usability. Compared perhaps to a guidance counselor, you have probably had little or no training in test administration. You may sometimes find it profitable for a teaching aide to administer a test for you. As you select or construct a test you should keep this factor in mind.

Simple directions increase the ease of administration and make it possible for untrained persons to give a test or rating device. Directions that are concisely and precisely written are much preferred to directions given orally. It might be desirable to read aloud the written directions for students who are slow learners. An example of how to answer a question increases the degree of simplicity and understanding. You might fieldtest directions by asking several students not in your class to read them for clarity.

Evaluation devices keyed to time allowed increase ease of administration. A test that requires more time than is available makes administration difficult because students are frustrated and want to know how much the penalty will be for not completing the test. An evaluation device that requires less time than allowed causes unrest in the classroom and students tend to doubt its usability.

Ease of scoring an evaluation device increases the degree of usability. A teacher is frequently required to give tests at a specific time and so may be scoring papers for four or five classes in a very brief time. Even when this is not the situation, she will probably have at least one device or test per class per week. This makes ease of scoring imperative.

An inflexible key facilitates scoring. This eliminates subjective decisions which require time and contribute to errors. An inflexible key also contributes to objectivity, another desirable characteristic. The easiest type of evaluation techniques with which to use an inflexible key is an objective test. However, a reasonably inflexible key can be developed for other types of tests and devices.

Answers recorded in the margin or on an answer sheet contribute to ease of scoring. Students may tend to be more accurate when recording the answers in the margin rather than on an answer sheet. On the other hand teachers may prefer the answer sheet when it can be scored on a machine. Answers recorded in various places on a test make accuracy of scoring difficult and require more time for scoring.

Scoring devices help to achieve accuracy and speed. As mentioned above answer sheets can be machine scored. A scoring device can be developed by punching holes in an answer sheet where the correct answer should be. This device is then placed on the answer sheet making counting correct answers very easy and quick. A scoring device to use when answers are in the margin is explained in Chapter 9.

Reasonable cost can determine the usability of a particular evaluation device. This is perhaps the least important of all the aspects of usefulness.

Cost does indeed make a difference but usually a teacher can find a way to reproduce tests and devices regardless of cost. You need to be wary so as to prevent the cost of reproduction from outweighing all other considerations.

Cost of buying standardized tests may be a determining factor in choosing a particular test. If you teach in a school where buying such tests is prohibited, you may reject this as a possibility. Moreover, standardized tests have other disadvantages and the prohibitive cost may be a plus in disguise.

Reproduction of a test may be a cost to consider. Mimeographing or other means of reproduction may be impossible in the school where you teach. Usually a certain number of pieces of paper is allotted to each teacher. Do not fall into the trap of eliminating objective tests because of this rule. One test can be developed with separate answer sheets for each class. Cost of reproduction is a major consideration but not necessarily a deterrent to usability.

Objectivity

Objectivity is the extent to which personal judgment is eliminated from the rating or scoring situation. A test or device is not likely to be fair to students unless it can be scored with reasonable objectivity. The coefficient of objectivity is the statistical measure used to determine the degree of objectivity. There are, however, practices that contribute to objectivity which are discussed in the following paragraphs.

A test possesses objectivity when it can be scored with an inflexible key. This is true only if the answers recorded on the key are correct and if there is only one possible answer for each question. However, objectivity has no meaning unless the test evaluates in terms of a selected objective.

An inflexible key is easily developed for an objective test; the very nature of the questions makes this possible. Multiple choice, matching, and true-false test items have only one possible answer. The short answer items, either in completion or in question form, do not promote objectivity to quite the same degree because the key is likely to contain more than one correct answer. The objective test is certainly appropriately named for it does possess the highest degree of objectivity of all evaluation instruments.

An inflexible key is difficult to construct for an essay test. As you will find in Chapter 7, there are two types of essay tests: restricted and extended response. The restricted response calls for short answers usually of a certain number. An inflexible key is possible for this type of essay question. When you ask for a certain number of a total list, you can put the entire list on the key and accept any on the list. The extended response essay question usually asks for discussion, explanation, or justification. An inflexible key is nearly impossible for such items. This means that other characteristics such as validity and discrimination have taken precedence over objectivity.

A rating device possesses objectivity when different judges can arrive at similar scores. Rating devices are used when observing performance or behavior, as well as when rating products. Rating devices are explained more fully in Chapter 11. Frequently, rating devices are used only by the teacher or in cooperation with the student whose product or performance is being evaluated. Objectivity of devices can be ascertained by comparing the ratings of several judges. However, you may not find this procedure necessary when using rating devices with your own classes.

The more options on a rating device the less likely is objectivity. Some rating scales have as many as seven options and the very nature of people prevents a high degree of agreement among judges. Scorecards frequently have a different number of points for each characteristic. If one item rates as many as twenty-five points, you can readily see how difficult it would be for several judges to reach agreement. It is necessary to have enough options to differentiate—usually three to five.

Precise descriptions increase the degree of objectivity of a rating device. Listing a characteristic with one word does not tell what is really expected; therefore, judges are not as likely to agree and neither are the student and the teacher. An example is the word "crust" on a rating device for a baked product. If the device really promotes objectivity, there will be descriptive paragraphs and preferably more than one. Even though you may not wish to use a panel of judges to determine objectivity, you will want to develop rating devices that insure a degree of objectivity.

Discrimination

Discrimination of a test or other evaluation instrument indicates the extent to which the scores spread the students in a group along a scale. If there is a satisfactory degree of difference between the high-achieving and the low-achieving students, then the evaluation is said to be discriminating. The place of a student with his peers on a scale of scores may be more significant than how he rates against a one hundred percent or some other norm established by a standardized testing procedure.

The degree of discrimination is influenced by the type of evaluation device. It is also influenced by the teaching-learning that has taken place. An evaluation instrument that tends to possess objectivity is usually discriminating. When you read about validity in the last section of this chapter you will understand how that characteristic also influences discrimination.

Objective tests are usually more discriminating than essay tests. The reason is that objective tests tend to produce a wider range of scores than do essay type tests. The inflexible key helps to produce this wider range. A teacher may unconsciously rate students more alike than not when scoring essay questions.

Rating devices tend to be highly discriminating. Perhaps the reason is that there is a range of scores from which to choose. Persons using rating devices tend to compare students in the class and therefore the high-achievers would normally score higher than the low-achievers. Here again objectivity of the instrument influences the degree of discrimination.

Teaching effectiveness can alter the degree of discrimination. One teacher had low scores in a cluster on an objective test. He knew that the students had a range of abilities and that there was another reason for this cluster of low scores. He analyzed each test item, eliminated the very poor items from the test, and tried teaching the same information to the next class in a more effective way. The results were more high scores in a wider range which meant the test was more discriminating.

Discrimination can be expressed in a variety of ways. You will want to choose one that is appropriate for you. If you are one of those teachers who prefers not to use mathematical computations, you will probably choose to look at the range. However, if you enjoy and understand statistical concepts you may choose to compute the index of discrimination or the standard deviation.

A range of actual scores is considered to be a very usable measure of discrimination. A range is the span between the lowest and highest scores. For example, on a test with 120 items the highest score was 108 and the lowest was 59. The teacher felt that the test was reasonably discriminating. On another test of 125 items she had scores of 118 to 98. Since the class contained a range of abilities, she did not consider this test to be discriminating.

Scores can be plotted on a graph so that the range takes on a curved appearance with a high peak that slopes on both sides. The more bell-shaped the curve, the more discriminating the test or rating device probably is.

Standard deviations can be shown on the same kind of curve. The difference is that the curve is perfectly bell-shaped and is called a normal probability curve. By the very nature of standard deviations, a third of the cases in any normally distributed group will fall outside the two standard deviations adjoining the mean. The example of the normal probability curve (Figure 5-1) will help you to understand. If you wish to compute standard deviations, you should consult a statistics reference.

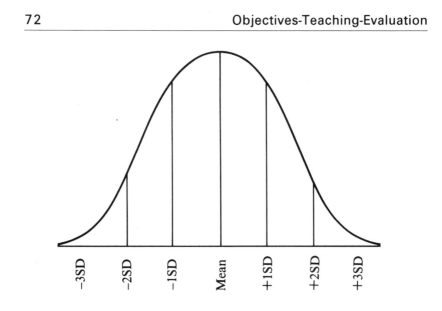

FIGURE 5-1

An index of discrimination can be computed for individual test items. This can be done by comparing the highest fourth with the lowest fourth of the students tested. Percentages of students who answered each item correctly are computed for the top fourth and the lowest fourth of the papers. At least fifty papers should be used if at all possible. The method for computing the index of discrimination is explained in detail in Chapter 10.

Reliability

Reliability indicates the accuracy with which the evaluation instrument measures whatever it is meant to measure. It can also indicate the consistency of the test or device. The reliability of a test can be expressed in terms of the statistic, coefficient of reliability. This is a numerical value which indicates how consistently an evaluation instrument measures whatever it does measure. Reliability can be determined by comparing students' ranks when they are given the same test a second time or by comparing their ranks on the even-numbered items in the test with the odd-numbered items. There are several simple suggestions that can increase reliability whether you compute the coefficient of reliability or not. These are discussed below in four major groupings.

Adequate sampling of content tends to produce tests with high reliability. Short tests are apt to have a low degree of reliability. One of the most effective ways to increase the reliability of a test is to add more items, providing these are of the same kind and quality as those already contained in the test.

A reliable test covers all aspects of the unit, module, or course that has been taught. This is not to say that you cannot test a *part* of a unit or course; rather it means you should not omit any aspect. An example is a unit in food preparation which has many questions on nutrition but few if any on principles of preparation. This usually occurs when it is easier to develop test items for one aspect than another. Chapter 6 explains how to develop a grid which will prevent the omission of important aspects of the content covered.

A test that is limited to one or more closely related content areas is usually more reliable than one which covers several unrelated content areas. Whenever semester examinations are required, it is most difficult to obtain reliability. A test that covers personal money management, clothing selection, and food preparation cannot be expected to possess reliability. Students have difficulty remembering over a long period of time and thus become frustrated. One teacher solved this problem by identifying the unifying concepts in the three units and using those as the basis for problem-solving questions. She used weighing values, decision making, and personal appearance for the three units previously named. This is not to indicate approval of tests that cover more than one aspect but rather to indicate a solution for a required long-range test.

Emphasis should be placed on the most important aspects in order to insure reliability. The emphasis can be readily determined by using the objectives covered in the unit. Another indicator is the amount of time used to cover a particular major objective or goal. A common error is in spending fifteen percent of the time teaching nutrition, sixty percent on food preparation, fifteen percent on buying and storing food, and ten percent on serving food, and then devoting sixty percent of the test to nutrition, twenty percent to preparation, and ten percent to each of the other two aspects. Using a properly developed grid can prevent this situation.

Reliability is influenced by types and quality of test items. The number of types as well as the form makes a difference. Quality of the test is influenced by phrasing, misused words, and terms that are too technical. It is most important for questions to be stated in language that a student can quickly comprehend.

A test with too many test forms will not have high reliability. Each form requires a different set of directions and a reorientation in students' thinking, which in turn affects reliability. Nor is using only one form considered desirable since the students are likely to find the test monotonous. It is generally agreed that three different forms of test items represent the number most likely to produce reliability.

Some forms of objective questions produce more reliable tests than do other forms. The three types that possess the highest degree of reliability are multiple choice with four choices, matching questions that are short and homogeneous, and cluster true-false. The forms that reduce the reliability of a test are long matching questions and ordinary true-false. All of these forms are selection type questions which are discussed more fully in Chapter 8.

Difficulty, discrimination, and objectivity affect reliability. You have already read the definitions for discrimination and objectivity. The paragraphs below will indicate how these two characteristics affect reliability. Difficulty is simply how hard or how easy a test item or a test as a whole is for students to answer. Chapter 10 explains how to determine the difficulty index and the difficulty of a test as a whole.

The majority of items on a test should be of average difficulty if a test is to be reliable. How difficult a test or an item is cannot really be determined until a test has been administered and scored. However, certain forms are considered less difficult than others. Matching of not more than eight and multiple choice are less difficult than most other forms. Reliability is increased when the easiest form is placed first on a test and when test items are arranged according to difficulty within each form of questions.

Reliability is increased when all items discriminate between the high-achievers and the low-achievers. One way to increase reliability is to cull out or reverse items that prove to be nondiscriminating. These would include those that no students missed, those that most students missed, and those that an equal number of excellent and poor students missed.

Lack of objectivity will tend to result in low reliability. Subjective scoring, rating, or ranking may be so highly desirable in some evaluation instruments that lowering the reliability is relatively unimportant. The inflexible key that insures objectivity also increases reliability.

Directions and legibility are major influences on reliability. These determine the speed with which students can answer questions and the degree to which they grasp the meaning of what they are doing. Since reliability indicates accuracy, it is easy to understand how the more quickly and accurately students answer questions the more reliable is the instrument.

The reliability of a test is higher when the directions are clear and adequate. Directions should explain what is to be done, how the questions are to be answered, and where the answers are to be placed. Examples frequently make directions clearer. Key words that are underlined also increase understanding. Poorly reproduced tests are a real hindrance to reliability. Time is lost when corrections have to be read or students need to ask questions for clarity.

A rigid time limit increases the degree of reliability and so does a test that many students do not finish. This is one reason why standardized tests usually have specified times and why people do not finish the tests. Here again, you may wish to sacrifice reliability rather than frustrate your students. If you should wish to increase reliability of a test, you could shorten the time allowed for answering the questions.

Validity

The validity of an evaluation instrument indicates the degree to which it measures what it claims to measure. A valid test or device must be directly related to the objective or objectives upon which the instruction has been focused. A valid instrument measures the extent to which selected objectives have been attained. Validity is the most important characteristic of an evaluation instrument and for this reason it has been left to last. It also involves reliability, objectivity, and discrimination.

Validity may be classified in four types. These types are content, predictive, concurrent, and construct. Each of these has a specific purpose and will be explained in the following paragraphs. Some of these will have more usefulness for you than others.

Content validity is the degree to which the evaluation instrument measures the subject matter content and the behaviors under consideration. It is assumed that the objectives incorporate the subject matter content and/or the desired behaviors. Content validity is of primary concern in determining achievement. The simplest and most useful way to determine content validity is to develop a grid or table of specifications based on objectives and compare the percent of items for each with the percent indicated in the grid. Chapter 2 explains in detail how to develop a grid.

Predictive validity which is criterion-related indicates how well test performance predicts some future performance. The procedure is to compare scores with another measure of performance obtained at a later time. One way you may wish to use predictive validity is to compare an earlier test on scholastic aptitude given to your students with their scores on your test. An interesting and valuable procedure would be to compare test scores with performance as a homemaker several years later.

Concurrent validity is very similar to predictive validity since it is also criterion-related. The difference in test performance is compared with some other *current* performance rather than one in the future. You may wish to compare scores in home economics with scores in another subject matter field such as math, English, or science. A correlation coefficient can be used for both predictive and concurrent validity.

Construct validity is the extent to which test performance can be described in psychological terms. The procedure is to determine experimentally what factors influence scores on the test. For example, you may want to use scores on a test of problem-solving questions not only to predict skill and knowledge in personal relationships but also to infer ability in reasoning or decision making. Construct validity as well as concurrent and predictive validity will not be as useful to you as content validity. However, these are types of validity that you should understand, and you should even consult a reference in statistics to help you when you desire to use one of these.

Caution should be exercised when using the term "validity." This is true in all the above described characteristics of evaluation devices. Perhaps caution is more urgent for validity since it is the most important of all the characteristics.

Validity is a matter of degree. You should refrain from referring to validity on an all-or-none basis. Results are not referred to as valid or invalid but rather in terms of degree. You should use the terms "low validity," "moderate validity," or "high validity."

It is the results of an evaluation instrument that possess a degree of validity. A common error is referring to the test or device as valid. If you wish to be very accurate, it is the validity of the interpretation of the results that you are discussing.

Validity is always specific, never general, in nature. A rating device may possess a high degree of validity for indicating attitude toward food but a relatively low degree of validity for predicting success as a chef. An objective test may be very valid for revealing knowledge of food preparation principles but have a very low degree of validity for predicting interests as a homemaker in preparing food. The most important thing for you to remember is that validity refers to the *degree* to which an instrument measures what it is supposed to measure.

Summary

This chapter has reviewed the characteristics desired in evaluation instruments. For the teacher who realizes the great importance of adequate and appropriate testing and rating devices, the following points will serve as a guide:

- the five basic characteristics of all evaluation devices are usability, objectivity, discrimination, reliability, and validity;

- validity is the most important of all the desirable characteristics;

- an evaluation instrument must possess usability in order for a teacher to find it helpful;

- an instrument that is easily administered is more likely to be used by a teacher;
- simple directions increase the usability of an instrument;
- an inflexible key insures usability, objectivity, and reliability;
- answers recorded in the margin or on an answer sheet increase usability;
- objectivity is the extent to which personal judgment is eliminated from the scoring situation;
- discrimination indicates the extent to which scores differentiate between low-achievers and high-achievers;
- objective tests are usually more discriminating than essay tests;
- rating devices tend to be highly discriminating;
- teaching effectiveness can alter the degree of discrimination;
- discrimination can be shown in a range of scores, the index of discrimination, or standard deviations;
- reliability is the accuracy with which the evaluation instrument measures whatever it does measure;
- adequate sampling of content tends to produce high reliability;
- short matching and multiple choice items are more reliable than are long matching and ordinary true-false;
- the majority of items on a test should be of average difficulty;
- reliability is increased when all items are discriminating;
- directions and legibility are major influences on reliability;
- validity indicates the degree to which an instrument measures what it is supposed to measure;
- validity is more directly related to objectives than any of the other characteristics;
- content validity is the degree to which the evaluation instrument measures the subject matter and behaviors under consideration;
- both predictive and concurrent validity indicate how well test performance relates to future and present performance respectively;
- construct validity is the extent to which test performance can be described in psychological terms;

– validity is a matter of degree ranging from high to low;

– validity is always specific and never general.

STUDENT ACTIVITIES

1. Rate each of the above statements of belief according to the way you believe about each, using a scale of (1) strongly agree, (2) partially agree, (3) do not agree.

2. Write as many conclusions as you can about how you will use the information in this chapter.

REFERENCES

Arny, Clara Brown. *Evaluation in Home Economics.* New York: Appleton-Century-Crofts, Inc., 1953.

Fleck, Henrietta. *Toward Better Teaching of Home Economics.* New York: The Macmillan Company, 1968.

Gronlund, Norman E. *Measurement and Evaluation in Teaching.* New York: The Macmillan Company, 1971.

Hall, Olive A., and Paolucci, B. *Teaching Home Economics.* New York: John Wiley and Sons, Inc., 1970.

_____. "What Is A Good Evaluation Device?" *Tips and Topics in Home Economics* IV, no. 3 (February 1964).

Part II PAPER AND PENCIL TESTS

INTRODUCTION

A paper and pencil test is one of several ways to evaluate cognitive objectives and is the one most frequently used by teachers. It is used to evaluate knowledge and intellectual skills and sometimes to evaluate affective objectives. Although a written test cannot effectively appraise psychomotor skills it can evaluate the principles that accompany these skills. The teacher who is required to administer a test to each of her classes at the end of a grading period finds the written test a useful technique. The two types of paper and pencil tests are essay and objective, each of which has its own advantages and disadvantages.

There are six steps in the process of using a test. The first is identifying the objectives that can and should be evaluated by such a means. The second step is listing the subject matter content the test should cover. The third step is developing a grid or table of specifications that indicates the percent of test items for each objective and content area. The fourth step is selecting or constructing individual test items and arranging these into a test. The fifth step is administering the test, and the final step is analyzing the results.

An essay test is made up of free-response questions to which students compose their own replies. Although all students must record similar answers to essay questions, there will be minor differences in wording, sequence, and even in content. Essay questions are particularly useful for interpreting data and for integrating ideas.

81

This type of question also helps students to think, to express their own reactions, to increase writing skill, and to improve English usage. Essay questions are usually easier for the more able student than for the less able.

The values and limitations of essay questions are approximately equal. The choice of whether to use essay questions rather than objective test items should depend on which is the most appropriate for the objective being evaluated. There may be teacher preferences for the choice that is made which include time available for scoring, ability level of students, and number of students who are being tested. The construction of essay test items is not easy nor does it require the minimum of time that it once was thought to require. There are key words to use and excellent guidelines to follow to insure the quality of essay questions just as there are rules to follow when constructing other types of evaluation questions and devices.

Objective test items can be classified as one of two types. The first type requires the student to supply or recall the answer and the second type requires the selection or recognition of the answer. Examples of supply questions are free-response, completion, and association. Free-response items are sometimes called short answer questions. Examples of selection questions are true-false or alternate response, matching, and multiple choice. Objective tests that are effective are arranged in a logical order, have clear directions, provide spaces for recording answers, and provide for identifying information. As a teacher you will find it advantageous to keep a file of test items and to analyze each as to difficulty and discrimination.

The essay test was at one time considered to be the most desirable, if not the only, method for formally testing knowledge held by students. It was then replaced by the objective test which was considered a much more precise way of measuring the learning that had taken place. At the present time, each has its own function and both are used when appropriate. More time is required to construct an objective test than an essay test but less time is needed to score the papers. The possibility of an inflexible key for the objective test provides for lack of subjective judgment. These are but a few of the advantages and disadvantages of these two methods of evaluating progress toward objectives.

The essay test is the focus of Chapter 6; Chapters 7 and 8 provide information about the supply and selection types of objective test items; Chapter 9 provides guidelines for preparing an objective test; and ideas for analysis of objective tests are contained in Chapter 10.

Chapter 6 ESSAY TESTS

The appropriate time to use essay questions is a teacher's personal decision. Understanding the values, limitations, and major purposes should help you to choose whether or not to give your students essay questions. The two major purposes are interpretation of data and integration of ideas and concepts.

The two forms of essay questions are restricted response and extended response. Examples for each will be given for both the cognitive domain and for personal qualities. Certainly you are already very aware that essay questions can fill in the gap that exists in the affective domain when a teacher has been limiting questioning to objective test items.

Values

Essay questions require the student to express himself in his own words, using information from his own background and knowledge. This is the essence of all the values of using essay questions.

Students are required to express ideas when answering essay questions. If only "pat" responses are needed to answer essay questions, this major advantage is lost. Exact and precise answers should be reserved for short answer recall questions. Essay questions should be designed to elicit a student's own ideas or a synthesis of ideas expressed by others.

Originality is a key element in expressing one's own ideas. Objective test items do not provide opportunities for being original or for expressing even an unoriginal idea. Essay questions can and should capitalize on this opportunity for originality.

Essay questions help to develop the skill of organizing ideas around a central theme. Being able to express oneself so that major ideas are clearly communicated to others is another skill promoted by the essay test.

Expressing ideas is usually done in writing whenever essay questions are used. This provides a technique for developing writing ability and refining the use of correct grammar and punctuation. Perhaps it is not the responsibility of the home economics teachers to teach English but it can provide her with an opportunity to help students further develop this ability.

Essay questions require students to integrate ideas. It is of utmost importance for students to recognize the relationship between what they already know, what they are learning, and how this applies today as well as in the future. Recognizing the relationship of one major concept to another is essential if ideas are to be integrated.

Essay questions permit answers to be qualified. This is certainly not true of any form of objective question where answers are either right or wrong. A student answering an essay question has an opportunity to explain his answer. He may wish to modify, expand, or refute a position implied by the question. As a teacher you may wish to ask essay questions that not only permit but also require students to qualify their answers.

Essay questions allow students to form generalizations that are their own. This is essential for students to be able to transfer learning from one situation to another. Generalizations also expand the retention level of students in a way that memorized and recalled principles cannot. This is one of the major advantages of essay questions.

The proposed problem in an essay question is usually a life-like situation. This enables the student to apply what he has been studying to a situation somewhat like his own. Sometimes essay questions are based on problems identified by the students and the answers may be personal and individual in nature.

Essay questions are adaptable to all areas of home economics. They are particularly appropriate for family and child development where the content is based on the social sciences rather than the physical sciences. Any area where personal values and goals are involved will lend itself very effectively to the use of essay questions.

A minimum of time is needed to construct essay tests. Many teachers choose essay questions over objective test items for this reason. It should be pointed out, however, that it does take time to construct quality essay questions and to determine how these are to be scored.

The preparation of an essay test utilizes very little time or effort when compared to other evaluation techniques. One reason is that an essay test usually contains a limited number of test items, since much time is required of students to answer each question. Directions are usually brief and are prepared for all questions on the test. Sometimes each question is so phrased that directions are included in the context of the question.

Another time saver is that an essay test does not require reproduction in quantity. It is true that some teachers have their essay tests mimeographed so that each student may have a copy. If this service is not available, a teacher usually writes the questions on the chalkboard.

As was pointed out in an introductory paragraph, the choice of whether or not to use essay questions does not depend upon the relatively small amount of time required to construct the questions. The most important value is that students have an opportunity to express and integrate ideas.

Essay questions eliminate guessing on the part of students. This is a decided advantage over most forms of objective questions. A student must know something about the content he is including in his answer. It is true that he can "filibuster" but this is usually discernible by the teacher or anyone else who reads the answer.

Essay questions are also useful for diagnosing incorrect interpretation. Since a student can not effectively guess, errors in understanding become quickly recognizable. This makes it easier to know what to reteach both the individual student and the class as a whole.

Essay questions are discriminating in that they do not permit guessing. A student must know the content covered by the question. The more able student will not only know the answer but also will be able to interpret, organize, and relate the content much more successfully than the less able student.

Limitations

The values and disadvantages of essay questions really cancel each other out. The appropriateness for the objective is truly the only criterion upon which the choice of an evaluation technique can be based. After you read the following limitations, you should be able to recognize when and when not to use essay questions.

Scoring of essay test items tends to be extremely unreliable. There is no way to develop a key that is objective or inflexible. The scoring of essay questions is always subjective and therefore likely to be inconsistent. You, like all other teachers, have no doubt experienced frustration as you evaluated essay questions knowing full well that you had not been able to do this adequately.

Essay questions are apt to be scored differently at various times. The same teacher can rate an essay question one day and again a week later and the scores are more likely to be different than alike. There are many factors that influence the way you score essay questions. One is your fatigue level, another is your mood, and a third is the way you are relating to your students at that moment. All of these factors vary from day to day—perhaps from hour to hour—and there are really few controls that you can exercise to stabilize this fluctuation.

Any two people will score essay questions differently. No one has the same standards or expectations as another person; these may be similar but will vary to a degree. Most home economics teachers do not find this limitation one that they cannot control since no one else will be evaluating the questions. However, when essay examinations are administered as qualifying exams and read by a team of evaluators, this can be a very serious limitation.

Reliability can be increased by following three simple but important rules. The first is to define the objective and relate the essay question to it. The second rule is to establish scoring criteria that are realistic and easy to use. The third rule is to frame the question so that it can be easily understood and so that it clearly states what kind of answer is expected. Specific suggestions for carrying out these three rules are given later in this chapter.

Scoring of essay questions is very time-consuming. This is in direct contrast to objective type testing which can be done quickly and almost without thinking. Students can be used to check objective tests but cannot be expected or permitted to do the same for essay questions. You, the teacher, must assume this responsibility and it does require time if done accurately and fairly.

The inability to develop an accurate and adequate answer key is one of the major reasons scoring essay questions requires so much time. Time is needed to identify the possible or expected answers before beginning to score the questions. Frequently it is necessary to add or delete answers from the original list after scoring has begun. This necessitates rereading and scoring those papers you have already read. This lack of an objective scoring key is not only time-consuming but also frustrating.

The amount of time needed varies with the number of questions, the number of papers, and the fatigue level or alertness of the evaluator. The teacher who has four or five classes which have been given essay tests during the same period of time frequently finds the task an impossible one. The result is hurriedly read papers and inadequate scoring. An essay test should be scheduled only when a teacher knows she has adequate time to evaluate each question effectively. Most teachers who do not use essay questions are greatly influenced by this time factor.

The content that can be sampled by essay questions is limited. The time allotted for an examination in most school situations is an hour or less. Even when more time is available, many students in secondary schools are unable to concentrate on a test for a longer period of time. Since essay questions do require considerable time to answer only a limited number can be asked.

Only a few objectives can thus be evaluated by any one essay test. If a wide variety of evaluation techniques are being utilized this disadvantage can easily be offset. The brief and restricted type of essay question may sample a wider range of content but not permit a great deal of integration of ideas by the student.

The limited sample of content may be a real disadvantage to students. For example, a student may know most of the content covered in a unit of study but not know one or more of the essay questions included on the test. Another student may be lucky and know the answers but very little else. While these are the extremes, they illustrate an important disadvantage.

The inability to evaluate all or most of the objectives decreases the validity of the test. A grid or table of specifications can be developed for an essay test in much the same way as for an objective test. This technique tends to increase the validity of an essay test. A combination of objective and essay questions on one test would also increase validity.

Essay questions may penalize the less able students. Students within the normal range of ability can respond effectively to essay questions but those who are not so capable find this type of testing most difficult. Many of these students have difficulty reading as well as writing. The objective type test is also difficult but not to the degree of the essay test. At least a teacher can read the objective questions and help these students to identify the correct answer.

The less able student lacks the vocabulary to answer essay questions whether asked orally or in written form. He may even lack the vocabulary needed to read and comprehend the question. You may feel that such a student does not belong in a class with the capable students. The truth is that he *is* there and essay questions add one more penalty to those he already has.

The inability to form grammatically correct sentences and to arrange these sentences into a paragraph makes it most difficult for the less able student to answer essay questions. Where even the basics of such skills do not exist, it becomes an impossibility for the teacher of home economics to use essay questions.

The less able student writes slowly. He may be able to formulate a brief answer to an essay question but unable to complete the entire test. He thinks slowly and is incapable of organizing his ideas. The patient teacher may decide to teach some students to organize ideas and thus write with more skill. Many of the less able students cannot master even the rudiments of such a skill.

You may have by now decided that essay questions are not appropriate for slow learners and that you will choose another form for testing them. However, in spite of the limitations of essay questions, they are advantageous for use with most students when evaluating certain objectives.

Restricted Response Items

Essay questions should be used primarily for evaluating those aspects of learning that cannot be measured by objective questions. This should say to you that simply recalling knowledge is not an appropriate use of essay questions. This puts a definite limitation on the use of restricted items which usually require a short answer of a definite type. However, you will find restricted test items useful particularly with students with limited communication skills. Such items can also be preparation for answering the more detailed extended response type of essay question.

A restricted response question should indicate the limits expected when recording the answer. This helps the student to formulate a definite, focused answer to the question and to relate it to the objective being tested. This same limitation makes it easier for the teacher to accurately score the question as well as to predetermine the possible and acceptable answers.

The content is usually limited by restricting the scope of the question. The more specific the question, the more exact will be the answers. Examples are:

1. List the differences in cooking by dry heat and moist heat.

2. Name the advantages of using a meat thermometer.

3. Describe the appearance of a medium rare steak that has been broiled.

4. List the probable physical characteristics of a child with rickets.

The most important aspect of such questions would be accepting flexibility in the wording of answers so as to prevent memorization.

Specifying a number is an excellent way to impose a restriction that is helpful to both the students and the teacher. Frequently, students will ask how many answers are expected. The first example given above could have "three" substituted for "the." The second and fourth examples could easily have a specified number. A teacher would profit by asking for one or two less than the maximum number. Students would not be frustrated by struggling to list every advantage, difference, or characteristic. This too would decrease the tendency to memorize.

The form of the question imposes another restriction. The first major word should tell the student the form for recording the answer. In the examples given above, *list* and *name* indicate outlining of certain points whereas *describe* implies sentences. Because they are in the restricted form all of these imply brief and concise answers.

Space allowed for the answer is another way of limiting the answer. If a test is reproduced in quantity, space for answers can be provided on the same sheet. The major disadvantage is that some students write so large that the space would be inadequate. If that is true, you might just indicate to those students that they can use the same amount of space on the back.

Restricted response items are appropriate for evaluating cognitive learnings. You must remember that the lower levels of cognition can be evaluated very effectively by objective test items. While each of the examples given below could easily be converted, they are recorded to indicate the entire scope of the cognitive domain. As you read each one, critically appraise the possible effectiveness with your own students.

Knowledge and comprehension can be evaluated by using restricted essay questions. Definitions, facts, rules, and criteria can be listed or named to indicate the knowledge held. Comprehension can be requested when students are asked to describe, discuss or explain. The last three examples require comprehension.

1. Define values, attitudes, and goals.

2. List the characteristics desirable in a meal.

3. Describe the behavior of the child you observed at the nursery school.

4. Give an example of conduct that would be considered mature for an eighth grader.

5. Review the steps you followed in making the cake.

Essay questions can be used to evaluate application of knowledge. You probably think of application as being action and, therefore, in the psychomotor domain. You are correct in this but you can also apply knowledge to solve a problem by answering a question. Examples of application essay questions are:

1. Interpret the directions on the guide sheet by stating the next three steps you will take.

2. Using the principle you learned in making white sauce, explain how you would thicken a stew.

3. Explain what you would do if you found a child hurt on the playground.

Application of knowledge questions can easily parallel a skill that has been developed. One danger is in asking students to explain on paper a process that can be more easily and appropriately demonstrated. Examples are threading a machine, putting in a sleeve, making biscuits or muffins.

The analysis level can be effectively evaluated by essay questions. As a home economics teacher you certainly have used analysis questions to evaluate laboratory lessons in both foods and clothing. Case problems are frequently used in family and child development and in management as a basis for analysis. Such questions provide a means for students to link facts and principles to actual situations. The follow examples are designed for the purpose of analysis:

1. Analyze the story about the conflict between Tom and his parents in order to determine the causes.

2. Identify two undesirable characteristics in the muffin pictured and explain what causes these characteristics.

3. Analyze the picture of the living room and list three qualities that make it appear livable and attractive.

The above questions are associated with visual materials but the same kinds of questions can be used with laboratory experiences, field trips, and observations.

Synthesis and evaluation can be achieved through essay questions. These two final levels of the cognitive domain are not always utilized when teaching high school students since they require considerable intellectual ability. Synthesis is the putting together of parts to form a new whole whereas evaluation involves judgments and summarizing. The examples given below are relatively simple and should help you in wording questions at these two levels. The first question is intended for synthesis and the second for evaluation:

1. Think about an imaginary young couple who have just married and are furnishing an apartment; list three major decisions they will need to make.

2. Summarize what you have learned about parent-teenage relationships by listing five guidelines you plan to use in your own life.

These two questions should not be questions used before but should be entirely new to students so that they have the opportunity to synthesize and to judge or to summarize.

Restricted response items are appropriate for evaluating personal qualities. These qualities include values, goals, attitudes, and interpersonal relationships. Since these are qualities that vary from individual to individual, most of the essay questions you or I will use cannot have absolute correct answers.

Essay questions provide an effective technique for weighing values. One of the challenges that teachers of home economics continually confront is helping students to recognize and weigh their values. Since values are personal and individual, it is necessary to construct essay questions that do not have right and wrong answers. This implies that such questions should not be used for grading purposes.

The ordering of values by individual students can be aided by essay questions. Values are arranged in a hierarchical system by each individual and the order of values within this system varies with circumstances. Essay questions can assist students in identifying the position of their values at the current time. It is also possible to help students to see how values vary with the family life cycle. Examples of essay questions that are concerned with weighing values are:

1. Name five values that you hold and then arrange them in order of importance to you.

2. Arrange the following in order of importance to you: an automobile, good-looking clothes, stereo and records, money for dating, a savings account for an education, money for a vacation. Place a zero (0) by any of these that are not important to you.

3. Identify three values that are probably more important to a young married couple than to a teenager. These may be material resources or personal characteristics.

Values are directly related to goals and students need to be helped to recognize this relationship. An essay question can focus upon the establishment of goals based on values held. Another type of essay question can be used to focus upon the ordering of values according to immediate or long-range goals. Examples are:

1. John is graduating from high school, planning to enter college in the fall, and has a job for the summer. He has decided not to go on a week-long trip to the beach with three of his friends although he wanted very much to go. Which of John's goals do you think caused him to make this decision? Which of his values do you think were in conflict and which one did he place first?

2. Mary has identified wearing pretty clothes as one of her top values. Others values she has identified as hers are going to cosmetology school and helping her younger and crippled brother to achieve. Which of these values would involve a long-range goal and which a short-range goal?

These two questions are based on "mini-case studies." Most essay questions related to goals and values would need to be based on such descriptions. The more realistic the case studies or situations, the more your students will be able to see themselves in the situation. The three-way relationship between values, goals, and decisions which is obvious in the above questions should be utilized as you work at wording essay questions for your own students.

Attitudes are observable and can be identified as desirable or undesirable. Frequently a class in home economics identifies the attitudes that are desirable in a classroom situation, at home with other family members, on a date, and in a marriage, as well as in other situations. Essay questions can be used to identify attitudes. The following are examples of such questions:

1. Anna and Tom have been married five years. She is completing her master's degree and expects to go back to teaching next year. Tom drives a truck and delivers soft drinks. Tom wants Anna to give up teaching, have a baby, and live on his small income. Anna will not agree because she knows she will be left at home without transportation and outside interests. What would you say is Tom's attitude toward the role of women in today's society? What is Anna's?

2. Johnny makes poor grades although he is very intelligent. He skips school whenever he has an opportunity. He dresses in unpressed and soiled clothes, rarely smiles, and has no interests or hobbies except playing his guitar. What would you say is Johnny's attitude toward himself?

Another type of restricted essay question that can reflect an attitude is the open-ended question, such as "I dislike reading because _____ __," "I like boys because _____," "I dislike school because ____ _____," and "I dislike sewing because _____."

Interpersonal relationships are very appropriate for restricted response essay questions. Examples are:

1. List five ideas for improving relationships with your parents.

2. Name five suggestions for cooperating with others in your laboratory group.

3. Suggest three ways to make friends in a new situation.

4. Name five ways to improve relationships with younger siblings.

Such questions will be most useful in assisting students to relate to what has been discussed and studied in family relationships. You may not wish to use these for grading purposes.

Extended Response Items

Essay questions that require an extended response provide an opportunity for students to express their own opinions and to organize facts in the manner that they desire. This has the advantages of flexibility, individuality, and creativity. On the other hand, it is most difficult for the teacher to assign a rating or score. Some teachers choose not to use extended response items for this reason whereas other teachers design a scoring system to use.

Extended response items should provide for latitude. If a question does not provide for this kind of flexibility, the major advantage has been lost. A teacher might as well use objective type items or restricted essay if she wants a particular answer reported in a specific manner.

A student should be free to answer a question in his own way. The extended essay should be so stated that a student can pursue the topic in a manner that seems logical to him so long as he can justify his position. This is the major purpose of such questions and you should not only state the question in this manner but also be willing to accept answers differing from the way you would have answered the question.

Extended response questions should evaluate ability to organize ideas. This may say to you that this type of question should be given to students that have the ability to organize and record ideas. The very young or below average students may find extended response too difficult. On the other hand, the older or brighter students will find them challenging.

Suggestions can aid students more effectively to answer extended response items. One teacher reminds students that they have so much time to answer a certain number of questions. She also suggests that near the end of the time allotted for each question, the student write a final paragraph and move on to the next question. Another teacher includes in his directions the suggestion that the student make an outline of major points before beginning to write. These kinds of suggestions prevent frustration and result in better answers.

Cognitive learning can be evaluated by extended response essay questions. The levels of knowledge and comprehension do not lend themselves to use with extended response questions. The other four levels are more appropriate and become increasingly so as they progress through application, analysis, synthesis and evaluation. At least one example is given for each of these levels.

Application of knowledge is frequently evaluated by performance or case studies. Such questions are usually similar to experiences students have had in the classroom. Since skill is developed in answering extended response questions, you will find it helps your students to begin with an application question before trying to answer one that is more difficult. The following is an extended response question at the application level:

1. The following menu was planned to be served as a luncheon to which mothers of the class have been invited.

Baked Pork Chops
Escalloped Tomatoes   Pear Salad
Hot Rolls   Butter
Jello

Explain how the above menu does or does not meet the characteristics of a desirable menu, and tell how you would change it.

The analysis level may be evaluated with a very simple to a very complex question. The example given below is rather simple but, if a new situation for the student, serves easily for the purpose of analysis.

2. Elizabeth is a tenth-grade student. She has an 18-year-old brother and a 13-year-old sister. As long as she can remember, the family has been having trouble meeting expenses although her father brings home $500 a month as a salesman. In addition to their regular household expenses, they are buying their home and make monthly payments of $112. They are paying $90 a month on a car and $105 on a motor boat. They also pay a part-time maid $75 a month to help with the housecleaning, washing, and ironing. There never seems to be enough money for everyone's needs, wishes, and wants. This leads to frequent quarreling and ill feelings. What seems to be the main source of trouble in this family's financial situation? What suggestions could you offer that might help them?

Questions at the synthesis level need to be more difficult than at the two previous levels. They should require putting together two or more concepts. The following could serve as a synthesis question:

3. Jan's husband gave her $92 which he received from overtime work. They need to improve or purchase a chair and sofa for the living room. While the children were small they bought cheap furniture before they were permanently located. The children are now teenagers. Jan teaches and belongs to a credit union. She is now paying $25 per month at the rate of 1% monthly interest on an unpaid balance. This will be paid up in one or two months. What would you advise Jan to do and why?

Evaluation questions frequently are used at the end of a unit or a series of lessons since they involve summarization. The following are questions designed for final evaluation:

4. Describe how you would decorate a living room and list the reasons you chose the furnishings, fabrics, and colors that you did.

5. List and explain five guidelines that a young couple could follow in order to have a happy marriage.

Personal qualities can be evaluated by extended response essay questions. The two areas in which these questions seem to be the most applicable are relationship problems and problems of management involving values and goals. Case studies can provide a base for such questions and insure better results.

A relationship problem usually has several factors that need to be considered. The questions asked should require students to analyze and react to all aspects of the problem. Following are examples:

6. Jean and Jane are twins but are very different. Jean is blonde, feminine and dainty whereas Jane is dark, tomboyish, and athletic. They share a room but

disagree constantly about the condition of the room and the way it is decorated. The twins also differ in the grades they make at school since Jean studies and Jane does not. However, Jane excells at sports and is a star basketball player. What do you consider their major problems and what suggestions do you have for them that would improve their relationship?

Management problems exist throughout life and as a home economics teacher you will want to help students to solve such problems. Extended essay questions are one way to do this. The following is an example of such questions:

7. May and John are planning to be married. May would like to have a large wedding. Her monthly income is $300 before deductions. Her parents have told her they will pay for the reception, but she will have to pay the other expenses. What should May do? What are May and John's long-term goals? Short-term goals? Plan May's wedding for her and include the cost.

Interpretation of Data

Essay questions are perhaps the most successful evaluation technique for interpretation of data. Throughout a person's life he must interpret what he reads, sees, and hears. You, as a teacher, should feel a responsibility for providing evaluation experiences that will contribute to interpretation skill. The essay question provides one way to do this. The complexity of the question can be keyed to the intellectual ability of the class as a whole. Very simple questions can be used with very young students as well as with the less able students.

Essay questions provide a way to test application of principles. The knowledge and understanding of principles provides the base necessary for application of these principles. All too often students are required to recall or recognize a principle without being given an opportunity to make an application. Knowledge in itself is not sufficient for everyday living and it cannot be assumed that students will be capable of making the application without assistance. The essay question is one way of applying knowledge.

Identification of principles that have been used in a process is most appropriate in a home economics class. The area of food and nutrition contains many principles that need identifying. The student who prepares a food without recognizing the principles involved will not readily transfer this learning to another food preparation. Examples of essay questions that identify principles are:

1. Explain the preparation principle that caused your muffins to rise.

2. Identify three principles of preparing green leafy vegetables.

3. List four guidelines for selecting a dress fabric.

4. Name five suggestions for improving brother-sister relationships.

5. List three principles that should help a teenager to better manage his time.

Illustration of principles is a verbal means of application. Illustrations are a part of the comprehension level of the cognitive process that overlaps into the application level. Home economics teachers frequently use illustrations in their teaching. Examples of essay questions that require examples or illustrations are:

1. Give an example of cooperation in a family.

2. Describe a dress that meets the criteria for attractiveness.

3. Explain what happened to the meat when the temperature was too high.

4. Describe a room that illustrates balance.

5. Give an example of poor money management.

Comparison of two situations is a means of applying principles. Comparing is a positive process seeking to identify how two things are alike. Contrasting is the opposite in that the purpose is to determine how two situations are different. Essay questions such as these can be used for this purpose:

1. Compare renting and owning a house.

2. Contrast budgeting and not budgeting by listing the advantages of each.

3. Compare the democratic family with the autocratic family.

4. Identify the possible differences in the health of a person who eats adequately and one who does not.

5. Compare the possible effect a well-groomed person and a poorly groomed person will have on a prospective employer.

These are but a few examples of essay questions that can be used for evaluating application of knowledge. The questions could be the same for students of different ability levels but the expected answers would vary in their complexity and amount of detail.

Essay questions can be used to analyze cause and effect. The reasons why something occurs or does not occur are an essential part of understanding principles. Students can sometimes answer the "why" more easily than recalling the principle. Actually they are identifying the principle but in a life-like situation to which they are relating.

The relationship of an occurence and its cause can be used as a basis for an essay question. Such relationships are frequently used in objective type questions such as multiple choice and cluster true-false. One way to obtain possible alternates for an objective question is to use student answers to the question in essay form. Case problems or situations coupled with essay questions form an excellent evaluating procedure. Examples of essay questions dealing with cause and effect and based on case situations are:

1. Analyze the budget of the newly married couple previously described and identify why it is not realistic; include omissions as well as items which are over or under budgeted.

2. Look at the pictures of two muffins and tell why one is a success and the other is not.

3. Explain why the above illustrated skirt hangs crooked and the floral design leans to one side.

4. Give the possible reasons why the children in the picture who are all nine years old are different in height and weight.

5. List the causes of marital difference that you see as you view the motion picture about June and Tom.

An appraisal to determine what is desirable can be based on the cause and effect relationship. Frequently the same decision is not desirable for all persons. Whenever this kind of choice is the intent of an essay question it becomes necessary to accept the decision and evaluate the causes or reasons for the choice. Essay questions that appraise situations are similar to these:

1. If you were babysitting with a three-month-old baby and he awoke crying, what would you consider to be the cause, and what would you do to make the baby comfortable?

2. If you needed a warm jacket for everyday wear and an outfit to wear to a dance but your money was limited, which would you choose as the most desirable and why?

3. If you were double-dating and the others wanted to go to a place that your parents considered "off-limits," what would you decide was the most desirable action for you?

Essay questions that analyze cause and effect can be based on trends. For example, data indicating the rise in the cost of living could be explained by identifying the reasons. The same type of question could be asked about the marriage and divorce rates.

Essay questions can provide a means for organizing facts in a logical order. One danger of this kind of question is that students may attempt to memorize facts. The ordering of information should be flexible enough so that the process outlined is that of the student. The variations from the teacher's listing should be reasonable and relatively unimportant.

Describing a process is a very adaptable technique in all areas of home economics. The process may be one of management, or of a homemaking task, a manual skill, or a leadership skill. Each of the following examples is designed for one of these purposes:

1. How would you plan to use your time on a day that is free to do as you wish?

2. What are the steps you would follow in cleaning a bedroom?

3. What are the general steps you should follow in making a blouse?

4. What are the steps in conducting a business meeting of a Future Home-maker chapter?

One danger to avoid is asking for details that are too specific to be worthwhile or for a process difficult to describe. For example, does a student need to list the steps in threading a machine in order to use it? My answer is "no" and I hope yours is the same.

Developing a plan requires organization that is realistic. Essay questions would indicate whether or not a student really understood how to plan. Usually such evaluation questions follow rather than precede the actual development of plans. Examples of such questions are:

1. How would you go about planning a home-degree project?

2. What would you include in a plan for a party?

3. What steps would you need to follow to plan a budget?

4. How would you go about making an inventory of your clothes?

5. What should be included in a plan for being well-groomed?

These questions are designed to ascertain the general procedures and could be considered correctly answered if the important elements were arranged in a logical order.

Summarization is a major use of essay questions. To answer such questions requires a skill which must be developed. As a teacher you can begin to help students gain this skill by asking this type of question orally and guiding the class or an individual to answer it. If this is done, it becomes easier for students to summarize on a test.

Listing major points in a discussion, a motion picture, a book, or an article is a standard procedure for almost every teacher. Certainly such a question is adaptable to all areas of home economics. Several examples are:

1. List the major points from today's class discussion about dating.

2. Write down three issues presented in the motion picture either as you view the picture or afterwards.

3. Summarize the major points in the novel you read for Family Development.

4. Outline in brief form the article you read on the teenage drug problem.

The summarization of data can be requested through essay questions. Perhaps one of the limitations of most people is the inability to interpret data and verbalize its meaning. The same technique applies in a lesser degree to reading labels. The following are examples of this type of essay question:

1. Explain the table on ages when marriage and divorce occurs.

2. Interpret in a few sentences the table on education and earning power.

3. Interpret the information given on the label on a can of tomato paste.

4. List what you learned from the hang tag removed from a rain coat.

The stating of conclusions and generalizations has become essential in the teaching of home economics. This is really a technique for summarizing what has been learned that is of importance to the students. A teacher may ask students to state their conclusions about any type of lesson and again at the end of the unit. Stating conclusions is a skill and students need help in learning how to do this. Therefore, you should first do this orally and, preferably, as a class group. Examples of questions are:

1. State in sentences what you learned about preparing tough cuts of meat.

2. What are the conclusions you have drawn about the relationship of food to health?

3. List five guidelines that will help you to decide about clothing purchases.

4. State the major conclusions you have made about parent-teenage relationships.

5. Summarize in concise statements what you have learned about guiding the play of children.

6. State your own conclusions about spending your allowance.

The interpretation of data questions has centered around application of principles, cause and effect, organizing in logical steps, and summarization. These are a select few of the ways that essay questions can be used for this major purpose. You will be able to find many others.

Integration of Ideas and Concepts

A higher degree of intellectual activity is required to integrate ideas than to interpret data. Almost without exception the interpretation of data is a cognitive process. The integration of ideas or concepts is as much if not more concerned with the affective domain as with the cognitive domain. The following paragraphs will attempt to utilize both domains and will focus upon making judgments, weighing values, and solving problems.

Essay questions are appropriate for evaluating the ability to make judgments. Involved in such questions are criteria and standards for behaviors, products, and performances. Knowledge of these criteria and standards is cognitive in nature. The judgment is an intellectual skill that goes beyond mere knowledge and involves to some degree a person's own values.

Judgments are often made in terms of criteria for behavior. The criteria, if personal and not prescribed, represent an integration of concepts from many sources. The teacher concerned with the student not only making his own judgments but also establishing his own criteria will word essay questions in an individualistic manner. Usually such questions are based on described situations such as the following examples:

1. What guidelines would you use to decide what is the thing to do when many of your classmates are planning a protest march without obtaining a parade permit?

2. State the basis upon which you would decide whether or not to attend a party where alcohol was likely to be served.

3. List the reasons why or why not a teenager would choose to cheat on an examination.

There are many questions that might be more appropriate for your students than the ones given above. You would choose those which would have the most meaning to your students and which would reflect the current issues faced by young people.

Judgments in terms of standards for products is an inherent part of home economics. Products in foods, clothing, and housing have always been considered evidence of skills developed in these areas. Evaluation has usually been accomplished by using devices such as checklists, scorecards, and rating scales. Another technique would be essay questions. Examples are:

1. Which standards of an acceptable meal did you meet and which ones did you not meet as well as you would have wished?

2. Identify the parts or units of your dress that are constructed in an acceptable way; then list those parts that could be improved and tell how.

3. Evaluate the room you used for a home improvement project by listing the ways in which you were successful and then naming the activities which were not as successful as you desired.

Standards for performances are as relevant in home economics as are standards for products. Essay questions based on these standards are directly related to the cognitive as well as to the affective and the psychomotor domains. Examples of such questions are:

1. Evaluate your performance as a member of the discussion group by listing the ways an excellent member should participate and indicating how well you performed in terms of the ways you listed.

2. Analyze the way you and your partner worked together in the foods laboratory by stating the behavioral standards you met and those you did not meet.

3. Evaluate your contribution to the FHA chapter meeting by listing first the positive actions you took and second the negative or neutral positions that you exhibited.

Problem-solving skill can be increased by answering essay questions. Probably the most important skill that home economics teachers can develop in their students is that of problem solving. Regardless of the technical and scientific advances that will continue to occur in home economics, every homemaker and every person must make decisions concerning the use of resources and relationships within the family as well as with individuals.

Essay questions can be based on a problem centered in a school situation. Young high schoolers frequently have personal problems to solve or decisions to make. Essay questions can help these young students develop a positive attitude toward and some skill in making their choices. Examples of a school-centered problem are:

1. Jan is making poor grades in chemistry and knows she must find some help if she is to pass the course. What alternates do you think she has? Which one would you choose and why?

2. Tommy is the quarterback of the football team but has difficulty with his history teacher, an older woman who prefers scholarship to athletic excellence. Tommy knows that his attitude is reflected in his insolent behavior and failing grades. He also realizes that he must change the situation if he is to be eligible to play football. What suggestions would you make to Tommy?

Essay questions are appropriately focused upon present day home situations. Similar to present-day school situations, these should be as realistic as possible. Most teenagers have problems involving their parents and their siblings. Questions such as these are appropriate for use:

1. Ken is going to the school dance and sets up the ironing board to press his slacks. His older sister comes into the room, sees him pressing and says, "I'll do that. You shouldn't be ironing!" He returns with, "But you don't press them right. I know how I like them to look." What does this say about this boy's attitude toward the male role? What does this say about his sister's attitude? What do you think could be done to improve understanding between this brother and sister?

2. Jack has just returned home after a Saturday afternoon of shopping. His parents have been upset with his appearance and dress but have not said anything to him. His mother begins the conversation by saying that his hair is too long—he's beginning to look more like a girl than a boy. His father is surprised at the brightly colored and patterned clothes and the necklaces Jack is wearing to school and questions him about them. Jack's father is also

amazed to learn that Jack shops alone and actually enjoys buying clothes. What does this say about him as a person? Does he think of himself as the agressive male in the traditional sense? What are Jack's parents' attitudes about dress and appearance? What probably has influenced their attitudes? What has influenced the development of Jack's attitudes? How do you think these attitudes affect Jack's relationship with his parents?

Present-day social situations can provide a basis for essay questions. Decisions of a social nature that must be made by teenagers are numerous and vary widely. The clue for you is to determine the ones that are the most pertinent for your students and base your essay questions on those social issues. The following are examples of such essay questions:

1. Karen had a date with Tom two weeks ago and hasn't heard from him since. She would like to see him again, so when she goes to her girlfriend's house she decides to call him. Would Karen be right in calling at all? Could she just call and chat, or talk about school work? Should she mention some activities which she would like to attend and hope he will take the hint and ask her out? Could she ask him out if she had been given tickets to a certain show in town? What are the rules? Can a young woman initiate a date?

2. Mary Jane wanted to get a part-time job to earn some extra money after school. Her father has always repaired the family car and Mary Jane watched, helped, and became quite capable. Because she was so skillful with cars she was able to get a part-time job at Carl's filling station. She wears coveralls, pumps gas, greases cars, and generally gets her hands dirty. She enjoys math and physics in school and hopes to go on to college to study to become an engineer. What is your reaction to a girl doing this type of work? What about the way she dresses? How do you feel her parents are reacting? For young men—if you were dating this girl how would you feel? What would your parents' reaction be to this girl? For young women—if Mary Jane were a friend of yours how would you feel about her working at this type of job? Would you do it yourself?

Essay questions can be used to discuss problem situations related to the future. Older teenagers are usually concerned with finding a job, getting married, and achieving adult status. These questions are examples of future-oriented problems:

1. Sally and John have become very serious and plan to get married. Sally's parents disapprove of John because he is selfish and inconsiderate. They are afraid Sally will be unhappy. Sally finds John ambitious, physically attractive, fun to be with, and she is anxious to be married. What should Sally do to help her parents understand why she wants to marry John? What should her parents do to help Sally be more aware of John's undesirable traits?

2. Jim is graduating from high school in June and ranks in the top ten percent of his class. He does not have the money to go to college. He thinks his choices are enlisting in the Marines, borrowing money to go to school,

working his way through college, or waiting to be drafted. What do you think he should do and why?

Essay questions are very valuable in getting students to solve problems by an integration of the ideas and knowledge they possess. If you have a group of students who are not able to answer such questions on paper, you could use these for class discussions. Their uses could range from an initial class activity to a final evaluation.

Suggestions for Test Construction

There are rules for constructing essay test items as well as for a test as a whole. Since these two vary slightly, two lists will be given. Each is as important as the other. You may follow all the rules or decide not to follow one or two. These suggestions are to help you.

If you wish to construct essay questions that are appropriate for your students follow these suggestions:

(1) Use words that are specific such as *explain, contrast, present proof, state conclusions, list guidelines, name steps.*

(2) State the limitations for the discussion of the question.

(3) Use essay questions only when objective questions are not appropriate.

(4) Ask questions that are based on specific objectives.

(5) Phrase questions so that the student understands clearly what he is to do.

(6) Indicate approximate time limits for each question.

The test as a whole should follow these rules:

(1) Select questions that place emphasis on interpreting data or integrating concepts.

(2) State the consideration that will be given to sentence structure, spelling, and punctuation, as well as to subject matter.

(3) Arrange questions from simplest to most complex.

(4) Assign a specific value to each question in advance or state that each question will receive the same amount of credit.

(5) Do not use optional questions except in unusual circumstances.

(6) Provide as many hints or helps as possible so that students do as well as they are able.

Scoring Essay Questions

The following suggestions are made to help you score essay questions more accurately and quickly:

(1) Develop a key by listing major points to be covered in each question.

(2) Decide how much credit each question will receive.

(3) Decide how many points, if any, will be subtracted for spelling and punctuation.

(4) Evaluate one question on all the papers before going to the next question.

(5) Cluster papers into three to five piles ranking from high to low in order to check for similar quality.

(6) Score papers anonymously to prevent subjectivity on your part.

(7) Rotate the order of evaluating papers so that a different paper is rated first for various questions.

(8) Take rest breaks frequently to prevent fatigue and thereby inaccurate scoring.

Summary

This chapter summary will be stated as conclusions about use of essay questions. Essay questions:

- require students to express their own ideas;
- require students to integrate ideas and concepts;
- are adaptable to all areas of home economics;
- do not need to be reproduced in quantity;
- eliminate guessing on the part of the students;
- are helpful in diagnosing incorrect interpretations;
- are usually discriminating because they do not permit guessing;
- tend to be unreliable because an objective key cannot be developed;
- require much time to score;
- sample a very limited amount of the content covered;

- may have limited validity because all objectives cannot be evaluated on one test;
- penalize the less able students;
- provide a means of testing application of principles;
- can apply principles by comparing two situations;
- can be used to analyze cause and effect;
- can be appraised to determine what is desirable,
- can provide a means for organizing facts into a logical order;
- can describe a process;
- are a major means of summarizing what has been learned;
- are appropriate for evaluating the ability to make judgments;
- may be based on judging standards of products;
- provide an effective technique for weighing values;
- can point out the relationship between values and goals;
- can increase problem-solving skill;
- should be specifically stated;
- should be arranged from simplest to most complex.

- may be in either the restricted response or the expanded response forms;
- restricted response items should have limits such as content, number, and form;
- restricted response items can be used to evaluate at all levels of cognition;
- restricted response items are appropriate for evaluating personal qualities such as values, goals, attitudes, and interpersonal relationships;
- extended response items should provide the latitude for students to organize ideas in their own way;
- can be used to evaluate application of knowledge, analysis, synthesis, and evaluation utilizing extended response forms;
- extended response items are particularly useful in evaluating problems involving relationships;
- can be used to evaluate problems of managing resources utilizing the extended response forms;

– should have a key developed for each question;

– should be evaluated by reading one question on all papers before evaluating the next question.

STUDENT ACTIVITIES

1. Explain how the values and the limitations of essay questions cancel out each other.

2. Construct an essay question that interprets data for each of the following:
    a. tests application of principles
    b. applies principles by comparing two situations
    c. analyzes cause and effect
    d. appraises what is desirable
    e. organizes facts in a logical order
    f. describes a process
    g. summarizes what has been learned

3. Construct an essay question that provides for integrating concepts for each of the following:
    a. evaluates ability to make judgments
    b. judges standards of a product
    c. judges standards for a performance
    d. weighs values
    e. arranges values in a hierarchical system
    f. relates values to goals
    g. provides for decision making or problem solving

4. Write a justification for using essay questions.

5. Construct one restricted response essay question for each of the following:
    a. knowledge
    b. comprehension
    c. application
    d. analysis
    e. synthesis
    f. evaluation

6. Construct one restricted response essay question for each of the following:
    a. values
    b. goals
    c. attitudes
    d. personal relationships

7. Construct one extended response essay question for each of the following:
    a. application
    b. analysis
    c. synthesis
    d. evaluation
8. Construct one extended response essay question for each of the following:
    a. personal relationships
    b. management problems

REFERENCES

Ahmann, J. Stanley and Glock, M. D. *Evaluating Pupil Growth.* New York: Allyn and Bacon, Inc., 1959.

Arny, Clara Brown. *Evaluation in Home Economics.* New York: Appleton-Century-Crofts, Inc., 1953.

Gronlund, Norman E. *Measurement and Evaluation in Teaching.* New York: The Macmillan Company, 1971

Hall, Olive A. and Paolucci, B. *Teaching and Home Economics.* New York: John Wiley and Sons, Inc., 1970

Chapter 7 OBJECTIVE TEST ITEMS: SUPPLY TYPES

Test items that require students to remember and record information are supply questions. This is a logical name since the student must not only know the information but also recall it from memory. These items may be classified as free response, completion, and association test items.

Free response and completion are really the same type since the difference is grammatical rather than in type of answer. The free response asks a question whereas completion requires the placing of a missing word or phrase in a blank in order to finish a statement.

Association test items are used for homogeneous material. A list of blanks are filled in by associating one concept with another. Examples are causes to effects, products to uses, stages to ages, and persons to responsibilities.

These three test forms are similar in three ways. First, each requires the recall of information by students. Second, each demands a short answer. A word or a phrase is sufficient to answer the test items but these must be the same as those of the teacher if the answer is to be considered correct. Third, supply test items rarely test for any level of learning other than knowledge of terms, facts, and principles. This means that such items have less flexibility and are limited as to use when compared to recognition and essay questions.

Advantages and Disadvantages
of Supply or Recall Items

Every type of objective question has certain advantages and limitations. This is true of each of the three types of supply test items. Collectively, these items have more limitations than do selection questions. However, their particular advantages make these questions very usable to evaluate certain kinds of knowledge and information.

Supply test items can effectively test in the knowledge area. The requirement of an answer consisting of a word or phrase limits to a great degree the use of supply questions. This may say to you that application of information should be tested using another form of test item. The same is true to some degree for testing understanding of principles and facts. However, teachers frequently wish to test recall of knowledge and when they do may find supply items very useful.

Knowledge of terminology can be evaluated by supply test items. Definitions of terms is basic information which students must know if they are to comprehend and apply principles and guidelines. Selection items, particularly matching, may be used for the same purpose but do not require the same level of knowledge as supply items. Completion and free response are both short answer questions very useful for evaluating knowledge of terms.

Knowledge of specific facts can be evaluated by supply test items. Association items lend themselves to testing specific facts even more so than free response. The facts may be given and the association to other concepts may be recalled by the students. Since the answer must be brief, the fact is supplied.

Knowledge of principles can be evaluated by supply test items. Free response and completion items are frequently used to test knowledge of principles. Supplying the key word that has been omitted in a completion can indicate knowledge of a principle. Providing the answer to a direct question can evaluate a grasp of a principle in the same way.

Knowledge of procedure can be advantageously evaluated using supply test items. Free response is perhaps more adaptable than completion for testing knowledge of procedure. Which step follows another is such a question. However, you must be careful in stating such items to be certain that the required answer is short.

Other types of questions such as recognition and restricted essay are also used to evaluate various bits of knowledge. As a teacher you must decide which is the most appropriate type of test items for the knowledge you wish to evaluate and for the intellectual level of your students.

Supply test items usually contribute to discrimination and reliability. Discrimination, as you remember, separates the more able students from the less able. Reliability of a test indicates its accuracy of measurement and its self-consistency. These two characteristics exist, however, only when tests are well constructed.

Accurate information is demanded by supply test items. A student must know the exact answer provided the item is not so worded that more than one answer is possible. The accuracy of the answer produces a discriminating effect since the better students are more apt to answer the question correctly than are poorer students. The demand for accuracy also tends to increase reliability since the possibility of a variety of misinformation is curtailed.

Guessing is at a minimum when answering supply questions. A student who does not know the answer to a supply question is less likely to make up an answer than he is to randomly choose an answer in a selection question that he does not know. This factor increases both discrimination and reliability. Students who have difficulty with writing, memorizing, and spelling are also not as inclined to guess as students with more highly developed intellectual skills.

Supply questions permit a wide sampling of knowledge. Almost every type of knowledge can be tested by this type of question. This is not true of the more complex intellectual abilities. Terms, definitions, facts, principles, procedures, computations are examples of knowledge particularly adaptable to supply questions. Associating one concept to another is also easily tested by use of such questions. Examples are products to uses, causes to effects, stages to ages, persons to responsibilities, and reasons to actions.

In summary, reliability and discrimination factors are two advantages of supply questions. Usability in testing for knowledge is probably the most important advantage. Supply items are also relatively easy to construct. They are adaptable to almost every subject area and therefore can be used to sample a wide variety of learnings. There are, however, several disadvantages which are discussed in the following paragraphs.

Supply test items require memorization by students. This is considered by many teachers and students to be the chief disadvantage of supply items. The exact term or phrase must be remembered, written down, and spelled correctly. Most students of less than average ability frequently find these questions frustrating and feel that recall questions do not indicate how much they know. Home economics is more often taught by a problem-solving or project procedure which is really inconsistent with recalling memorized information.

Students with limited ability to remember are penalized. Retention of knowledge is an intellectual ability not accomplished by many students who otherwise understand and apply the principles. The author had an experience in her early years of teaching that clearly illustrates this point. A student was unable to name the basic food groups which at that time were seven. She had studied the information in eighth grade health and home economics, and in ninth grade biology and home economics. The student was told she must name these seven groups if she were to pass. This was a foolish mandate for she was unable, after study, to do this. She asked the teacher who in the class planned the best menus and had the best home projects in food preparation. The teacher readily admitted that she did, and needless to say, the student received an acceptable grade without recalling the exact composition of the basic seven food groups.

Students with limited vocabulary are penalized by supply questions. All too often students from the lower socioeconomic level not only have limited vocabulary but also use different words than do the students from a higher level. Furthermore, each culture has words, phrases, punctuations, and "sayings" that are peculiarly its own. These differences make it difficult for students to respond to test items constructed by a teacher whose background is different from theirs. It is equally difficult to memorize definitions, facts, principles, and other items of knowledge since these students must first associate their own terminology with that written in the book and that of the teacher before memorization can take place.

Supply test items are time-consuming in their demand for the exact word. A student may know the answer but have difficulty remembering what it is. All too often a student uses the association technique to remember the words rather than really knowing the information. For example, the three Cs for vitamin C, scurvy, and citrus fruit. A fond memory from my own childhood is using the letters h-o-m-e-s to recall the Great Lakes. Try it and see that it works. Have you ever frantically searched your memory for a particular word? If you have, you know how a student feels when the minutes tick by and the answer continues to evade his memory.

Scoring of supply test items is less objective than scoring of recognition items. This is the second major limitation in the use of test items that recall information. An inflexible key is almost an impossibility. An alert student frequently records an answer that is correct but not the one selected by the teacher. However, it must be pointed out that inflexible keys have been developed for all three types of supply questions. This can occur when the test constructor develops items that can have only one possible answer. Most teachers do not have the ability to construct test items of this caliber.

A variety of answers are possible for many supply items. For example one home economics teacher asked "How long is a yard?" Her answer was thirty-six inches since her class was in a clothing construction unit where one is more apt to use inches rather than feet. Of course this is obviously a poorly constructed item. It does, however, illustrate how difficult it is to word test items that have only one possible answer.

Answers are sometimes only partially correct. This tends to be more the case with questions requiring a phrase than with those needing only one word to answer or complete. Whenever this occurs scoring not only becomes less objective but also time-consuming. This can be avoided by providing sufficient information and by carefully wording the question. Clues can be provided in the question itself or in the space provided for the answer.

Supply items should be used only when the correct response is a single word or phrase. The requirement of more words makes scoring more difficult and reduces the degree of objectivity. A completion question that contains more than one blank is not only difficult to score but also confusing to the students taking the test.

Recognition or selection questions, which are explained in the next chapter, can have only one correct answer selected from two or more possible answers. The difference in the construction of the two types of questions provides the degree of objectivity. However, ease of scoring is not the only reason for choosing one form over another. Supply items do discriminate, are usually reliable, and are most effective in testing retention of knowledge. The key to the successful use of both supply and selection questions is the way they are constructed.

Free Response and Completion Test Items

Both free response and completion questions require a word or phrase for an answer. Both demand recall of information and test for facts and terms rather than application. The only difference is that free response is a question and completion contains one or more blanks. Students generally find free response easier to answer than completion whereas the teacher finds that students are apt to write more than is required for free response.

The construction of free response and completion items determines their usability. This is, or course, true for every form used to evaluate progress toward objectives. However, certain rules of construction are particularly applicable to free response and completion:

(1) Write statements or questions where only one correct answer is possible. More than one answer lessens the objectivity of the test, tends to confuse students, and prevents the question from being as discriminating as it could be.

(2) Omit the key word rather than a trivial detail. For example, omit the term and write the definition. Ask yourself what is the most important word in the sentence and use it for the answer. This suggestion is as applicable for free response as for completion. In

fact, a very useful way to determine the word to be supplied for the blank in completion is to word the test item as a question.

(3) Be specific in asking for the kind of response desired. An example is "Oranges are a _____fruit." The answer could refer to cost, nutritive value, type of fruit, season, meal or some other factor. Answers that are computational should have the type numerical unit indicated such as feet, inches, or pounds, ounces.

(4) Use only one blank for completion. When more than one is desirable, be sure that the meaning is clear and not lost in the mutilation of the sentence. Usually a completion test item that has more than one blank can be asked more effectively as a free response. The test item, "The primary colors are _____, _____, and _____," could instead be worded "What are the three primary colors?"

(5) Avoid giving clues in the word preceding the blank, such as *a, an, was, were, is, are.* Sometimes clues are given in the context of the sentence or question. This occurs all too often in definitions. A student with an excellent vocabulary can answer such questions without having studied the content covered by the test item.

(6) Place the blank at or near the end of the completion test item. This helps students to answer the question more rapidly. Whenever this is not possible, place the blank near the front. First wording the test item as a free response can help you to do this correctly. Blanks placed in the middle are very confusing and are apt not to be desirable test items.

(7) Do not lift statements verbatim from textbooks and references. A statement taken out of context frequently loses its meaning. This will avoid requiring students to memorize a text. It will also avoid statements that are general and vague.

(8) Have all response lines the same length. This applies to free response as well as to completion since you may wish to place a line after a question as well as in a sentence. When lines are the same length, they do not provide a clue to the answer.

(9) Set up a key with correct answers. List possible alternates whenever applicable. It is most desirable to formulate the key as items are constructed so as to prevent errors. A clever idea is to list words that will be the answers and then construct test items to match these words.

(10) State directions clearly and concisely, underlining key words. Using language familiar to students will help them to answer the questions more quickly and accurately. Completion and free re-

sponse test items should be separated with different directions given for each. However, it is unusual for both types to be used on the same test.

Free response and completion are not as desirable types of test items as are the recognition forms. However, they can successfully be used to test for various forms of knowledge at the lowest or first level of cognitive objectives. Without these kinds of basic or fundamental knowledge, students cannot answer more complex questions. Free response and completion items can successfully test for knowledge if correctly worded. Selection items can also do this but are not as discriminating as supply items. A student must not only know but also be able to recall and record the term.

Free response and completion can test for knowledge of terminology. Definitions and terms are vital to every area of home economics but are more often tested in the areas of food and nutrition, clothing and textiles than in family and child development. Perhaps the reason is the scientific basis as opposed to the psycho-sociological basis. Regardless of the area the form is much the same. Examples with appropriate objectives are given below.

EXAMPLE 1

OBJECTIVE: *to define methods of cooking food.*

Directions: Answer the following questions by writing the word in the blank that best completes the sentence.

1. To cook by dry heat, usually in an oven, is to_____.
2. To bring a liquid to a temperature just below the boiling point is to_____.
3. To cook in hot fat over direct heat is to_____.
4. To cook under a direct flame is to_____.

EXAMPLE 2

OBJECTIVE: *to define methods of mixing ingredients.*

Directions: Answer the following questions with one word. Record the answers on your answer sheet.

5. What is the term that means to mix dough with the hands?
6. What is a person doing when he removes the outside covering of a piece of fruit?
7. What is the process of combining fat and sugar?

It is probably obvious to you that knowledge of definitions or terms can also be evaluated by using recognition questions such as matching. Furthermore, the examples given above illustrate that completion items read more smoothly than do short answer items.

Knowledge of specific facts can be effectively tested using free response and completion. Alternate choices (true-false) are frequently used for this purpose but are less desirable because they are sometimes tricky. As a home economics teacher, you will have many specific facts that you want students to know. These facts are necessary for problem solving and for background information in skill development. These facts may be scientific, economic, sociological, or psychological in nature. However, they are always related to families and individuals in their application. Examples with appropriate objectives are given below.

EXAMPLE 3

OBJECTIVE: *to identify the functions of food nutrients.*

Directions: Answer the following questions by writing the word in the blank that best completes the sentence.

   8. The food nutrient that has building body tissues as its chief function is____ .

   9. Body processes are regulated by a group of a nutrients called____.

  10. The chief function of carbohydrates is____.

  11. Body growth is aided by a group of nutrients called____.

EXAMPLE 4

OBJECTIVE: *to identify purposes of characteristics of fabric.*

Directions: Answer the following questions with one phrase or sentence. Record the answers on your answer sheet.

  12. Which characteristic of fabric determines if a garment hangs straight?

  13. Why is the selvage edge of fabric woven?

  14. How is a true bias made?

One difficulty with using free response to test knowledge of facts is that answers may vary and yet be correct. You may decide to use completion or some form of recognition question. Students with below average ability may find these test items difficult to answer. You will want to choose those kinds of questions best suited to the intellectual skills of your students.

Free response and completion can test simple computations. This is a skill that homemakers need and to which home economics teachers can contribute. Estimating fabric yardage for garments, draperies, slipcovers, and the like is one need for computational skill. Another instance is in doing equivalent measurements in food preparation.

Free response lends itself very well to testing computation.

EXAMPLE 5

OBJECTIVE: to determine the amounts of fabrics needed to redecorate
a room.

Directions: Answer the following questions with <u>one</u> word. Record the
answers on your answer sheet.

15. How many square feet would you need to carpet a room 10′ x
12′?

16. How many yards would you need for draperies in a room with four
windows 72″ long if you needed two lengths for each window?

17. How many yards of 36″ fabric would you need to make four
pillows 10″ x 10″?

A problem situation can be used effectively to test equivalent measurements using completion.

EXAMPLE 6

OBJECTIVE: to alter a recipe for use with a smaller group.

Directions: Mary is having a party for twenty-five and wishes to use a
punch recipe for seventy-five people. Record how much she
will need in the following recipe.

For 75	*For 25*
4 c. sugar	18._____c. sugar
2 c. water	19._____c. water
2 c. lemon juice	20._____c. lemon juice
2 1/2 c. orange juice	21._____c. orange juice
6 c. pineapple juice	22._____c. pineapple juice
4 qt. ginger ale	23._____qt. ginger ale

Completion, as well as free response, can test computation but test items that are related to a problem or situation have more meaning than those not based on such information. Home economics lends itself extremely well to the use of test items of this sort.

Association Test Items

Association items are sometimes called identification because they relate or identify one concept to another. As in other recall questions, association items require recall of facts in a very precise manner. They are useful in relating products to use, causes to effects, stages to ages, and persons to responsibilities.

The construction of association test items assists students in relating one concept to another. Most of the suggestions given for completion and free response are also pertinent for association items. Those rules that are particularly helpful are discussed in the next paragraphs.

(1) Use homogeneous groupings. The wording of the question should make this evident. In other words do not mix knives with pots and pans. A student is likely to become frustrated when required to move from one set of concepts to another in the same question.

(2) Label each column of concepts. Examples would be uses and knives, ingredients and purposes, persons and responsibilities. This not only aids the student but also assists you in following the rule given above.

(3) Both columns should consist of brief words or phrases. Sentences that are long and involved should be saved for other types such as completion, short answer, and multiple choice.

(4) Use not more than six or eight groups of concepts. This increases the reliability of the test and prevents a feeling of defeat on the student's part.

(5) Use concepts that can be related to only one other concept for the same purpose. This increases the objectivity of the test. If it is at all possible to have more than one answer, be sure to place alternates on the answer key.

(6) Count the answer correct if spelling error is minor. The exception would be when accurate spelling is an objective of the test. All too often students fail to do well on a test because they were evaluated on factors unrelated to the objectives for the test.

(7) State directions clearly and concisely. An example is "After each food write the nutrient for which it is an excellent source." Be sure to use words that are in the vocabularies of your students.

Association test items are discriminating and frequently valid. However, it must be pointed out that they have the distinct disadvantage of demanding memorization. Rarely can they be used for problem questions since they do not require application, analysis or integration of facts and principles.

The relationship of products to uses can be tested with association questions. Products can be interpreted to mean something that is produced either by the homemaker or for her use. Equipment, food products, clothing, furnishings are the most usual kinds of products to be used in association questions.

An example of equipment as related to use could involve knives and their purposes, scissors and their uses, pots and pans and their uses, cleaning equipment and their major functions.

EXAMPLE 7

OBJECTIVE: to identify the purpose of each type of scissors.

Directions: Write the name of the scissors opposite each use listed in the first column. A particular kind of scissors may be named more than once.

Use	Kind of Scissors
cutting out garment	1.
cutting edges	2.
finishing raw edges	3.
cutting buttonholes	4.
clipping seams	5.
removing stitching	6.
clipping embroidery threads	7.
cutting off corners of seams	8.

Association questions are appropriate for this kind of information since students are required to remember the use of a piece of equipment in order to appropriately select it. Another arrangement would be to display the various types of scissors and ask students to identify the purpose for each one. Each pair of scissors would have a number that corresponded with a test item number.

EXAMPLE 8

OBJECTIVE: to identify the purpose of each type of knife.

Directions: After carefully studying the exhibit of knives, write the purpose of each opposite the letter that corresponds with the letter on the knife.

Knife	Purpose
9. A	9.
10. B	10.
11. C	11.
12. D	12.
13. E	13.
14. F	14.

This is a more complicated question than the first one since the student must recognize the knife as well as know its purpose. The name should give a clue to its purpose before both of these are tested. An example would be a paring knife or a carving knife.

Association items can test relationship of causes to effects. Since home economics is based to a large degree on scientific principles, it is natural to teach and test for the relationship of cause and effect. Subject content that lends itself especially to evaluating cause and effect by association includes care of clothes, food preparation, and household tasks. However, other areas can be used for association test items.

Textile facts and principles affect the methods of caring for clothing. A question that will test for this kind of information is illustrated below.

EXAMPLE 9

OBJECTIVE: *to recognize reasons for selecting particular methods of cleaning garments.*

Directions: Write the reason in the column to the right for choosing each method of cleaning.

Method of Cleaning	*Reason*
Laundering wool with cold-water soap	15.
Permitting to drip dry	16.
Pressing on wrong side	17.
Omitting bleach from laundering	18.
Using ice to remove chewing gum	19.
Soaking blood spots in cold water	20.

Methods of food preparation also lend themselves to testing for cause and effect as the following questions would indicate.

EXAMPLE 10

OBJECTIVE: *to identify the effect of methods of food preparation on vegetables.*

Directions: Write the effect in the column to the right for each listed method of food preparation.

Method of Vegetable Preparation	*Effect*
Cooking without a cover	21.
Adding soda	22.
Cooking in large amount of water	23.
Cooking until mushy	24.
Serving as soon as cooked	25.

Association test items to test for scientific principles or cause and effect are not easy to construct or simple for students to answer. Yet, it is important for students to know why various methods are considered appropriate.

Multiple choice and alternate choice can be used for this purpose but these types of questions require recognition. Supply questions are more similar to life situations than are either multiple or alternate choice.

Association test items can test relationship of stages to ages. The life cycle and the ages of children are often used for association questions. Identification of a particular characteristic of a stage as related to age provides an evaluation of family development.

The following is an example of the relationship of stages to ages for children.

EXAMPLE 11

OBJECTIVE: *to identify the usual age for young children to behave in particular ways.*

<u>Directions:</u>   In the column on the right, write the age (1 to 6 years) when a child usually behaves in the manner listed on the left.

Behavior	Age
Runs and hops more than walks	26.
Can use several hundred words	27.
Enjoys companions	28.
Prefers to be alone	29.
Pretends at play	30.
Has difficulty concentrating	31.

The family life cycle is divided into various stages. The names of the stages frequently imply the approximate age of the adults in the family. An example is given below.

EXAMPLE 12

OBJECTIVE: *to recall the name given to each stage of family life cycle.*

<u>Directions:</u>   Write in the column on the right the name of the stage in the family life cycle that corresponds to the task description on the left.

Task Description	Stage of Family Life Cycle
Caring for needs of children	32.
Providing for teenage needs	33.
Establishing a home	34.
Off-spring beginning own life	35.
Having first baby	36.
Relinquishing job for retirement	37.

The above question could be reversed by naming the stages and asking students to define or to list a task; however, since this requires more words and there are more possible correct responses, the test is less objective.

Association questions require students to record information and therefore are discriminating. You may wish to use other types of questions for students who do not recall such facts with ease or accuracy.

Summary

The following are conclusions about and principles for the construction of supply type objective tests:

- supply test items require memorization by students;

- free response and completion require the same type of answer;

- supply test items demand a short answer of one word or phrase;

- knowledge of definitions, facts, and principles can be effectively tested by supply items;

- supply items are usually discriminating and reliable;

- scoring of supply test items is less objective than that of recognition items;

- completion items should have only one blank placed near the beginning or end of the sentence;

- free response and completion can test simple computations as well as terms, methods, functions, and processes;

- association items relate one concept to another;

- relationship of products to use, causes to effects, and ages to stages can be identified by using association items;

- supply items are more difficult for students to answer than are recognition questions.

STUDENT ACTIVITIES

1. Write a general set of directions for (a) free response items, (b) completion items, and (c) association items.

2. Construct examples of free response that evaluate:
    a.   knowledge of terms
    b.   knowledge of specific facts
    c.   simple computations

3. Construct examples of completion that evaluate:
   a. knowledge of terms
   b. knowledge of facts and principles
   c. simple computations

4. Construct examples of association items that test the relationship of:
   a. products to uses
   b. causes to effects
   c. stages to ages
   d. persons to responsibilities

5. List rules for constructing supply items and evaluate your own examples using the rules.

6. Write a justification for using supply test items.

REFERENCES

Ahmann, J. Stanley and Glock, M.D. *Evaluating Pupil Growth.* New York: Allyn and Bacon, Inc., 1959.

Arny, Clara Brown. *Evaluation in Home Economics.* New York: Appleton-Century-Crofts, 1953.

Gronlund, Norman E. *Measurement and Evaluation in Teaching.* New York: The Macmillan Company, 1971.

Hall, Olive A. and Paolucci, B. *Teaching Home Economics.* New York: John Wiley and Sons, Inc., 1970.

Vaughn, K. W. "Planning the Objective Test." *Educational Measurement,* 1951, pp. 159-84.

_____. "Test Construction," and "Hints for Improving Tests." *Tips and Topics in Home Economics* IV, no. 3 (February 1964).

_____. "Evaluation Instruments: Purveyors of Meaning to Students." *Illinois Teacher* V, no. 4 (December 1961), pp. 170-88.

Chapter 8 OBJECTIVE TEST ITEMS: SELECTION TYPES

Objective test items that require students to select the correct answer are classified as recognition questions. Although students need to know the correct answer in order to be sure of selecting the right response, recognizing rather than recalling information enables students to make higher scores.

The forms of recognition items are matching, multiple choice, and alternate response. The third form is frequently called true-false of which there are modified forms as well as the unmodified form. Matching items consist of two parallel columns with each word in one column being matched to a word or phrase in the other column. A multiple choice item consists of an incomplete statement or question and a list of four or five suggested solutions. Alternate response items consist of a statement which the student is asked to mark true or false, right or wrong, agree or disagree.

It is obvious that the major similarity in these three forms is that knowledge is a matter of recognition and therefore does not require the correct spelling or writing of an answer. Another similarity is that the degree of objectivity is very high since an inflexible key can usually be established.

A major difference is in the levels of knowledge that can be evaluated. Matching can successfully test terms and definitions, but it cannot evaluate intellectual skills. Such skills can be tested by multiple choice and by modified alternate response. Another difference is in the amount of space required. Matching requires a minimum and multiple choice a maximum amount of space.

An objective test frequently contains two if not all three of these forms. Both multiple choice and alternate response are used with problem-solving questions. Questions of this type are also called interpretive exercises. Intellectual skills that require application and analysis of knowledge can be effectively tested using problem-solving questions. This is probably the greatest advantage of recognition questions over supply questions.

Advantages and Disadvantages of Selection Test Items

Selection questions have some of the same advantages as supply items. Objectivity can be established to an even greater degree. Knowledge at various levels can be evaluated even though problem situations must accompany a set of objective-selection items before intellectual skills can be evaluated.

Selection items permit a wide sampling of knowledge. This type of question can be quickly and easily answered and this makes it possible to have many test items on one test. All of the forms can test for facts, principles, and terms. Those that are based on a problem situation can test for application and analysis of knowledge.

Recognition items can be used in all areas of home economics content. The definitions of terms pertinent in an area make excellent matching questions and are usable for multiple choice or alternate response questions. Facts and principles, whether scientific or sociological, can be used for both multiple choice and alternate response. Application of knowledge is more successfully evaluated by multiple choice and alternate response than by matching. It does not matter whether the area is food and nutrition, textiles and clothing, housing and management, or family and child development, recognition questions work equally well.

Selection test items can provide an indication of whether or not students have a grasp of the subject matter that has been covered. Essay questions cannot do this as well because of the time factor. Supply questions can evaluate students' knowledge but not to as great a degree as selection items. They take somewhat more time and are not as adaptable to all kinds and levels of knowledge.

Relationship of one concept to another can be evaluated by selection questions. Matching and multiple choice do this exceptionally well. Human relationships may also be the basis for a multiple choice question when a problem situation is a part of the question. The relationship of one principle to another may be used for either alternate response or multiple choice.

Selection questions possess a high degree of objectivity. The amount of subjective judgment is at a minimum. More than one person can check the same papers and arrive at the same total score provided there are no numerical errors. The objectivity is such that students can check answers as accurately as the teacher.

An objective and inflexible key can be established. There should be only one correct answer to each question and it is recorded on the key. For most teachers this is the greatest advantage. However, you must remember that errors can be made in constructing the key as well as in scoring. Student complaints about scores should be checked for this reason.

Objectivity contributes to discrimination because of the lack of subjective judgment. Selection questions do, however, permit guessing on the part of students. A student stands a fifty percent chance of getting an alternate response correct if he guesses and a twenty-five percent chance with multiple choice. Perhaps this still discriminates since better students usually make more intelligent guesses than do poorer students.

Selection questions are easy for students to answer because they are objective. Essay and supply questions are more difficult because of the memorization and recall that may be needed. Selection questions are frequently easy for the teacher to construct. Because they lend themselves to so many cognitive levels, they are easier than other forms.

Response set varies according to the type of selection question. A response set is a consistent tendency to follow a certain pattern in responding to test items. Some students choose the third response to all multiple choice when they do not know the answer. Many students choose true over false. The pattern varies from student to student. Careful test construction can prevent one student having an advantage over another because of his particular response set. You need to vary your answer in a random fashion whether multiple choice, matching, or alternate response.

Selection items are frequently time-consuming to construct. This may just be balancing one period of time against another. Time used to construct recognition items may be saved in scoring the papers. Time saved in constructing essay is definitely used in reading and determining a score. Time available is a factor but the objective being measured should be of major significance.

The difficulty in finding plausible answers affects the time required. Matching questions either lend themselves to the terms to be evaluated or they do not. Therefore, finding plausible answers is not a problem when constructing matching questions. Finding plausible answers does become an acute problem in multiple choice, however. Three believable distracters are frequently very difficult to find. Some test makers use only two plausible answers and one that is obviously not the answer—but this is not a worthy practice. Even then it may require considerable time to construct a multiple choice item. Alternate response items are difficult if the information to be tested does not really lend itself to this form of question. When this occurs, it would be advisable to pick another form of test item.

There is a probability of clues being present if test items are not carefully constructed. The prevention of clues requires time as well as skill in test construction. Reading and rereading a test is necessary in order to avoid giving clues to answers. Using an advanced student or another teacher for pretesting is an excellent way to eliminate clues although this process does take time.

Multiple choice and modified forms of alternate response are more time-consuming to construct than are matching items. You must keep in mind their advantage in testing for application and analysis. This in itself should be sufficient reason for the additional amount of time. Well-constructed selection items can be filed for further use and in this manner you can cut down on the amount of time used to construct an objective test.

Space needed varies according to type of selection question. All three types do require more space than do essay questions. Only matching requires as little space as identification questions and only unmodified alternate response items require as little as completion and short answer. The space requirement is really a disadvantage only when having tests reproduced is a problem.

Multiple choice utilizes much space. The stem uses from one to five lines and the choices, four additional lines. The same problem situation could result in four test items rather than one if the form is a modified alternate response. However, multiple choice may be by far the best form to use for problem or interpretive questions.

Matching items are spatially very economical. Four to eight questions make up one set of matching. Each question utilizes one line of space. Since there is not a description of a problem situation, four times as many answers can be obtained as in a multiple choice item.

Various forms of alternate responses require different amounts of space. The unmodified form requires the least and the cluster true-false usually requires the most since these are based on a problem situation.

Although use of space is a disadvantage for using recognition questions, it should not be a determining factor. Selection items have many advantages and should be used whenever appropriate.

Matching Test Items

Construction of matching test items usually consists of a stimulus list and a response list arranged in parallel columns. The stimulus list, sometimes called a list of premises, includes definitions, descriptions, phrases, or single words. The response list consists of single words or very short phrases. Matching questions are limited to measurement of terminology, specific facts, and simple associations. Matching test items are most appropriate for identifying the relationship between two things. Students usually like matching questions and find them relatively easy to answer.

The rules for constructing matching test items can make the task simple and effective. Each of the following suggestions may apply to other types of questions but is particularly applicable to matching. There is a brief explanation for each rule which should help you to develop matching questions to successfully evaluate the objectives for which they are designed.

(1) Directions need to explain clearly how the matching response is to be answered. This needs to be done although the basis for matching is usually obvious. Directions should be brief and precise. Since frustration and testing time will both be saved, test scores will be higher.

(2) Each column should be given a descriptive label. This reinforces the directions. If labels are long and awkward, you may decide to use "Column A" and "Column B."

(3) The items in each matching exercise should be homogeneous. This is the most important yet most violated of all rules given for matching questions. When only a few items that are related or similar can be found, another form of question should be used.

(4) Four to eight items are generally enough for one matching exercise. Less than four is hardly worth the effort and more than eight is confusing and time-consuming. This is a flexible rule but one should have a sufficient reason to expand the list. Many teachers consider ten items the maximum number that can be effectively used in one matching exercise. This is certainly not to say that you can have only one set or exercise. You may have as many as you have need to use in any one test. Three sets of eight provide twenty-four questions but think how confusing all of these in one set would be.

(5) There should be an unequal number of responses and premises. Usually the response list has one or two more items than the stimulus list. However, a shorter response than stimulus list can be used with the directions clearly stating that an answer may be used more than once. Having the same number in both lists contributes to guessing.

(6) The responses should be arranged in a logical order. Numbers and dates should be placed in sequence. Terms and other words or phrases should be arranged alphabetically. This eliminates the possibility of clues and contributes to speed in answering the question.

(7) Capital letters or arabic numbers should be used to label the items in the response list. This helps to make students' answers clear. Lowercase letters such as *b* and *d* are easily confused.

(8) The items in the response list should be shorter words than those in the stimulus list. These should be placed on the right side of the page. Students can find the answer more easily when it is brief and teachers find it easier to maintain homogeneity.

(9) All the items for one matching exercise should be placed on one page. Turning pages back and forth causes confusion and wastes time.

Matching test items effectively evaluate knowledge of terminology. This is probably the most effective use of matching questions and is used the most frequently. As has been pointed out, matching test items cover the same levels and kinds of knowledge covered by free response and completion items.

Examples 1 and 2 give appropriate objectives and directions and should help you develop sets of matching for use with your own students.

EXAMPLE 1

OBJECTIVE: *to define the various methods of cooking foods.*

Directions: Match the definitions in the left-hand column with the terms in the right-hand column by writing on the answer sheet the <u>letter</u> corresponding to the term beside the number representing the definition.

Definition	*Term*
1. To cook by dry heat, usually in an oven.	A. bake
2. To bring a liquid to a temperature just below the boiling point.	B. boil
3. To cook in hot fat over direct heat.	C. scald
4. To cook slowly just below the boiling point.	D. broil
5. To cook under direct flame.	E. fry
6. To cook in a liquid at a temperature above the boiling point.	F. sear
	G. simmer
	H. steep

EXAMPLE 2

OBJECTIVE: *to define methods of mixing ingredients.*

Directions: Match the definitions in the left-hand column with the terms in the right-hand column. Write the <u>letter</u> of the term beside the number on the answer sheet.

Definition	*Terms*
7. To combine fat and sugar, mixing well until light and fluffy.	A. cut in

EXAMPLE 2 (continued)

Definition	*Terms*
8. To mix dough with the hands.	B. fold
9, To combine fat with dry ingredients using a pastry blender or two knives.	C. knead
10. To mix food with a circular motion for the purpose of blending.	D. cream
11. A method of combining ingredients with egg whites to incorporate air.	E. roll
12. To mix two or more ingredients together.	F. combine
	G. stir

Terms are important for students to know. Principles are not understandable if the terms used in the principle are not in the students' vocabulary. Matching questions not only evaluate knowledge of terms but also reinforce the learning of these terms.

Matching test items evaluate knowledge of specific facts. These must be simple facts and answers must be brief. If the information to be tested does not meet these two criteria, another type of question should be used. Facts, as you already know, are another first level of knowledge. Yet without an understanding of these, it is very difficult to analyze problems or apply information to problems.

Examples 3 and 4 are matching questions that can be used to evaluate specific facts.

EXAMPLE 3

OBJECTIVE: *to identify the correct method for storing various types of garments.*

Directions: Match the clothing in Group I with the method of storing or caring for them in Group II. Each method may be used more than once or not at all. Write the letter corresponding to the method beside the appropriate number on the answer sheet.

Group I: Clothing	*Group II: Method of Care*
13. Sweaters	A. Hang in closet with clamp hangers
14. Skirts	B. In bag, rack, or box
15. Knitted suits	C. Fold and place in drawer or on shelf
16. Long coats	D. Hat box
17. Hats	E. Hang on hook or nail
18. Shoes	F. Hang on heavy wooden hangers
19. Belts	G. Leave in belt loops on dress
20. Dressy shoes	H. Hang on padded hanger
21. Silk blouses	I. Hang by buckle on dress hangers

EXAMPLE 4

OBJECTIVE: *to select the correct thread thickness for a particular sewing task.*

Directions: If you would use a double thread for doing the following, mark an *A* on the answer sheet; mark *B* if you would use a single thread.

Sewing Task	*Thread*
22. Sewing on a button	A. Double thread
23. Hemming a skirt	B. Single thread
24. Tacking down a facing	
25. Sewing on snaps	
26. Basting	
27. Making tailor's tacks	
28. Hand gathering	
29. Sewing on hooks and eyes	

Matching exercises can be used to identify relationship of one concept to another. Concepts are major ideas related to each other in whatever ways one concept can be joined to another to further expand learning. Matching questions can teach as well as evaluate such relationships.

Example 5 relates these concepts to one or more other concepts found in the process of management, and Example 6 relates qualities of color to the usual psychological effects.

EXAMPLE 5

OBJECTIVE: *to relate various aspects of management.*

Directions: Write the <u>letter</u> representing each term in Column B by the number on the answer sheet that <u>best</u> represents the word in Column A.

Column A	*Column B*
30. time	A. goal
31. choice-making	B. management
32. possessions	C. resource
33. aim	
34. organization	
35. skills	
36. money	
37. purpose	
38. energy	

EXAMPLE 6

OBJECTIVE: *to identify psychological effects of colors.*

Directions: On the answer sheet, record the letter corresponding to the effect of a color beside the number corresponding to the color or color combination. An answer may be used more than once.

Color		*Effect of Color*	
39.	Black	A.	cool
40.	Blue	B.	neutral
41.	Gray	C.	warm
42.	Green		
43.	Orange		
44.	Purple		
45.	Red		
46.	White		
47.	Yellow		

Multiple Choice Test Items

A multiple choice test item is generally considered to be the most usable form of all types of objective questions. It tests a wide range of knowledge, is usable for problem questions, is objective, and is usually discriminating. The required space and the difficulty in finding plausible distracters are the major disadvantages.

The rules for constructing multiple choice are guides to aid a teacher in developing the items. You will want to refer to these suggestions as you develop multiple choice questions in order to make them as effective and useful as possible. Multiple choice consists of a stem which may be a sentence, an incomplete statement, or a direct question followed by a series of alternative responses.

(1) The stem should present a problem except when testing vocabulary. The problem may be in a paragraph or asked as a question. Paragraphs are used with the more complex situations. Questions are used when testing facts and principles.

(2) Four responses are generally used. Each one should be plausible. Some teachers use ridiculous items for one of the four. This author feels that this is almost an insult to students. Another acceptable but frustrating response is *all of the above* or *none of the above*. If you cannot construct four plausible answers, perhaps some other type of question should be used. Five choices are acceptable but give very little advantage. Three choices have been proven statistically inadequate.

(3) Correct responses should be arranged in random order in succes-
sive items. This is to lessen the effect of guessing. One college
freshman who was exempted from English on the basis of her test
scores had answered all items *c* without reading the questions.

(4) All unnecessary words should be eliminated from the stem. This
saves space and makes the statement clearer.

(5) Clues to the answer should be eliminated from the stem. These are
usually words like *the, a, an* which are more appropriately placed
before each response.

(6) Responses should be placed in column form rather than in a paragraph. This promotes clarity and speed in answering. It is true that
paragraph listing saves space but is hardly worth the disadvantages
that result. Students are also apt to make better scores.

Multiple choice items can be used to evaluate terms. You have already
realized that matching is the most spatially economical when evaluating
terms. You and your students might prefer multiple choice items and in that
instance you would use them. If definitions are not brief enough to use with
matching, you will find multiple choice very useful.

Examples 7 and 8 illustrate the use of multiple choice for testing knowledge of terms.

Multiple choice items are used to evaluate knowledge of simple facts.
This use is adaptable to every area of home economics. The only difficulty
is that of overuse. Applying knowledge and solving problems are far too

EXAMPLE 7

OBJECTIVE: to name the parts of the sewing machine according to
               purpose.

Directions: The following are multiple choice items. Choose the best
               answer. Write the letter of your response on the answer
               sheet.

   48. The part of the machine which pushes the fabric along is called the
        A. Presser foot
        B. Feed dog
        C. Treadle
        D. Throat plate

EXAMPLE 8

OBJECTIVE: to identify the words used in describing a table setting.

Directions: The following are multiple choice items. Choose the best
               answer. Write the letter of your response on the answer sheet.

   49. An "individual cover" designates
        A. All the dishes on the table.
        B. The linen and silverware on the table.
        C. All the appointments used by one person.
        D. The glasses and china on the table.

important for all multiple choice items on a test to be used in this way. So, don't let yourself fall into that trap. Examples 9 and 10 test very simple facts and are similar to those you use.

EXAMPLE 9

OBJECTIVE: *to recognize the functions of various food nutrients.*

Directions: The following are multiple choice items. Choose the best answer. Write the letter of your response on the answer sheet.

50. Leafy green and yellow vegetables furnish the body with
      A. Fat
      B. Vitamin A
      C. Vitamin D
      D. Protein

51. The chief function of fat in the diet is to
      A. Furnish energy
      B. Build body tissues
      C. Aid in digestion
      D. Remove waste materials

52. Proteins are important for
      A. Giving us heat and energy
      B. Helping us to grow
      C. Helping us to have better eyesight
      D. Regulating body processes

53. Our best source of calcium is
      A. Meat
      B. Fortified margarine
      C. Milk and milk products
      D. Whole grain cereals

54. Iron is needed in the body to
      A. Develop good teeth
      B. Build red blood
      C. Help prevent night blindness
      D. Keep hair from turning gray

EXAMPLE 10

OBJECTIVE: *to identify effective ways of cleaning floor coverings.*

Directions: The following are multiple choice items. Choose the best answer. Write the letter of your response on the answer sheet.

55. The best way to clean small deeply tufted rugs is by
      A. using a vacuum cleaner
      B. using a carpet sweeper
      C. shaking
      D. sweeping with a broom

56. The best regular treatment for a waxed floor is to use
      A. a dry mop
      B. oiled mop
      C. a broom
      D. soap and water

Multiple choice are very useful in evaluating application of knowledge.
This level of learning follows knowing simple facts and is not as complicated
as problem solving. Very young high school students will do well on this
type of question and many will find it challenging. You should use this type
question before using the more complicated problem or situational question.

Examples 11 and 12 are simple and fairly easy samples of tests of applying
knowledge and could be used to evaluate facts if you have taught the
information as such.

EXAMPLE 11

OBJECTIVE: *to apply information to questions about development of*
                 children.

Directions: In the blank on the left of the question, place the letter of the
                best possible answer.

___ 57. Johnnie is not developing as he should. He is eight months old and
        is not sitting alone. His mother should not worry because
        A. She did not develop rapidly and children usually follow their
            parents.
        B. All babies grow and develop in the same order, but each does
            so at his own rate.
        C. The age at which babies achieve their steps in growth are the
            same for all children.
        D. His actions compare with the child next door.

___ 58. Mrs. Smith has a very bow-legged baby. She might have prevented
        this if she had given the baby
        A. Strained cereals
        B. Strained vegetables
        C. Corn syrup
        D. Fish liver oil

EXAMPLE 12

OBJECTIVE: *to select the correct pattern size.*

Directions: In the blank to the left of the question, place the letter of the
                best possible answer.

___ 59. Kitty is 16 years old. She is 5'3" and rather slim, but well-developed.
        Misses sizes are too long-waisted for her; junior sizes are too short-
        waisted and sometimes too tight across the chest. She should try
        A. Misses Petite size
        B. Junior Petite size
        C. Teen size
        D. Misses

EXAMPLE 12 (continued)

___ 60. Rose is 14 years old. She is 5'6" and has a slim, well-developed
         figure. Teen and Junior sizes run too short-waisted for her. She
         should try
         A. Misses
         B. Misses Petite
         C. Tall size
         D. Junior Petite

*Problem-solving or situational questions are ideal for the use of multiple
choice test items.* In the author's opinion, no other use of objective test
items is as important as problem solving. This type of question may range
from relatively simple to very complicated or sophisticated. It does take
time to construct multiple choice based on a problem or situation. For this
reason, you would be smart not only to keep such test items in your file but
also to determine their difficulty index and their discriminatory level.

Examples 13 and 14 should provide a pattern for you to follow as you
develop your own problem or situational questions.

EXAMPLE 13

OBJECTIVE: *to choose acceptable ways to guide the behavior of children.*

Directions: In the blank to the left of the question, place the letter
                representing the best possible answer.

___ 61. Mrs. Smith wants Jane to learn to share her toys with other children.
         When Jane is selfish, her mother should
         A. Take her toys away from her for a time.
         B. Give some of her toys to her friends to play with.
         C. Send her to bed without her supper.
         D. Suggest how she and her friends can use the toys together.

___ 62. When Jimmy's mother calls him to come in, he is usually too busy
         playing to mind her. The best thing for his mother to do is
         A. Give him a five minute warning, then go and bring him in.
         B. Call him, and then go inside and pay no attention to him.
         C. Tell him how badly she feels when he is naughty.
         D. Go out and bring him in; then make him stay in the rest of
             the afternoon.

___ 63. If John has trouble getting along with other children his mother
         should
         A. Remove him because the other children have been unkind to
             him.
         B. Try to discover and treat the causes of the difficulty.
         C. Tell him he has to learn to fight for his rights.
         D. None of the above.

EXAMPLE 14

OBJECTIVE: *to select ways to manage time effectively.*

Directions: The following items are multiple choice items. Write the letter
               of the correct response in the blank on the left.

____64. Jane has an hour before her date arrives. She has not cleaned the
         living room as she promised her mother; she must bathe and dress,
         and she has not studied her French lesson. Which of these is the
         best solution to her problem?
         A. Break her date and do her assignments.
         B. Do the dusting, dress quickly, and come in early from her
             date to study her French.
         C. Get her mother to do the living room and take a chance on
             getting her French at school.
         D. Apologize for the living room, make an excuse for French, and
             spend her time dressing.

____65. Helen's mother works and she is responsible for keeping the house
         clean but she never seems to get all the jobs done. Which one of the
         following ideas is not very good?
         A. Make a list of all the jobs that need to be done.
         B. Continue cleaning but do it less thoroughly.
         C. Plan to do certain jobs on certain days.
         D. Try out various ways of doing different jobs.

____66. Eleanor realized one morning that it takes her too long to dress and
         one reason was probably the way her room was arranged. What
         should she do first?
         A. Move the furniture around to see if she could make more room.
         B. Draw the room on paper.
         C. Write down the steps in getting dressed.
         D. Use a plan-a-room kit with miniature models.

Alternate Response or
True-False Test Items

There are, in general, two types of alternate
response. The first one is the unmodified or "regular" true-false. This is the
type with which you are probably the most familiar. The unmodified form
is of doubtful use in testing achievement in home economics. Many authorities in the field of evaluation recommend that the use of this form of test
be discontinued. It does, however, provide an excellent teaching-learning
technique. A lively discussion can result from unmodified true-false items
that present an issue. This author shares the following conclusions about

the use of unmodified ture-false or alternate response. You will want to draw your own conclusions.

The modified forms of alternate response are cluster true-false, rephrasing false statements, crossing out the incorrect word and substituting a correct one, and two-choice. Cluster true-false are series of statements based upon a situation which must be considered in making each decision. You can easily see how this type of alternate response lends itself to problem-solving questions. Rephrasing false statements to make them true is used less frequently than cluster because it is more difficult for students to answer and less objective to score. Crossing out the false word and substituting the correct word is a type of test item that is very limited in its use but at the same time highly discriminating. The two-choice type is really selecting between two alternatives and is not answered true or false. You, as a teacher of home economics, may find cluster true-false the most usable.

The rules for constructing true-false vary for each form but are similar to other types of recognition questions. The suggestions given in the following paragraphs are written to indicate the form to which the rules refer. Read and follow these carefully if you should decide to use alternate-response. The general rules will apply to all forms including the unmodified form.

(1) Statements should be constructed so that they are unequivocally right or wrong. This is difficult but very necessary. You may wish to ask one or more students to answer and criticize the questions before you use them in a test.

(2) The number of false items should be approximately the same as the number that are true. This prevents an answer set from resulting and decreases the degree of guessing. This is not a "hard-fast" rule. It is one that can be broken if it seems desirable to do so.

(3) The directions should indicate that students reply to every item in cluster true-false. Otherwise the scorer will not know whether the student considered the item false or did not make a decision.

(4) The stem of cluster true-false should contain a specific situation containing all the details that are needed to answer correctly.

(5) Statements that are to be rephrased should be brief and should center around one idea rather than several. Since these are difficult and time-consuming to answer, brevity is necessary.

Terms and definitions can form a basis for alternate response items. The unmodified form is frequently used for this purpose even though it has many disadvantages. A more acceptable form is crossing out the incorrect word and substituting the correct one. You may find matching a more usable form of question for use with terms than either of these. The choice is yours.

Example 15 contains a series of unmodified true-false and Example 16 uses substitution of the correct word.

EXAMPLE 15

OBJECTIVE: *to recognize the insurance terms that are used frequently.*

Directions: Before each statement that is true, place a plus (+) and before each statement that is false, place a zero (0).

_____ 67. The major risk-bearing agency in modern society is the insurance company.

_____ 68. The person to whom the proceeds of an insurance policy are payable in case of loss is called the insurer.

_____ 69. The transfer of a property insurance policy from one owner to a new owner is called an assignment.

_____ 70. Homeowners policies are also referred to as "all risk" policies.

_____ 71. Insurance that provides protection against damages to one's own car is property damage insurance.

EXAMPLE 16

OBJECTIVE: *to define insurance terms that are used frequently.*

Directions: Before each statement below place a plus (+) if the statement is true. If the statement is false, place a zero (0) before the statement, cross out the word or words that make it false and write the word or words that will make it true in the blank after the false statement.

_____ 72. The amount paid to the insurance company for protection is called an assignment._____

_____ 73. Both mutual and stock insurance companies sell nonparticipating policies._____

_____ 74. Bodily injury insurance provides protection against a damage suit on the part of a person injured by an automobile._____

_____ 75. Comprehensive personal liability insurance provides protection against damage to one's own car._____

The disadvantage of this form is the awkwardness of scoring. You may prefer the student to write the correct word above the incorrect word or in a blank preceding the statement. All three of these have the same disadvantage in scoring.

Alternate response items are useful in testing knowledge of facts. This is probably the most frequent use of true-false although students find them tricky. It is also easy for teachers to include clues that tend to give away the answer to alert students. One way to improve the use of alternate response items is to require students to rephrase those statements which are false.

Example 17 contains items that could be used as unmodified true-false but for which the directions require students to rephrase the false statements.

EXAMPLE 17

OBJECTIVE: *to recognize causes and effects of children's emotions.*

Directions: In the space at the left of each statement listed below, place a plus (+) before the statements that are true and a zero (0) before those that are false. If the statement is false, replace the false phrase with the correct one using the line below to write the correct statement.

_____ 76. A temper tantrum is more constructive than a fight because it does not hurt others.

_____ 77. Mild fears which cause children to be cautious are good for them.

_____ 78. Fears caused by television can be overcome through play.

_____ 79. Jealousy is easier to prevent than to cure.

_____ 80. Children enjoy fear in stories that end happily.

This type of modified true-false or alternate response requires students not only to know the information and recognize the error but also to write a correct form. Some junior high home economics students might have difficulty doing this whereas older students might be challenged. An objective key is almost impossible to construct and this makes scoring difficult for the teacher. You might decide to include a limited number of such items on a test. Another use might be a daily test containing a few questions. These would then provide an excellent way to reteach and reinforce learning.

Alternate response items can be used to evaluate application of information. The unmodified form is generally a poor choice for evaluating application of information. The modified forms of cluster true-false and two-choice are more adaptable than many other types. Examples 18, 19, 20 are of these two types, with cluster true-false presented in 19 and 20.

EXAMPLE 18

OBJECTIVE: *to recognize errors in threading a sewing machine.*

Directions: Read the situations and the responses written below. If you think the response is true, mark a + on the answer sheet. Mark a 0 if you think the response is incorrect. Answer all questions.

If a machine fails to sew or make a good stitch the reason may be:

81. Needle has dull point.
82. Bobbin is not in right position.
83. Thread is not the right size.
84. Machine is not threaded correctly.
85. Stitch regulator has been moved.

EXAMPLE 19

OBJECTIVE: *to choose clothes that are appropriate for the person and the occasion.*

Directions: Read the situations and the responses written below. If you think the response is true, mark a plus (+) on the answer sheet. Mark a zero (0) if you think the response is incorrect. Answer all questions.

Jane has to choose a school outfit. Which of the following would be attractive school outfits?

86. A green taffeta dress with a low neckline and a velvet belt.
87. A bright floral polished cotton with rhinestones decorating bodice.
88. A blue-checked gingham shirt-waist dress.
89. A cotton blouse and wool skirt.
90. A light blue cotton dress with matching lace jacket.

Betty who is rather short and plump, has chosen a solid color blouse with a striped skirt for school wear. The stripes in the skirt are horizontal.

91. The horizontal lines of the skirt will tend to make Betty appear shorter.
92. Betty should have chosen a striped blouse to match the skirt.
93. A skirt with vertical stripes would have been a better choice.
94. If Betty had chosen a solid color skirt to match the blouse, this would have made her appear smaller.

EXAMPLE 20

OBJECTIVE: *to select foods that require a minimum amount of time to prepare.*

Directions: In the column on the left record the letter representing your choice. Answer all questions.

Jane is planning a menu for the family's night meal. She wishes to use as small an amount of time as possible. Which food in each pair would require the least amount of preparation and cooking time?

Food		A	B
_____ 95.	Green beans	Frozen	Fresh
_____ 96.	Potatoes	French fried	Baked
_____ 97.	Steak	Sirloin	Chopped
_____ 98.	Bread	Corn muffins	French bread
_____ 99.	Salad	Tossed	Head lettuce
_____ 100.	Dessert	Ice cream	Apple pie

EXAMPLE 21

OBJECTIVE: *to evaluate a menu using established criteria.*

Directions: The following menu was planned to be served as a luncheon to which mothers of the class have been invited.

Baked Pork Chops
Escalloped Tomatoes   Pear Salad
Hot Rolls   Butter
Jello

Below are several statements about the menu. Some are true, some are false. Mark a plus (+) on your answer sheet by the ones which are true and a zero (0) by the ones which are false. Answer all questions.

101. The meal is high in energy foods.
102. There is a variety of textures in the meal.
103. There is an agreeable variety of flavors in the meal.
104. The meal is rather colorless.
105. The meal is rich in vitamin B.

Some of the following suggestions would improve the meal. Mark a + on your answer sheet by the suggestion you think would improve the meal and a 0 by those which you think would not improve the meal.

106. Substitute applesauce for the pear salad.
107. Substitute fresh tomatoes for the escalloped tomatoes.
108. Add creamed peas to the menu.
109. Substitute lime sherbet and cookies for the jello.

Cluster true-false and two-choice are nearly always based on a situation. This provides the means for applying what students have learned to a situation that is similar to those at school and at home. Alternate responses items that are application and problem questions are more valid than any other use of this form of recognition items.

Problem-solving situations can be effectively evaluated by cluster true-false. These are very similar to application questions using alternate response. The same advantages exist and the same disadvantages that accompany unmodified true-false. Example 21 indicates the similarity but is a more detailed and complicated problem than are problems that evaluate application of knowledge.

Problem solving or decision making exists in every area of home economics. You, as a teacher, have probably used questions such as the one above in a food course. This type is particularly helpful in evaluating learning in family and child development. These can be used for teaching-learning situations as well as for evaluation.

Summary

This chapter, like the preceding one, will be summarized by stating conclusions for constructing objective test items. In general, these conclusions are concerned with recognition items and are those of the author. Perhaps, most of them are similar to your conclusions about this form of test question. We can conclude that:

- selection items require less memorization by students than do recall items;
- selection items are objective and relatively easy to score;
- selection items can be used to test many levels of learning;
- selection items are usable in all areas of home economics;
- selection items are time-consuming to construct but require a minimum amount of time to score;
- matching and alternate response items require a minimum amount of space, whereas multiple choice require maximum space;
- each set of matching questions should consist of homogeneous items arranged in two labeled columns;
- matching questions should consist of four to eight items with an unequal number in either the response or premise list;
- the stem of multiple choice items should generally present a problem or situation;

- four responses are usually considered sufficient in a multiple choice item;

- correct answers to multiple choice items should be randomly arranged;

- modified alternate response are more reliable and discriminating than is the unmodified form;

- alternate response items should be constructed so that they are unequivocally right or wrong;

- approximately the same number of alternate response items should be right as are wrong;

- symbols such as + and 0 are more acceptable than are T and F for answers to alternate response items.

STUDENT ACTIVITIES

1. Write a general set of directions for:
   a. matching items
   b. multiple choice items
   c. unmodified alternate response
   d. cluster alternate response
   e. two-choice items

2. Construct examples of matching test items that evaluate:
   a. knowledge of term
   b. knowledge of specific facts
   c. the relationship of one concept to another

3. Construct examples of multiple choice test items that evaluate:
   a. knowledge of terms
   b. knowledge of specific facts
   c. application of knowledge
   d. solving of problems

4. Construct examples of modified alternate response items that evaluate:
   a. knowledge of terms
   b. knowledge of specific facts
   c. application of knowledge
   d. solving of problems

5. List rules for constructing selection items and evaluate own examples using these rules.

6. List advantages of using selection test items.

REFERENCES

Ahmann, J. Stanley and Glock, M. D. *Evaluating Pupil Growth*. New York: Allyn and Bacon, Inc., 1959.

Arny, Clara Brown. *Evaluation in Home Economics*. New York: Appleton-Century-Crofts, 1953.

Gronlund, Norman E. *Measurement and Evaluation in Teaching*. New York: The Macmillan Company, 1971.

Hall, Olive A. and Paolucci, B. *Teaching Home Economics*. New York: John Wiley and Sons, Inc., 1970.

Chapter 9 PREPARATION OF OBJECTIVE TESTS

The preparation of an objective test is as important as the writing of individual test items. No matter how well-constructed the questions are, faulty arrangement of items on the test can cancel out their effectiveness. This chapter will explain four steps in the preparation of an objective test. The first step will be the development of test items, which is a summary of suggestions given in the preceding two chapters. The second step is the arranging of items on a test. Writing directions and providing for the recording of answers is the third step. The final step is the construction of an answer key. Suggestions for each of these steps are included.

Developing Test Items

An excellent practice is to write each possible test item on a 5" x 8" card. This size card provides sufficient space for the instructional objective, key, item analysis information, and notes on effectiveness of the item. If a 3" x 5" card is used, such information can be recorded on the back of the card.

The following are some specific suggestions for developing test items:

(1) Select the type of test item that is most appropriate for the specific objective being evaluated.

(2) Use short and definite statements.

(3) Use simple and familiar language.

(4) Include only one independent idea in each question.

(5) Use the content rather than the form as the indicator of the correct answer.

(6) Avoid wording that provides clues to the answers.

(7) Construct items that require students to apply rather than merely to recall their knowledge.

(8) Use techniques that will discourage guessing.

(9) Avoid the use of trivial items.

(10) Include only homogeneous content in an item.

(11) Be certain that there is only one correct answer.

(12) Use correct grammar.

A very profitable habit is to construct test items periodically, such as twice a week, while your exact presentation of a topic is fresh in your mind. This can help you to relate the content, as well as the type of test item, to the method of instruction. Another advantage is that the time needed to construct test items is not concentrated but rather spread over several weeks. It also provides time to review the test items to see if they meet the suggested criteria given above.

Arranging Items in a Test

If you have been clever enough to record test items on cards periodically as suggested, you will be ready to select those questions which you wish to use and arrange on a test. More consideration can be given to the arrangement of questions when these have already been formulated.

The entire test should be keyed to the grid which should be the first step in preparing a test. A grid or table of specification was described and illustrated in Chapter 3. This is a preplan for the test and deviation from this plan is to be expected. A grid does provide a guide for developing a test directly keyed to the objectives being evaluated.

The relating of the test items actually used to the grid is a simple and rewarding process. This is made easier whenever test items are recorded on cards. To begin, cards are stacked according to the concepts to be included on the test. Each stack is then separated according to level of learning. For example, the grid for an objective test in Chapter 3 has two levels, knowledge and application, and ten concepts. The sorting of cards would result in twenty piles. If your test contained 120 items then you should have twelve items for personal food needs, six of which are knowledge items and six of which are application.

An example given below is a partial reproduction of the grid in Chapter 3 but illustrates how the actual percentages of items are recorded and how deviations can occur. The percentage in parentheses is the anticipated one.

Concepts	Knowledge	Application	Total
Personal Food Needs	(5) 6	(5) 5	(10) 11
Daily Food Requirements	(5) 5	(5) 4	(10) 10
Food Preferences and Prejudices	(0) 0	(5) 4	(5) 4
Nutritional Contributions of Snacks	(0) 0	(5) 5	(5) 5
Food Away from Home	(3) 3	(5) 5	(8) 8

The grouping of test items should be logical and to the advantage of the student. Poorly grouped questions can have a very decidedly adverse effect on the scores students make on a test. Too many groups, lack of homogeneity, and complexity of arrangement can work against rather than for students.

Not more than three types of objectives test items should be included on one test. You remember from the two preceding chapters that there are six major types with variations among at least two of these. More than three types cause confusion by forcing a student to go from one set of directions to another. On the other hand a major test should contain more than one type of test item so as to avoid boredom. More than one type also gives the student a chance to answer the type question which he handles best.

All test items of a particular type should be grouped together. For example, if a test contains three sets of matching, one set should follow another. This kind of grouping needs only one set of directions for each type of question. Students will answer more questions and probably receive higher scores if like test items are grouped together.

Test items covering similar content should also be grouped together. This may sound in conflict with the rule given above but should be considered secondary. If more than one type of question is used to cover the same concept, the content is arranged within the framework of the type. For example, if daily food requirements and personal food needs are included in a group of cluster true-false questions and a group of multiple choice questions, those for one concept precede those for the other concept in the true-false and again in the multiple choice question.

The arrangement of test questions within a grouping should be from the simple to the complex. Successfully answering one question gives the student a feeling of security and he will be more likely to answer the remaining questions correctly. If you have not analyzed the test items, you may not know which are the easier questions. The only alternative is an educated guess.

The sequence of items on a test should be arranged so as to ensure ease of answering and scoring. The teacher as well as the student can profit if a test is orderly and concisely arranged. The grouping of test items by type contributes to this sequence as does numbering, randomizing of answers, and paging.

All items should be numbered consecutively throughout the test with arabic numbers being used. Different parts of the test should not be labeled. Each test item in a set of matching questions should be numbered separately. This rule also applies to cluster true-false. The last number used in a test represents the total number of items. When one point is given to each item, this also represents the total score.

Groups of test items should be arranged so that the easiest type of question is first and the most difficult last. Although authorities don't always agree on the order of difficulty, many do believe that recognition questions are easier for students than are recall questions. Matching is probably the least complicated with true-false, multiple choice, free response, and completion following in that order.

All parts of a question should be on one page. When one part of a question is on the bottom of a page and the remainder on the top part of the next page, time is lost in turning the page back and forth. Students are apt to make mistakes and become frustrated.

Test items should be arranged at random so the responses do not fall into a regular sequence. This holds true for multiple choice and true-false more than for the other types. An alert student can easily recognize a pattern of answers and rely on that sequence for either answering or double-checking his decisions.

Errors can be eliminated by reviewing and editing a completed test. No matter how carefully constructed, a test can be improved, items stated more clearly, and clues eliminated by reviewing each test item as well as the test as a whole. You can review the test yourself after a few days have passed, ask a fellow teacher to review it, or ask a former student to read it for errors. A useful technique is to take the test as though you were a student.

Some of the questions you need to consider when reviewing a test are:

1. Can any test items be altered so that the test balances as nearly as possible with the grid?
2. Is the test as a whole consistent with the range of abilities in the class and will it be discriminating?
3. Are there any test items that provide a clue for an answer to another item?
4. Does the wording in any item provide a clue to the answer?
5. Is the intent of the item clear?
6. Are the items free from grammatical errors?
7. Have all unnecessary words been eliminated from the items?

Reviewing a test requires time and a small amount of effort. This means that reviewing must be included in your planning for developing a test. The teacher who hurriedly makes out a test just before it is to be reproduced is likely to make unnecessary errors. At least one day of "cooling-off" time is needed between constructing and reviewing a test. It is worth the extra time.

Equivalent forms of the same test are not difficult to construct and have several uses. If you have test items recorded on cards it is much easier to pair questions than if you do not have them recorded. A grid is also helpful in developing two equivalent tests. Two different tests are considered equivalent when they cover the same content and have the same length, validity, and reliability. The average score for each test should be approximately the same.

Equivalent forms have several uses. Make-up tests may be the one in which you have the most interest. They can also be used when students must sit very close together. Equivalent forms can be used when you wish to measure gain with a pretest and a post-test.

There are at least two ways to develop equivalent forms. The first of these is very simple and involves arranging items in reverse order in the two tests. The only problem is that the second test cannot have items arranged in order of difficulty.

The second system is more difficult but also results in a better set of tests. It involves constructing test items in pairs or selecting two test items covering the same content from those already constructed. Pairs of questions can be developed by covering the same content using two different types of questions. For example, a set of matching questions can be converted to multiple choice. It is desirable to use the same two or three types on both tests since one type of question is usually easier than another type.

Writing Directions and
Providing for Answers

The writing of directions is equally important as constructing test items and arranging the items on a test. You may find it helpful to develop a set of directions for each of the types of both supply and selection questions. These may be usable without any alteration. In other instances a slight modification may be needed in order to relate the directions to the content of the questions that follow.

Each set of directions should cover the essential points. This is necessary if students are to begin immediately and understand exactly what is expected. These points include the purpose of the test, time allowed, basis for answering, and procedure for recording answers. Frequently a teacher finds it desirable to include directions about guessing.

The purpose of the test may be written or given orally. The test may have a title which indicates the purpose. Teachers frequently record objectives at the top of the test. This procedure makes it clear to both the teacher and the students the reasons for selecting the items included on the test. It is desirable for most types of questions to include the purpose in the directions preceding the group of questions.

Students need to be told the time allotted for the test. This can also be written or stated orally. Calling time or setting an alarm clock to go off periodically can be distracting. A clock that is clearly visible will help students keep track of time. A rough guide for the use of the teacher in timing a test is one multiple choice, two matching, or two true-false per minute. This applies to high school students of average ability. Younger or less able students will require more time.

The directions should tell a student the basis for answering and where to record his answer. Matching and multiple choice use the best answer of those listed as a basis. Cluster true-false use the basis of right or wrong. If guessing is penalized a student should be told not to guess and why.

The criteria for judging directions are excellent guidelines to follow. These are the essential ones:

(1) Adequate   (4) In student language

(2) Clear   (5) Key words underlined

(3) Concise or brief (6) Simple and direct

Examples of appropriate directions may be used as guides. Each type of test item has slightly different directions since the choices and the form of the answer vary. Where the answer is recorded also makes a difference. Examples are given in the following paragraphs for true-false, matching, multiple choice, and completion.

True-false or alternate response has two choices. The + and the 0 are more acceptable forms that T and F or writing out the two words. The first set of directions given below are the cluster true-false, and the second set is not based on a situation.

Directions: John is six, but he takes no interest in doing things for himself. He leaves his clothes scattered all over his room and his mother has to put them away. In the blank at the left, mark a + by each suggestion which you believe might be desirable for John's mother to use; mark a 0 by each one which would not.

Directions: To the left of each statement place a + if you think the statement is *true.* Place a 0 if you think the statement is *false.*

Matching questions are used to test knowledge and therefore are not appropriate for testing application. The two examples given below are different in that the first one has the purpose stated as identifying utensils. They also request answers to be recorded differently.

Directions: Match the utensils named in Column II to the kitchen utensils pictured in Column I. Print the letter of your answer in the blank provided. No answer should be used more than once. Some items in Column II will not be used at all.

Directions: Do not write on these pages. Mark your answers on the answer sheet provided. Match the definitions in the right-hand column with the terms in the left-hand column. Write the letter of the term by the number on the answer sheet.

Multiple choice questions may test either knowledge or application and the directions will imply which one. The first example is based on a situation and the second one is not. The answer for the first one is recorded on the test paper and for the second one on the answer sheet.

Directions: Record your answer in the blank on the left. Kitty is 16 years old. She is 5'3" and rather slim, but well-developed. Misses sizes are too long-waisted for her; junior sizes are too short-waisted and sometimes too tight across the chest. She should try:

A.   Misses Petite size
B.   Junior Petite size
C.   Teen size
D.   None of the above

Directions: The following are multiple choice items. Choose the best answer. Write the letter of your response on the answer sheet.

Completion questions may be either supply or selection. A list of possible answers make the questions selection. Answers may be written in the blanks scattered throughout the question or in the blanks on the right. The first two sets of the following directions indicate that possible answers were supplied. The third set of directions indicates a recall of information.

Directions: Select from the list on the right the correct word or words to fit in the blanks. Put the letter that represents the correct word before the statement where the word fits. All of the words will not be used.

Directions: Mrs. Greene was spending a week in the hospital and Sue had to do the family laundry. When Sue went into the laundry room she was faced with numerous boxes, bottles, and cans with which she was very unfamiliar. Please help Sue through her "Washday Blues" by selecting the most appropriate answers from the column at the right. An answer may be used once, more than once, or not at all.

Directions: Write the word that best completes each sentence in the blank provided.

Answers can be recorded in a variety of ways. The directions given above indicate placement on an answer sheet or on the test paper. These two places also have variations. The choice should be based on ease for the student and convenience for the teacher.

The answers that are recorded on the test paper are most frequently written in blanks that have been provided. Usually these blanks are on the left side of the page and placed in front of the numbers. The answer may be circled. Multiple choice lends itself best to circling and alternate response may also be answered this way. Sometimes answers are underlined and at other times checked. The last two methods are awkward and easily misunderstood.

An answer sheet can usually be more rapidly scored than the test paper. A type of answer sheet with which you are familiar is the one which can be machine scored. The student is asked to mark between two narrow, short lines the letter for the answer he chooses. The answer sheet looks similar to this portion of an illustration:

	A B C D			A B C D			A B C D
1.	▪ | | | | | |		21.	| | ▪ | | | |		41.	▪ | | | | | |
2.	| | | | ▪ | |		22.	▪ | | | | | |		42.	| | | | | | ▪
3.	| | | | | | ▪		23.	| | | | ▪ | |		43.	| | | | ▪ | |
4.	| | | | ▪ | |		24.	| | | | | | ▪		44.	| | ▪ | | | |

Another form of answer sheet requires the student to write his answers by the appropriate number. A portion of such an answer sheet which has been used follows:

1. A	21. C	41. +	61. *fruits*
2. C	22. F	42. O	62. *meat*
3. D	23. D	43. O	63. *milk*
4. C	24. E	44. +	64. *vegetables*
5. B	25. A	45. O	65. *bread*

Circling can be used on answer sheets as well as on test papers. This form uses more space than any other type, as you can see by the following example:

1. Ⓐ B C D	21. A B ©D	41. Ⓣ F
2. A B ©D	22. A Ⓑ C D	42. Ⓣ F
3. A B C Ⓓ	23. A B C Ⓓ	43. T Ⓕ
4. A B ©D	24. A Ⓑ C D	44. Ⓣ F
5. A Ⓑ C D	25. Ⓐ B C D	45. T Ⓕ

Identifying information should be supplied and directions are needed for this process. Usually these directions are given orally. The spaces are provided on the test paper or the answer sheet and usually at the top of the first page.

The most important identifying information is the student's name. This is so obvious that one wonders why it is even mentioned. If you are a teacher you know that students frequently do not write their names on papers. A space on the left upper corner of the first page will remind students to write their names.

Less important information is the name of the course, the period or section, and the date. This does become more necessary if a teacher has several sections of the same course. When a pretest-posttest situation exists, the date is essential.

Most teachers prefer a space to record the score. There may be a space provided at the bottom of each page as well as at the top of the first page or on the answer sheet. Page scores recorded on the bottom of each page along with the total score provide for checking the accuracy of determining a total score.

Preparing a Key

The key to an objective test should be inflexible —there is only one correct answer for each question. This makes the preparation of a key much simpler than one for an essay test which could have more than one possible answer for each question. The key should always be prepared in advance and, preferably, as the test is being constructed. The answer for each item will already be on the card if you use this system.

The answer key can be quickly converted to a scoring key. The form this scoring key takes depends on the type of answer sheet being used. The machine-type answer sheet is, of course, scored by a machine. The teacher-developed scoring key takes the same form as the test on answer sheet.

A strip scoring key can be developed for use when answers are recorded on the side of the test paper. A strip scoring key can be used by students, aides, or the teacher. The time needed to construct is minimal compared to the time saved in scoring a large number of papers. Accuracy in scoring is increased when a strip scoring key is used.

The first step in preparing a strip scoring key is to record the correct answers in the blanks provided on the left side of each page of an unused test. The handwriting should be very legible if the answers not printed or typed. The test can be used in this form by placing the edge of the scoring key next to the answers on the student's paper. This becomes awkward if the test covers more than one page.

A second step can be followed to make the strip scoring key more useful for a test with several pages. The columns of answers are cut away from each page. These are then pasted on a piece of cardboard. A file folder cut in half is an excellent background on which to mount the columns of answers.

Very few errors are made if the strips are reversed. Place the answers to page one on the edge, reverse the cardboard sheet and paste the answers for the second sheet on the opposite side. Other pages can be pasted to the back. This arrangement forces the scorer to turn the cardboard each time he moves to another page. One side of the strip scoring key looks like this:

_B_ 1.		32.	O
_C_ 2..		31.	+
_D_ 3.		30.	O
_A_ 4.		29.	+
_C_ 5.		28.	O
_B_ 6.		27.	O
_D_ 7.		26.	O
_C_ 8.		25.	+
_A_ 9.		24.	+
_B_ 10.		23.	+
_C_ 11.		22.	O
_D_ 12.		21.	O
_A_ 13.		20.	+
_B_ 14.		19.	+
_C_ 15.		18.	D
_B_ 16.		17.	A

An accordian-pleated key is appropriate for an answer sheet with answers in columns. The folding and unfolding is a little time-consuming but is much more accurate than using an unfolded answer sheet for scoring.

The first step is the same as for a strip scoring key. The correct answers are recorded on an unused answer sheet and checked for accuracy. The sheet is then creased between the first and second rows of answers so that the first column is folded under the sheet. The second crease is in the opposite direction so that the second column fits over the first column and is faced down on the third column. This process is continued until all columns are folded under, leaving the first column on top.

The accordian is unfolded and adjusted so that only the appropriate column of answers is visible. This column is placed against the same column of answers on the student's answer sheet. It is then a simple process to check those answers that are incorrect.

A scoring key can be produced for circled answers by cutting holes to fit over the answers. This is probably the most time-consuming method of developing a scoring key. Like all others methods it saves time in scoring and produces a higher degree of accuracy. The first step is similar to those for all other methods. An unused test or scoring sheet has the correct answers written on it.

After this step is completed the procedure varies for the answer sheet or for answers recorded on the test. If the answers have been circled on an answer sheet, the hole reveals the circle since it is larger than the circle. If answers have been written on a test such as completion, this will not work. The procedure is to cut holes in the same place on a clean sheet of paper and write the correct answer above the hole. Although this requires time and patience, the rewards are worth it.

Summary

The preparation of an objective test becomes easier as a teacher puts his conclusions to work as guidelines. It is hoped that you have drawn some conclusions as you studied this chapter. We can conclude that:

- test items should be recorded on 5" x 8" cards;
- test items should be concise, in student language, and appropriate for selected objectives;
- the content for a group of questions should be homogeneous;
- test items should be constructed periodically, such as twice weekly;
- an entire test should be keyed to an already developed grid;
- from one to three types of objective questions should be on one test;
- all test items of a particular type should be grouped together;

- test items covering similar content should be combined within a major grouping;
- test items should proceed from the simple to the complex;
- all items should be numbered consecutively on a test;
- all of one question should be on one page;
- errors can be eliminated by reviewing and editing a completed test;
- equivalent tests can be developed by pairing items as well as by reversing the order of test items;
- directions should include the purpose of the test, time allowed, basis for answering, and procedure for recording answers;
- answers can be recorded on the test or on an answer sheet;
- identifying information should be recorded on the test paper;
- identifying information should include the name of the student, the date, and the course;
- space should be provided for recording the total score on the first page;
- accuracy in totaling a score results when scores are recorded on the bottom of each page;
- a strip scoring key should be developed for tests with answers recorded on the left side of each page;
- an accordian-pleated key is appropriate for scoring an answer sheet with answers in columns;
- a scoring key can be produced for completion and for circled answers by cutting holes to fit over the answers.

STUDENT ACTIVITIES

1. Record on 5" x 8" cards a large number of test items in one area.
2. Develop an objective test that includes matching, multiple choice, and cluster true-false test items. Select items from those on the cards.
3. Develop another objective test that includes completion and free response test items. Select items from those on the cards.
4. Develop an equivalent test for the first test you develop.
5. Evaluate each of the tests by the criteria listed throughout the chapter.

6. Develop a strip scoring key for the first test.

7. Develop either an accordian-pleated key or one with holes for the second test.

REFERENCES

Ahmann, J. Stanley and Glock, M.D. *Evaluating Pupil Growth.* New York: Allyn and Bacon, Inc. 1959.

Arny, Clara Brown. *Evaluation in Home Economics.* New York: Appleton-Century-Crofts, 1953.

Gronlund, Norman E. *Measurement and Evaluation in Teaching.* New York: The Macmillan Company, 1971.

Hall, Olive A. and Paolucci, B. *Teaching Home Economics.* New York: John Wiley and Sons, Inc., 1970.

Chapter 10 ANALYSIS OF OBJECTIVE TESTS

There are many ways to analyze tests and test items. Some of these are complicated as well as sophisticated. Others are simple, easy to compute, and beneficial to the classroom teacher. You, like many classroom teachers, may not be inclined to do mathematical computations regardless of how profitable these may be. This chapter contains only three suggestions for analysis, all of which are not only useful but also easy to compute. These three are difficulty of a test as a whole, difficulty of individual items, and discrimination of individual items. The last section of this chapter discusses the development of a test file. The various analyses should be included with each test item that is filed.

Difficulty of a Test

The difficulty of a test as a whole is one that should be of great concern to you. No doubt there have been many times when you have blamed students for unusually low test scores. Maybe you have done some soul searching and blamed yourself for not teaching students so that they learned. The truth probably lay in the difficulty of the test. In the previous chapter you read that some types of items were easier to answer than others. You also need to be aware that you may have taught

information in a very different way than you tested it. Knowing the difficulty of a test can help prevent this situation from happening so frequently.

*The advantages of knowing the difficulty of a test are worth the effort of
discovering what it is.* Some of these advantages relate directly to the test.
Others are more directly related to students. There are also advantages that
point to teaching techniques or to curriculum improvement.

The major advantage in knowing the difficulty level of a test is to prevent
administering one that is too difficult or too easy. Your feelings of concern
occur more often when most students make low scores than when most
students make high scores. Either situation indicates that the test was not
geared to the ability level of students in the class.

Another advantage of knowing the difficulty level is that it provides an
incentive to improve the test. You need to know more than the difficulty
of a test as a whole to do this. Each item would need to be evaluated so you
can know which ones to change in order to adjust the difficulty to your
students.

Knowing the difficulty level helps a teacher to interpret the results of a
test. The actual score of an individual student is really not as important as
where that score fits into the range of scores. If a test has a high difficulty
level, a poor score is not so significant as it would be if the situation were
reversed. A teacher can make an adjustment if she knows that the test has
been either too easy or too difficult. A method for doing this is explained
in Chapter 16.

The difficulty level of a test plus the place of an individual student in the
range of scores can aid in diagnosing student difficulties. This is only one
evidence of the achievement level of a student but can be a very important
clue. Knowing that a student scores low on an easy test would lead a teacher
to conclude that the student probably has minimum intellectual ability. On
the other hand a student who has a high score on a difficult test is probably
very intellectually capable.

A test can frequently tell a teacher more about her methods of instruction
than it can about the ability of her students. Determining the difficulty of
a test provides clues for evaluating teaching techniques and for analyzing
whether or not the test items are compatible with the objectives of the
course. A close look at curriculum scope can be done at the same time. The
teacher should ask herself why certain scores were obtained and what she
could do to make the difficulty level more realistic.

*Difficulty of a test can be estimated by comparing the average score with
the possible score.* If you gave a test with 135 test items and the average
score was 52, you could be reasonably certain that the test was too difficult.
If you gave a test with 120 items and the average score was 101, you could
assume that the test was too easy. There are three measures of average that
you can use to compare with the possible score: the mean, the median, and
the mode.

The mean is probably the most appropriate of these measures for estimating the difficulty of a test, and so is the most commonly used measure of average or central tendency. The simplest and most direct way to determine the mean is by adding all of the scores and dividing by the number of scores. In other words, it is the arithmetic average. The mean can also be computed from grouped data. This method is more usable when you have scores from more than one class. If you wish to use this method consult a book on statistics. An example of the simple way to determine the mean is given below:

Scores: 92, 91, 89, 89, 88, 87, 86, 86, 86, 82, 81, 80, 78, 75, 74, 72, 65, 65.

Total: 1466 ÷ 18 = 81.4 = mean.

The median is the score at the middle of the distribution. It is called the mid-score because the same number of scores fall below it as above it. The median is used when extreme scores at either end should be repressed. If the range given above had 40 or 110 added to it, the median would be more useful than the mean. The median can also be computed from a frequency table using a formula. The simple method can be illustrated using the range in the above paragraph. There are eighteen scores; therefore the median falls between the ninth and tenth scores. These two scores are 82 and 86 which means the median is 84.

The mode represents the most frequently recurring value in a group. The mode is nearly always computed from grouped data arranged in a frequency table. If it were determined in a rough fashion from the range given above it would be 86. The three measures of average are the same in a perfect bell-shaped curve. It is obvious that the above distribution would not be bell-shaped since all three of these have several points difference.

Difficulty of a test can be estimated by noting the range and distribution of scores. The range is obtained by subtracting the lowest score from the highest score. It is the simplest and crudest measure of variability but it does indicate the difficulty of a test as a whole. In the example given above the range is 92 – 65 = 27. The distribution of scores is related to the range but provides more information about the difficulty of a test. The distribution of scores can be arranged in a frequency table or plotted on a curve.

A frequency table aids in recognizing the spread of a group as well as in obtaining measures of the average. The first step is to determine the range. The size of the interval is the next decision. There should be between 8 and 20 intervals. In the distribution given above, the range is 27 which divided by 3 gives 9 intervals. The third step is to decide the limits of the interval with the lower limit being a multiple of the size of the interval. In our example the first interval would be 63–65 and the last interval would be 90–92. The remainder of the process would be to set up the frequency table, record the scores in the table, and total the scores in each interval. The distribution given above is shown in Table 10–1.

TABLE 10-1

Interval	Tally	f
90 - 92	. .	2
87 - 89	: :	4
84 - 86	: .	$\frac{3}{2}$ 83.5 assumed median
81 - 83	. .	
78 - 80	. .	2
75 - 77	.	1
72 - 74	. .	2
69 - 71		0
66 - 68		0
63 - 65	. .	2
		$N = 18$

This table would lead one to believe that the test was not too difficult if the highest possible score was 100 and the class was of average ability. However, if the highest possible score was 120, you could conclude that the test was too difficult.

A frequency curve provides a visual picture of a distribution of scores. If a large number of scores are used it may be desirable to have larger intervals than on a frequency table. The more bell-shaped the curve the more normal is your own distribution. The data shown in the table above are plotted on the curve in Figure 10-1 but using intervals of five.

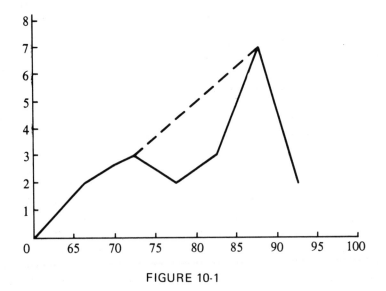

FIGURE 10-1

You can readily see that this is not a bell-shaped curve. If the curve were smoothed out as indicated by the broken line, it would still indicate that this test was not too difficult and might even have been too easy.

Difficulty of a Test Item

The difficulty of each test item has more significance than the difficulty of a test as a whole. After all, it is the difficulty of test items that determines the difficulty of the entire test. It is relatively easy to calculate the difficulty of each test item. This process can be done for you by a teacher aide or an advanced student. A record can be kept for each test item, thus providing you with a legitimate basis for deciding about further use of the test item.

Knowing the difficulty of a test item has many advantages. Once you have become aware of these you will realize that it is worth the effort required to determine the difficulty index. The time required to do the computation will be balanced by the time you can save in developing future tests.

The major advantage is perhaps the fact that you can prejudge a test as a whole. The process is simple when you can select most of the items for the test which have a difficulty index indicating that the majority of students will be able to answer the question correctly. This eliminates guessing how difficult the test item might be.

Equally important is the advantage of being able to arrange the items in order of difficulty. You have already learned that a test should begin with the easiest items and proceed to the most difficult. In order to do this as accurately as possible, it is necessary to know the difficulty index of each item.

Although the index of difficulty is not stable it does tend to rank in the same order when compared with other test items. This advantage can help you to know about where to place the item on a test. The more student scores involved in establishing the difficulty index, the more stable it is likely to be.

The difficulty index is the percentage of a group who answered the item correctly. This includes not only the items missed but also those that were not answered. The only thing a teacher needs to know is how to compute percentages if she is to find the difficulty index. This process is simple enough to be done by students.

The first step is to count how many students answered each item correctly. This needs to be recorded on an answer sheet or a piece of paper that has been numbered. It is important to be accurate when counting. A precaution is to separate the papers according to missed and not missed items, item by item. If you have student help, let one separate for item one, another count those not missed, and a third count those missed. Counting both provides a check on accuracy.

The second step is to divide the number of papers into the number who answered the question correctly. For example, of 25 students, 13 answered item one correctly making a difficulty index of 52. On the same test three answered item two correctly, making a difficulty index of 12. A third item was answered correctly by 21 students which gave this item a difficulty index of 84.

Most test items should be of average difficulty. This means that the difficulty index should be between 40 and 60. In the illustration above, the first item index is 52 or of average difficulty, the second is very difficult, and the third item has a very low difficulty index. This should say to you that item three should be placed first on a test and that very few of this level of difficulty should be used. The second item should be placed near the end of the test if used at all. The difficulty index for a test item should be recorded on the back of the card on which the item is written.

Discrimination of a Test Item

An item is classified as discriminating if sufficiently more good than poor students answer it correctly. The index of discrimination has the purpose of indicating how much difference is significant. An item is classified as nondiscriminating if approximately equal proportions of the good and the poor students answer it correctly. An item is classified as a reversal if more poor than good students answer it correctly.

Items may be nondiscriminating because of content, construction, wording, or type of item. Once a teacher has discovered that an item is nondiscriminating, it is essential to find out why. This may require the aid of students if you cannot reason why the item did not discriminate.

The content of the item may not have been really significant in the course. Sometimes teachers ask questions because the content lends itself to certain types of test items rather than because it was significant. The content of the item may not have been emphasized enough for students to remember it. All too often teachers ask questions in a way different from that in which the content has been taught: for example, naming the basic four food groups rather than analyzing a menu to tell what food group is missing. Items can also be nondiscriminating because they are too easy.

The construction of a test item can affect the discrimination of the item. Poorly worded directions can affect the ability of a student to answer the question correctly. Too many items in a set of questions can have a similar effect. This is particularly true in a set of matching items. Placing part of a question on one page and the other part on the next page makes a difference in how many students answer the question correctly.

Wording frequently gives away the answer and thus affects the level of discrimination. Derogatory words usually indicate an incorrect answer. Words such as *all, none, never, always* are clues that the statement is false.

An index of discrimination of fifteen percent is satisfactory. A sufficiently accurate estimate of the discrimination of a test item can be obtained by comparing the extremes of a group and ignoring the middle. The top third or fourth of the scores is thus compared to the bottom third or fourth. It is assumed that the middle third or half does not affect the index of discrimination. It is important to have at least fifty papers when computing the index.

The first step is to select the highest third and the lowest third of the papers. This is done after the papers are arranged in rank order. If you have a large number of papers you may use the highest and lowest fourths rather than thirds.

The second step is to record the errors on a previously developed form. The top third is recorded on the left side and the bottom third on the right. An example of how to record these is given in Table 10-2.

TABLE 10-2

Item	*Highest Third (N=20)* Tally	No. right	*Lowest Third (N=20)* Tally	No. right
1	✗✗✗ ∴	18	✗✗ ∵	12
2	∴	3	•	3
3	✗✗ ∷	14	✗✗ •	11
4	✗✗ •	11	✗	5
5	✗	5	•	1
6	✗ ∙ ∙	7	∷	4

The third step is to determine the percentage difference between those in the top third and those in the bottom third. Using the data from the tabulation in step two, Table 10-3 explains the procedure. Items 1, 3, 4, 5, and 6 are discriminating since the index is 15 or more. Items 2, 7, 9, and 10 are nondiscriminating since the index is less than 15. Item 8 is a reversal since more of the best third missed it than did those of the poorest third.

Other statistical measures can be used to express discrimination. One is the statistical significance which is usually acceptable at the five percent level. Another measure is a coefficient of discrimination which should be at

TABLE 10-3

	Highest Third (N=20)		Lowest Third (N=20)		
Items	Total	Percent	Total	Percent	Index
1	18	90	12	60	30
2	3	15	3	15	0
3	14	70	11	55	15
4	11	55	5	25	30
5	5	25	1	5	20
6	7	35	4	20	15
7	0	0	0	0	0
8	1	5	7	35	-30
9	3	15	3	15	0
10	2	10	1	5	5

least 20. If you are interested in these, you should consult a statistics reference for further information.

Development of a Test File

The relationship between analysis of objective tests and the establishment of a test file may seem vague to you. It will seem less so if you ask where the analysis data are to be recorded. The most appropriate place is with the test item. The next question is how it shall be recorded. Since one rarely uses a test more than once, recording data on the test seems foolish.

There are several advantages to having a test file. You may feel that this requires time and it does. On the other hand you may find the advantages worth the initial time needed. A file need not be large to begin with but should be set up so that it expands course by course and year by year.

The first advantage and perhaps the most important is that the test items can be used over and over. An inherited notion is that a test should never be given more than once. The reasons for this are obvious. However, there is no established taboo against using a test item a second, a third, and even a fourth time. The most convenient way to use test items more than once is to have each one recorded on an index card and filed so that they are very accessible.

The second advantage was referred to in the opening paragraph of this section. It is an appropriate place to record analysis data. Other kinds of data could be grade level for which it was designed and dates when the item was used. These data are particularly helpful in deciding whether or not to use the test item and where to place it on a test.

A third advantage is that it saves time when putting a test together. It is true that it takes time to develop and maintain the file. If the time required to do this were compared to the time saved in developing a test, one would find that time was being saved. Certainly frustration is eliminated and this in itself is a time-saver.

The index card should contain more information than the test item. The item, of course, is the vital part of the information recorded on the card. Everything else is related to it. However, the test item alone will not have all the advantages that were just listed.

The objective which the test item is evaluating should be recorded above the item. This is most important if you are relating an objective test to a grid or table of specifications. The major concept referred to in the objective should be underlined. This leaves no doubt as to where the item may be most appropriately used. An example of objective and an underscored concept is: "To establish criteria for selecting and storing fresh food."

The answer to the question should also be recorded. There are several ways this can be done. The most frequently used one is to record the answer on the back of the card. However, if the item is true-false or multiple choice the correct answer can have a ring drawn around it. Anyway you choose to record the answer is acceptable, but be sure you *do* record it.

The third type of information is the analysis data which are nearly always recorded on the back. The index of discrimination and the difficulty index can be recorded as soon as the test item is used the first time. Each time the analysis is done, the indices should be recorded and a date placed by them.

The grade level or course should also be indicated on the back of the card. It is conceivable that a test item can be used for more than one grade level but it is more appropriate for one than another. Knowing what is most suitable helps to decide when to use it for another level.

Each time a test item is used should also be recorded on the back of the card containing the test item. This may be evident when you record the analysis data. After several uses you may decide not to compute the difficulty index and the index of discrimination. Even though you make this decision, you should record the date of use on the back of the card.

Setting up a file is a simple process involving only a few steps. Beginning the file is perhaps the most important step. Once it has been started it is relatively easy to keep up to date. The more often the file is used, the more necessary it will become. A file may be started before the first test is given. Test items may be collected from texts, guides, old tests, and other teachers. These can be placed in the file without any of the analysis data. The beginning is in obtaining a file and a stack of index cards.

The second step is to place dividers in the file. These dividers will indicate subject areas. You may wish to separate clothing from textiles, food from nutrition, housing from home improvement, management of time from money management, family relationships from child development. The area dividers that you choose should be those that have the most meaning and usefulness for you.

The third step is to subdivide the subject area by concepts. This would require dividers smaller than the subject area dividers. In the area of food and nutrition you might have daily food requirements, food away from home, food service occupations, selecting food, storing food, food preparation, and table service, to name only a few.

Another division that is possible but not necessary is by course offerings. This helps when you are developing a test for a particular grade level. The most reasonable division would be first by grade or course levels; second, by areas; and third, by concepts. Whether or not you use this kind of division is a personal choice.

The most essential decision is the one to begin a test item file. It is hoped that by now you have made this decision and are ready to go buy a small file box and a package of index cards. Once this step is taken the rest is relatively simple. It is a decision you will never regret.

Summary

This chapter like the previous three will be summarized by conclusions. The statements that follow are all conclusions drawn by the author about analysis of objective tests. We can conclude that:

- the difficulty of a test as a whole should be estimated;
- a measure of central tendency or average should be computed and compared with the possible score;
- a range should be determined for a set of scores;
- a frequency table or curve should be constructed in order to effectively present the distribution of scores in a range;
- the difficulty index should be computed for each test item;
- a difficulty index of 40 to 60 should be used as a guide for selecting items for a test;
- the index of discrimination should be computed for each test item;
- an index of discrimination of fifteen percent or more should be used as a guide for selecting test items;

- test items should be analyzed to determine why they are not sufficiently difficult or discriminating;
- a test file should be begun and added to periodically;
- analysis data, answers, times used, and objectives should be included
  with test items placed in the file.

STUDENT ACTIVITIES

1. Estimate the difficulty of a test that you or someone else has given by:
   a. determining the range
   b. constructing a frequency table
   c. constructing a frequency curve

2. Compute a difficulty index for each item on the same test and indicate which
   items have a difficulty index:
   a. between 40 and 60
   b. above 60
   c. below 40

3. Compute an index of discrimination for each item on the same test and indicate
   which items:
   a. discriminate at the fifteen percent level or above
   b. do not discriminate
   c. are reversals

4. Develop a test file and:
   a. record each item included on the above named test on an index card.
   b. write an objective above each test item.
   c. write the answer on the back of the card.
   d. record the difficulty index and the index of discrimination with the date
      on the back of the card.

REFERENCES

Arny, Clara Brown. *Evaluation In Home Economics.* New York: Appleton-Century-Crofts, 1953.

Ahmann, J. Stanley and Glock, M. D. *Evaluating Pupil Growth.* New York: Allyn
and Bacon, Inc., 1959.

Gronlund, Norman E. *Measurement and Evaluation in Teaching.* New York: The
Macmillan Company, 1971.

Part III NONTEST DEVICES

INTRODUCTION

The previous parts of this book have discussed philosophy of evaluation, explained different types of behavioral objectives and their relationship to evaluation, and illustrated the development of objective and essay tests. Part III attempts to explain and illustrate the development and use of nontest devices and procedures which include rating devices, reporting forms, sociometric and audio-visual techniques.

Nontest devices and procedures are particularly applicable for the evaluation of personal qualities and homemaking skills; they do not easily lend themselves to the testing of knowledge. Neither do nontest devices result in a score or a grade in the same manner as do tests of knowledge. Devices that evaluate products and skills are much more adaptable for grading purposes than are those designed to evaluate personal qualities such as values, attitudes, and relationships.

Rating devices include checklists, rating scales, and scorecards. These are very useful in evaluating personal qualities. Rating scales and scorecards are used frequently to evaluate the products and procedures resulting from the development of homemaking and occupational skills.

Reporting forms include project reports, diaries and logs, questionnaires, anecdotal records, and autobiographies. Project reports can and frequently do evaluate personal qualities, skills, and knowledge. Whether or not a project does evaluate all three depends upon the questions or form of the report. Diaries and logs, along with questionnaires and autobiographies, reveal personal qualities far more often than any other type of learning.

Audio-visual techniques are usually incorporated with some other technique. Tape recorders, films, photographs, slides, and graphs are the more usual audio-visual techniques. As a group these are more usable for evaluating personal qualities than for evaluating knowledge or skills.

Chapter 11 describes the uses, advantages, and limitations of observational devices. Examples of checklists, rating scales, and scorecards are given to further illustrate the uses of observational devices. Chapter 12 is concerned with reporting forms which include project reports, diaries, logs, questionnaires, anecdotal records and autobiographies. The uses, advantages, and limitations of each of these are described and each is illustrated. Audio-visual techniques, rarely used for any purpose other than evaluating personal qualities, are explained in Chapter 13. Chapter 14 describes and illustrates sociometric techniques such as the sociogram, who's who, and roleplaying.

Chapter 11 OBSERVATIONAL DEVICES

The major uses of rating devices are evaluating personal qualities and appraising processes and products. Most of these devices, usable by students and by teachers, are particularly adaptable to self-evaluation. The types of rating devices that are discussed in this chapter include checklists, rating scales, and scorecards.

Checklists

A checklist is the simplest to construct and use of all the rating devices. A checklist can be defined as a list of characteristics or criteria which requires a simple check of whether or not each item on the list has been met. Frequently an in-between answer of *somewhat* is used with a *yes* and *no,* making a three-choice answer possible.

There are both advantages and limitations in the use of checklists. These do not really determine whether or not you decide to use a checklist. The determining factor is what kind of behavior you are attempting to evaluate and whether or not a checklist is the most appropriate technique.

Checklists can be developed and used as a part of the teaching-learning situation. Students can help develop a checklist by identifying the criteria that will be included. This means the items on the checklist are more readily accepted by the students as desirable. It also results in students' knowing what each of the criteria really means. Checklists are very easy for students to answer. The directions are usually simple and decision making is relatively easy compared to other rating devices. A student can readily see how well he is doing and draw his own conclusions about his progress and direction.

Checklists are easy and not too time-consuming to construct. For many teachers this is one of their chief advantages. A teacher can take a list of characteristics identified by students, edit for consistency of form, write a set of directions, and provide columns for checking. The result is a quickly constructed checklist. These same checklists are easy to interpret for the same reasons that they are easy to construct.

Checklists are extremely versatile: they are usable in a variety of situations in all areas of home economics and adaptable to all ages and to all levels of ability. Checklists can be used to evaluate groups as well as individuals. The same form can be used several times to evaluate similar or identical situations.

A disadvantage of checklists is that they do not readily lend themselves to scores or grades. It is not always necessary to have a score and so this need not be a serious disadvantage. When grading time arrives in a course where personal qualities and participation are of primary concern, a lack of scores could be a handicap in recording a grade that is representative of student performance.

Checklists provide only a surface evaluation. They may be lacking in reliability. The extent to which the evaluation is accurate depends upon how concrete the evidence is. Checklists for evaluating products are usually more reliable than those that are designed to evaluate personal qualities.

The disadvantages of checklists are far less important than are the advantages. This should imply that you will want to use them for evaluating personal qualities, processes, and products, particularly when you want students to do self-evaluation.

Construction of all checklists follow the same general procedures. The suggested guidelines discussed below should help you to develop your own checklists. They are arranged in order so that they are not only guidelines but also steps in developing a checklist.

(1) Each criterion or characteristic to be included in a checklist should be identified and described. This step is critical to the development of an effective checklist. The criteria should be related directly to the quality being evaluated by the checklist. The description of each criterion contributes to both the validity and reliability of the checklist. The usability of the device is perhaps

greater than either the validity and the reliability because of the descriptive statements.

(2) Each item should be carefully edited so as to provide for grammatical consistency. This means that each statement is similar to all other statements. A mixture not only confuses the respondent but makes a definite pattern of answers impossible to establish. Each statement should be stated in the same way. If the first criterion is stated as a sentence, then all the following criteria should be stated in the same manner. If phrases are used, then this should become the accepted pattern.

(3) All items should be stated in the same manner, such as positively or negatively. When one statement is positive and another negative with the desirable answer for both being "yes", nothing but confusion will result. Neither does a consistent pattern emerge which prevents a student from readily identifying weaknesses and strengths.

(4) Criteria or behaviors should be arranged in a logical manner. Items that are similar should be grouped together. A sequence should be observed when one exists. For example, when work habits in a foods laboratory lesson are evaluated, the behaviors should be listed in the same sequence that lab tasks occur with those behaviors that are general listed first.

(5) Directions should be concisely stated and placed before the list of criteria that are to be evaluated. It is helpful to draw a line under the word *directions* as well as any key words that are contained in the directions.

(6) Two or three columns should be provided for checking the appropriate answer. A simple *yes* or *no* frequently needs a middle column labeled *sometimes* or *somewhat.* An answer that may be *always* or *never* usually needs *occasionally* added. Answers are seldom that positive or that negative.

(7) Each of the columns should be labeled with an appropriate heading. Those given in the preceding paragraphs are the more usual ones. Sometimes *maybe* is used with *yes* or *no.* If a checklist is more than one page, the columns on all pages should be labeled.

(8) A blank should be provided for a total score when such a score is desirable. A total score can be converted into *excellent, good, fair, poor,* and even into letter grades. More often than not a total score is not needed since individual behaviors are being evaluated.

(9) A space should be provided for name of student, class period, course number, and date. This provides a permanent means of identification and prevents a checklist from becoming an item for "file thirteen."

Checklists are used to evaluate personal qualities, participation, products, processes, and projects. As has already been pointed out, these checklists are usable by both students and teachers, independent of each other or in cooperation with each other. Checklists are all similar in nature but different in the behaviors or criteria that are listed. Examples are given on the next few pages for each of the above named uses.

Personal qualities that can be evaluated using a checklist include interpersonal relationships, interests, opinions, attitudes, and appreciations. One or more examples are given for each of these in Examples 1 through 4.

EXAMPLE 1

OBJECTIVE: *to exhibit an ability to get along with others.*

What Kind of Friend Are You?

Directions: Place a checkmark (X) in the column that represents your usual behavior.

	Yes	*Sometimes*	*No*
1. Are you cheerful when with others?			
2. Do you refrain from borrowing money from your friends?			
3. Do you compliment others upon the good things they do?			
4. Do you seldom ask your friends to wait for you?			
5. Do you restrain yourself from repeating gossip you hear?			
6. Do you seldom resent it when one of your friends is friendly to someone else?			
7. Do you seldom make cutting remarks about others?			
8. Are you friends with people other than those who "rate" at school?			
9. Do you spend little time telling your troubles to your friends?			
10. Are you a good listener?			
11. Do you seldom quarrel with friends?			

EXAMPLE 1 (continued)

	Yes	Sometimes	No
12. Have you had one or more of the same friends for several months of this year?			
13. Do you have more than one friend?			
14. Are you seldom jealous of your friends?			
15. Do you make friends easily with both boys and girls?			
16. Do you trust your friends?			

EXAMPLE 2

OBJECTIVE: *to determine interests in children.*

An Interest Inventory for Planning

Directions: The questions below will help you decide what your interests are concerning children. Place a checkmark (X) in the column that best represents your answer.

	Yes	Sometimes	No
1. Do you like to babysit?			
2. Do you know how to be a good babysitter?			
3. Do you want to feel at ease with children?			
4. Do you like children and want to have them around you?			
5. Do you know what to expect from children of different ages?			
6. Do you want to know which toys are best for children of different ages?			
7. Do you want to know which games and stories children like?			
8. Do you wish to tell a story so it will be meaningful to children?			
9. Do you want to know how to direct children's play?			
10. Do you want to know how music affects a child?			
11. Are you interested in knowing which TV programs are exciting for children?			
12. Do you know what to do when a child cries?			
13. Are you interested in why a child has fears?			

EXAMPLE 2 (continued)

	Yes	Somewhat	No
14. Do you desire to know how to care for a child in a temper tantrum?			
15. Do you know how much a child should eat?			
16. Do you know how to dress a baby?			
17. Do you know how to change a diaper?			
18. Can you give baby his bottle or baby food?			
19. If an accident happens, do you know what to do?			
20. Are you safety-conscious regarding home accidents?			

EXAMPLE 3

OBJECTIVE: *to identify own attitudes toward children.*

Checklist for the Babysitter or Play School Participant

Directions: Check (X) your answer in the appropriate column.

	Yes	Sometimes	No
1. Am I interested in children?			
2. Do I show a desire to learn more about children?			
3. Do I try to cooperate with parents in handling their children?			
4. Am I willing to set a good example?			
5. Am I willing to supervise play intelligently?			
6. Do I show tolerance and patience?			
7. Do I desire to select toys and other play materials wisely?			
8. Do I try to help children to develop good play habits?			
9. Do I help children to develop habits of independence?			
10. Do I respect the rights and feelings of children?			
11. Do I try to find the reason why a child cries?			
12. Am I fair when a child quarrels with his friends?			

EXAMPLE 4

OBJECTIVE: *to indicate an appreciation for an attractive arrangement of accessories.*

A Checklist for the Arrangement of Accessories

Directions: Place a check (X) in the appropriate column.

	Yes	*Sometimes*	*No*

Selection of Accessories

1. Is it appropriate for the type of furnishings?
2. Are good art principles applied?
3. Is the size, color, and texture suitable for the room and family?
4. Does the accessory express the personality of the owner?
5. Is it useful or serviceable?

Use of Accessories

6. Is it arranged at the most attractive place?
7. Does the accessory complement flower arrangement?
8. Are the accessories used with good taste (neither too crowded nor too many)?

Participation by a student as an individual as well as in a group is important. Examples 5 through 7 are for class participation, home responsibilities, general conduct, and observation.

EXAMPLE 5

OBJECTIVE: *to participate in an acceptable manner in class.*

How I Rate as a Class Member

Directions: Using the numbered columns to indicate the sequence of weeks from one to no more than six, score yourself using a ✓ to indicate always, an X if you don't have a perfect score, and a 0 (zero) to indicate a need for much improvement. Score yourself once a week.

	1	*2*	*3*	*4*	*5*	*6*

1. Was I in place, quiet, and ready with pencil, paper, and notebook to begin class on time?
2. Was I prepared for class every day? Had I prepared my homework, reread my notes to refresh my mind? Would I have made a satisfactory mark had a quiz been given any day this week?

EXAMPLE 5 (continued)

	1 2 3 4 5 6

3. Did I contribute intelligently to class discussions, talking in a low-pitched voice and only when I had the attention of every member of my class? Did I bring up unrelated topics? Was I a good listener?

4. Did I follow directions given the class, thereby using my class time properly?

5. Did I refrain from primping and chewing gum in class?

6. Did I voluntarily make up missed work before coming to class?

7. Did I proceed with my work when the teacher was not with the class?

8. Did I wait for the class to be dismissed or the bell to ring before putting away my work?

9. Considering the above questions, was my class better because I was present?

EXAMPLE 6

OBJECTIVE: *to assume "home" responsibilities at school.*

Checklist for Evaluating "My Home Duties at School"

Directions: Place an (X) in the column on the right-hand side that best answers each question.

	Yes	*Sometimes*	*No*

1. Do you complete your housekeeping duties within time alloted?

2. Do you work in an orderly manner?

3. Do you cooperate within your group?

4. Do you have work organized to make cleaning easier?

5. Do you accept your share of responsibilities?

6. Do you practice quick, easy, and efficient methods of housekeeping?

7. Do you accept your duty willingly?

8. Did your experience in class help you with home duties?

EXAMPLE 6 (continued)

	Yes	*Sometimes*	*No*
9. Do you think home duties are necessary at school to have a neat, orderly department?			
10. Did you think demonstrations in class are unnecessary to complete homemaking practices?			
11. Do you think home duties at school are necessary for students?			
12. Did you learn anything by doing the duties?			

Suggestions:

Give suggestions for improving our methods of keeping the department clean, orderly and attractive.

EXAMPLE 7

OBJECTIVE: *to be well-mannered by following general conduct rules determined by class.*

A Checklist for General Conduct Rules

Directions: Place an (X) in that column that best describes your conduct in the food lab.

	Yes	*Sometimes*	*No*
1. Talked in low tones			
2. Did not call across the room			
3. Stayed in assigned kitchen			
4. Worked quietly with equipment			
5. Allowed others to do their own work			
6. Did not borrow from neighbors			
7. Refrained from telling others what to do			
8. Did not laugh at the mistakes of others			
9. Cooperated with partner			
10. Was courteous to others			
11. Started to work on schedule			
12. Did not demand too much of teacher's time			

Products that can be evaluated with checklists include purchased items, constructed items, equipment, and arrangements. Examples 8 through 10 illustrate these kinds of checklists.

EXAMPLE 8

OBJECTIVE: *to select ready-made clothing for myself.*

A Checklist for Buying Ready-made Clothing
(skirts, blouses, dresses)

Directions: Place a check (X) in the appropriate column on the right.

	Yes	No

1. Is the fabric of good quality?
2. Is it serviceable for my needs?
3. Does the label give adequate information about fiber content and care?
4. Is the workmanship of good quality?
5. Are the fastenings and placket serviceable?
6. Is the garment cut correctly according to the grain of the fabric?
7. Are plaids, stripes, and checks accurately matched?
8. Are the trimmings of good quality and the belt well made?
9. Is the price in line with the quality of the garment?
10. Is the hem wide enough for lengthening?
11. Is there ample seam allowance and are the seams finished to prevent raveling?
12. Is the fit perfect for me?

EXAMPLE 9

OBJECTIVE: *to acquire small equipment needed for clothing construction.*

1   *Are You All Here?*

Directions: See if you have all the necessary equipment for sewing. Put an (X) in the first column if you have the article at school today. Put an (X) in the second column if you have your name on the article or package.

	Have Equipment	Name on Article

1. Package of medium-sized needles
2. Package of sharp-pointed pins
3. Thimble that fits my finger
4. Pincushion that pins go into easily
5. Tape measure with numbers that start on opposite ends

EXAMPLE 9 (continued)

	Have Equipment	*Name on Article*
6. Scissors that are sharp-pointed and will cut cloth		
7. Thread to match material		
8. Thread to baste of contrasting color		
9. Sturdy box to hold sewing supplies		
10. Suitable pattern (name on each piece)		

Did you have X's in each column? If you do not have some article, please explain why you do not.

EXAMPLE 10

OBJECTIVE: *to evaluate a table setting that has been created by self.*

Checklist on Table Setting

Directions: Place an (X) in the appropriate column.

	Yes	*Somewhat*	*No*
1. Is the tablecloth or placemat on straight?			
2. Are the covers opposite each other?			
3. Is the centerpiece low and placed in the center of the table?			
4. Is there just enough silverware and china so that the table does not appear crowded?			
5. Is each individual cover set properly?			
6. Are the serving dishes arranged for the convenience of the host and hostess?			
7. Does each person have about eighteen inches for his cover?			
8. Are the chairs placed so that they will not have to be pulled out from under the table when each guest sits down?			
9. Have you remembered everything that should be on the table?			
10. Are the dishes far enough away from the edge of the table?			
11. Are all dishes free of finger marks?			
12. Is all the serving silver on the table and in place?			

Processes that can be evaluated using checklists include work habits, practices, and pressing habits. Examples 11, 12, and 13 illustrate each of these.

EXAMPLE 11

OBJECTIVE: *to use effective habits of work in the kitchen.*

A Checklist for Work Habits in Kitchen

Directions: Place an (X) in the column that best describes your work habits.

Yes   Sometimes   No

1. Wore an apron and a cotton dress
2. Washed hands before starting to work
3. Assembled all supplies before starting to mix
4. Used only the supplies needed
5. Followed the recipe accurately
6. Measured accurately
7. Turned on range at proper time
8. Kept working space clean
9. Wiped hands on hand towel
10. Used clean spoon for tasting
11. Rinsed utensils when finished with them
12. Scraped bowls and measuring cups clean
13. Used paper to catch scraps
14. Put away all equipment
15. Emptied garbage
16. Left kitchen spotless

EXAMPLE 12

OBJECTIVE: *to use effective practices when shopping for groceries.*

Check Your Shopping Practices

Directions: Answer each question by checking the appropriate column.

Always   Usually   Never

1. Were like foods listed together on your list?
2. Did you go up one aisle and down another as you came to them?
3. Did you check items off the list as you bought them?
4. Did you read labels?

EXAMPLE 12 (continued)

Always Usually Never

5. Did you refrain from buying more than one "extra"?

6. Did you buy only the quantity you needed?

7. Did you compare prices?

8. Did you buy familiar brands?

9. Did you select your own fruits and vegetables?

10. Did you refrain from "fingering" the food on the counters?

11. Were you considerate of other shoppers?

12. Did you stay within your food budget?

EXAMPLE 13

OBJECTIVE: to press clothing correctly.

A Checklist of Your Pressing Habits

Directions: Place an (X) in the appropriate column on the right.

Yes No

1. Did you read the label on the garment (or information on the bolt) to get information concerning pressing and temperatures?

2. Did you test the temperature of the iron on a seam or other hidden place before you began pressing?

3. Did you press with the grain of the material?

4. Did you press silk, wool, and most synthetic materials on the wrong side to prevent shine?

5. Did you use a press cloth or steam iron when necessary?

6. Did you press trimmings, collar and sleeves first, in order to prevent wrinkling of the body of the garment?

7. After pressing, did you check to see if any parts needed retouching?

8. Did you hang the garment on a hanger and close all fasteners?

9. Did you press rather than iron at all times?

10. Did you use the needle board when necessary?

Rating Scales

A rating scale has not only a list of characteristics but also multi-level descriptions for each characteristic. These descriptive levels make rating scales different from checklists or scorecards. Scores rather than checkmarks are used to indicate which descriptive level has been identified.

Advantages far outweigh the disadvantages of rating scales. If you do not construct your own rating scales but use those developed by others, you really have only advantages. Once you have developed and reproduced the rating scales you wish to use, you have eliminated the disadvantages.

A major advantage of rating scales when compared to other observational devices is that behaviors are precisely defined. The descriptive levels indicate very clearly the expectations at the highest, medium, and lowest levels. This means that both students and teacher can easily and quickly identify the behaviors that best describe a student in a given situation.

The descriptive levels provide a continuum and this is a decided advantage over the *yes-no* structure of a checklist. Some rating scales contain only two descriptive levels, but generally there are three levels. The descriptions are given odd number ratings with even numbers placed between so that a three-description rating scale has five possible ratings.

Students can readily see the lowest or most undesirable type of behavior as well as the top level. This aids students in knowing what is expected of them. It is possible to accomplish both self-evaluation and cooperative evaluation with a minimum of frustration.

A disadvantage of rating scales is that construction is time-consuming. The writing of the descriptive levels cannot be done hurriedly if they are to be both precise and concise. Each level must vary considerably from the others if a continuum is to exist. Rating scales also need to be pilot-tested before being used so as to eliminate errors and misleading statements. All of this takes time.

It is difficult to involve students in the development of a rating scale. They can identify the components of the overall framework but have considerable difficulty in distinguishing levels. The time needed also prohibits great involvement on the part of students. This chief disadvantage is that students are more willing to use and will more easily understand an observational device when they have been involved in its construction.

Construction of rating scales is done on a continuum base. As you have already read, this is the major difference between rating scales, scorecards, and checklists. Otherwise, rating scales should be constructed following the same guidelines as those given in rules (1) through (5) as well as (8) and (9) on pages 178-80. Go back and review these before reading the additional suggestions which follow.

(1) Each of the characteristics should stand apart from all others. Grouping of characteristics only confuses the rater. For example, well-groomed, appropriately dressed, becomingly dressed are three separate criteria although each has to do with appearance. A person could be two of these without being the third.

(2) Each level should contain words that clearly indicate the condition to be described. Ambiguous words are confusing. The descriptive levels should also be concise; eliminate repetition and unnecessary wording.

(3) The columns of descriptions should be labeled with numbers. The lowest level usually carries the rating of "1." The highest level of a two-column rating scale is then labeled "3," with a three-column device using "5." The even numbers of "2" and "4" are placed between the descriptive columns. This provides the rater with a definite score should he feel that the person being rated really comes between the two descriptions.

The Examples 14 through 18 explain these three guidelines in more detail.

Rating scales are used to evaluate personal qualities, products, processes, and projects. The section on checklists contains examples of many devices for evaluating the end results of these same behaviors. There will be far fewer rating scales in this section for evaluating personal qualities. Perhaps the reason is that personal qualities are more successfully defined with simple statements than in the section describing checklists.

Personal qualities that are readily evaluated by use of a rating scale are generally confined to interpersonal relationshipw. Example 14 is such a device. Rating scales for attitudes and appreciations can be developed but are difficult to distinguish between the various levels.

EXAMPLE 14

OBJECTIVE: *to determine how one rates as a family member.*

How I Rate as a Family Member

Directions: If your evaluation of yourself falls between the description labeled 1 and the description labeled 3, your rating will be 2. The same thing applies to a rating of 4. 1 is the poorest or lowest rating, 3 medium or average, and 5 highest or excellent. Total your score at the end.

	1	*2*	*3*	*4*	*5*	*Rating*
1. Moody, unhappy person.		Usually cheerful.		Cheerful, happy at all times.		

EXAMPLE 14 (continued)

	1	2	3	4	5	Rating

2. Completely disinterested in interests of other family members. / Partially interested in interests of other family members. / Extremely interested in interests of other family members.

3. Make no effort to understand parent's viewpoint. / Make some attempt to understand parent's viewpoint. / Make a sincere effort to understand parent's viewpoint.

4. Never discuss important matters with parents. / Sometimes discuss important matters with parents. / Discuss all important matters with parents.

5. Make no effort to have friends and parents know each other. / Make some effort to have friends and parents get to know each other. / Make a big effort to have friends and parents get to know each other.

6. Not dependable. / Usually dependable. / Always dependable.

7. Do unpleasant tasks unhappily. / Usually do unpleasant tasks willingly. / Carry out unpleasant tasks cheerfully and willingly at all times.

8. Take no advantage of opportunities parents give me. / Take some advantage of opportunities parents give me. / Take advantage of all opportunities parents give me.

9. Ask special favors that other family members do not get. / Sometimes ask special favors that other family members do not get. / Never ask special favors that other family members do not get.

TOTAL

Products that can be evaluated by a rating scale are the same as those for which a checklist or scorecard is appropriate. These are usually in the areas of clothing, foods, and housing. Examples 15, 16, and 17 illustrate this conclusion.

EXAMPLE 15

OBJECTIVE: to evaluate the fabric purchased for constructing a blouse.

Evaluation of a Blouse Fabric

Directions: In evaluating your choice of fabric for a blouse, rate each of the characteristics listed below by this scale: 5 excellent, 4 **good**, 3 average, 2 fair, and 1 poor. Total your score when you have finished.

	1	*2*	*3*	*4*	*5*	*Rating*
1.	The fabric is a poor color for your skin tone.		The fabric is a fair color for your skin tone.		The fabric is an excellent color for your skin tone.	
2.	The fabric is not at all appropriate for the pattern chosen.		The fabric is fairly appropriate for the pattern chosen.		The fabric is very appropriate for the pattern chosen.	
3.	The fabric is not at all appropriate for a blouse.		The fabric is fairly appropriate for a blouse.		The fabric is very appropriate for a blouse.	
4.	The fabric is not at all colorfast and fades a great deal in sun and water.		The fabric fades somewhat in sun and water.		The fabric is colorfast.	
5.	The fabric is very difficult to handle and sew.		The fabric is fairly easy to handle and sew but sometimes slips and puckers.		The fabric is very easy to handle and sew.	
6.	The fabric must have much special care.		The fabric requires some special care.		The fabric is very easy to care for.	

TOTAL

EXAMPLE 16

OBJECTIVE: *to evaluate the unit construction of a sleeve.*

Rating Scale for Sleeves and Armholes

<u>Directions:</u>   Rate each characteristic listed. If the evaluation falls between the description labeled 1 and the description labeled 3, the rating should be 2. A rating of 1 is the lowest score and a rating of 3 the highest.

1	*2*	*3*	*Rating*
1. Sleeve is placed too far forward or back; does not fit naturally.	Curved seam fits smoothly; free from pulling (sleeve).		
2. Curved seam does not fit smoothly.	Curved seam fits smoothly (blouse)		
3. Tucks and gathers in sleeve.	Sleeves are free from tucks and gathers.		
4. Raw edges left on facings.	Sleeve facing is suitable to material and type of garment and is finished correctly.		
5. Hand stitches show on right side.	Hand stitches are invisible on right side.		
6. Facing edges vary in width.	Facing edges are correct width.		
7. Dolman sleeves aren't reinforced under arm.	Dolman sleeves reinforced under arm.		
8. Hem or cuff uneven, too long or too short.	Hem of sleeve and cuff even in width and length.		

TOTAL SCORE
HIGHEST POSSIBLE SCORE

EXAMPLE 17

OBJECTIVE: *to evaluate a menu planned for a foods lab lesson.*

Rating Scale on Meal Planning

<u>Directions:</u>   Rate your menu by recording the rating that best fits, using 2 and 4 when you feel your menu is between the descriptions. Underline those phrases that best describe your menu. Total your score at the end.

	1	*2*	*3*	*4*	*5*	*Rating*
A. Menu						
1. Time	Meal elaborate;		Meal somewhat complicated;		Meal simple; could easily be	

EXAMPLE 17 (continued)

	1	*2*	*3*	*4*	*5*	*Rating*
		cannot be easily prepared in time available.	could be prepared in time but might rush worker		prepared in time available.	
2.	Cost	Excessive cost; foods out of season, too expensive for school use.	Moderate cost; some unnecessary expense involved.		Reasonable cost; no extra expense involved.	
3.	Contrasts	Little or no contrast in color, texture, flavor, temperature, shape and nutrients. Meal uninteresting.	Some constrast in either color, texture, flavor, temperature, shape or in nutrients. Meal rather interesting.		Good contrasts in color, texture, flavor, temperature, shape and nutrients. An interesting meal.	
4.	Suitability	Menu unsuited to both equipment available and energy involved in preparation.	Menu suitable either for equipment or for energy, but not for both.		Menu suited both to available equipment and for wise use of energy.	
5.	Order Lists	Not all foods needed are included; quantities not stated or not suitable.	Most of foods needed are included; quantities may be questioned for service of group.		All foods needed are included; in reasonable quantities for service of group.	

TOTAL

Processes can also be evaluated using rating scales. The simpler process probably should be analyzed by using a checklist whereas the more complicated lend themselves to the use of a rating scale. Example 18 is for a more complicated process.

EXAMPLE 18

OBJECTIVE: *to determine quality of a rearranged work area in a*
                 kitchen.

Rating Scale for Evaluating Arrangement of Work Areas

Directions: Place the rating you select in the last column on the right
                 under "Rating." If the rating falls between 1 and 2, it will
                 be evaluated as poor, 3 and 4 will be average, and 5 will
                 be excellent. Use a number for rating.

1	*2*	*3*	*4*	*5*	*Rating*

Kitchen Work Areas

1. Space limited for work areas. | Some space provided. | Adequate work space in all work areas.

2. Not enough cabinets for storage. | Cabinets for the essential storage, such as groceries, small utensils, and dishes. | Cabinets for all storage and counters of convenient heights.

3. Confusion and cross traffic; doors not located in proper area. | Three doors in kitchen adds some cross traffic, but located fairly well | Work area reasonably free of cross traffic because only two doors are used and are conveniently located.

4. Scattered appliances. | Appliances that are somewhat inconveniently located in the room. | Appropriate appliances arranged for convenience in different centers.

5. Unorganized but compact. | Work areas organized but rather rambling. | Work areas organized into reasonably compact centers; convenient.

Scorecards

The scorecard was apparently used in home economics before either the checklist or rating scale. It lends itself particularly to products and processes (see Examples 19 through 23), and since

EXAMPLE 19

OBJECTIVE: to evaluate the ability to operate a sewing machine.

Scorecard for Operation of Sewing Machine

Directions: Score yourself from 1 to the highest possible score. Ask
your teacher to do the same thing.

	Standard Score	My Score	Teacher's Score
1. Know the parts of the machine.	10		
2. Can thread machine quickly and correctly.	10		
3. Can thread bobbin.	5		
4. Can wind the bobbin.	5		
5. Can bring up the bobbin thread.	5		
6. Can regulate the stitch.	5		
7. Can stitch straight line using guide.	5		
8. Can hand-tie threads at end of stitching.	5		
9. Can machine-knot thread at end of stitching.	5		
10. Can backstitch evenly.	5		
TOTAL	60		

home economics places emphasis on skill development in performing home-making tasks, the early use of scorecards is understandable.

Advantages and disadvantages of scorecards balance out each other. Their usability is sometimes questioned because they lack objectivity and reliability. Scorecards can be used successfully to evaluate products and processes. They are more accurately used when the same person does all of the evaluations.

Scorecards are easy to construct. Teachers find that they can quickly list the characteristics desired and assign a standard score to each one. Most scorecards contain no more than a dozen items. The ease of construction is a definite advantage.

Scorecards can be used as a part of teaching-learning. Students can be involved in the development of a scorecard by assisting in the identification of the various characteristics. Texts and references can be used to find appropriate descriptive wording for each characteristic. Students can also help in deciding what the standard score for each characteristic will be. In this way they identify the standards for the product or process. When

EXAMPLE 20

OBJECTIVE: *to determine how well dietary needs are being met.*

A Dietary Scorecard

Directions: Record your score (1-10) for each of the food groups and arrive at total.

Foods	Each Day You Need	Score for One day	Your Score
Green and yellow vegetables	1 serving	10	
Citrus fruits or other vitamin C-rich foods	1 serving	10	
Potatoes and other vegetables and fruits	3 servings	5	
Milk & milk products	3-4 cups	20	
Meat, poultry, fish	1 serving	15	
Meat, poultry, fish, or meat alternates	1 serving	10	
Eggs	1 daily (4 per wk.)	5	
Whole grain or enriched bread or cereal	1 serving per meal	10	
Butter or other fats	2-3 tbsp.	5	
A good breakfast, including some form of protein, as milk or egg.		10	

TOTAL 100

scorecards are used as a means of self- or cooperative evaluation, further learning takes place.

A third advantage is that a scorecard can result in a grade. While most teachers prefer not to give grades, nearly all are required to do so. Students and parents understand grading a product or a process. Grades and scores do communicate a degree of success. So use a score for grading purposes if you desire.

The limited use of a scorecard is a disadvantage. Personal qualities, as a general rule, are not effectively evaluated by this device. Processes can be somewhat successfully evaluated. The best use of scorecards is in product evaluation.

Another disadvantage is the difficulty of arriving at a score for each individual item. If a standard score is 10, a person has ten alternatives from

EXAMPLE 21

OBJECTIVE: *to rate a piece of large equipment before making a purchase.*

Scorecard for Buying Large Equipment

Directions: In the column to the right, score each item 1 to 4 points. Determine your score by the characteristics of large equipment. Total your score by adding all the points together.

Characteristics	*Perfect Score*	*Your Score*
Appropriateness		
1. For family needs	4	
2. For family size	4	
3. For individual preferences	4	
4. For amount of money	4	
5. For design of other appliances	4	
6. For allotted space	4	
7. For color scheme	4	
8. For existing conditions of location in area	4	
Serviceability		
9. Easy cleaning	4	
10. Recognizable brand	4	
11. Reliable dealer	4	
12. Reliable guarantee	4	
13. Clearly stated instruction book	4	
Construction		
14. Feels steady and solid	4	
15. Interior smooth, without cracks and crevices	4	
16. Good insulation	4	
17. Motor is quiet when running	4	
18. Leveling feet	4	
19. Exterior made of durable material	4	
20. Interior made of resistant material	4	
21. Trays, racks, and dispensers made of rust-resistant material	4	
22. Conveniently located removable parts or vents	4	
23. Conveniently located controls	4	
24. Conveniently hinged	4	
25. Door or parts fit securely	4	
TOTAL	100	

which to choose. The inexperienced evaluator meets great frustration and even an experienced evaluator wishes for more direction.

Construction of a scorecard is relatively simple but there are definite rules to follow. The same rules apply for scorecards as for checklists and rating scales. Reread suggestions one through five, eight, and nine given for checklists (see pages 178-80) before reading the additional ones given below that pertain only to scorecards.

(1) The lists of described characteristics are usually stated in concise phrases. Sentences can be used but do require more space and more reading time.

(2) A standard score must be established for each listed characteristic. Sometimes the same standard score is given to each item which makes it easier for the evaluator. At other times, it seems desirable to have a different number of points for each characteristic. Whichever you decide, a standard score is a must.

(2) Space to record a score must be provided for each characteristic. Sometimes spaces are provided for student scores and for teacher scores. The second or third space can be included for a parent or classmate to score each characteristic.

Scorecards are useful for evaluating processes, products and projects. It is possible (standard) to evaluate some few personal qualities but scorecards are seldom used for this purpose.

EXAMPLE 22

OBJECTIVE: *to evaluate the dress being considered for purchase.*

Scorecard for Evaluating Dress

Directions: Score your dress from 1 to the maximum points given for each characteristic.

	Perfect Score	Score Pupil	Teacher
1. Color is appropriate for your coloring; becoming to you.	8		
2. Style is appropriate for your figure type.	10		
3. Fit of the garment is pleasing both in appearance and to wearer.	10		
4. All seams are straight and have the correct allowances.	5		
5. Hem is straight and stitches do not show on the right side; is correct width.	8		
6. Zipper smooth with no ripples; machine stitches are straight.	5		
7. Style of dress is correct for type of fabric used.	8		

EXAMPLE 22 (continued)

		Perfect Score	Score Pupil	Teacher
8.	Sleeves are sewn in smoothly with no puckers at top; are not too light or too loose.	8		
9.	Skirt and other parts of the garment are cut on grain; hangs gracefully.	10		
10.	Length of dress is appropriate for your figure type; is neither too long nor too short; is level all around; is becoming to shape of legs.	5		
11.	Hand stitching is neat; stitches do not show; correct hand stitch was used for place or position on garment.	7		
12.	Machine stitching is straight.	8		
13.	Darts come out to a smooth point; are not puckered at the point.	8		
14.	Stitching on belt is straight; buckle is neatly and correctly covered.	8		
15.	Fasteners are neatly sewn on; are correctly placed.	5		
16.	Facings are neat; do not show or tend to show.	9		
17.	Buttonholes are correctly placed and worked.	5		
	TOTAL	127		

EXAMPLE 23

OBJECTIVE: **to evaluate a meal prepared to serve to own family.**

Scorecard for a Family Meal

Directions: Score as follows: 5 excellent, 4 very good, 3 good, 2 fair, and 1 poor.

		Standard Score	Pupil Score
1.	Interesting and tasty menu	5	
2.	Suitable for season of year	5	
3.	Suitable for group	5	
4.	Nutritionally good	5	

EXAMPLE 23 (continued)

		Standard Score	*Pupil Score*
5.	Both hot and cold foods	5	
6.	Table properly set	5	
7.	Prepared in time allotted	5	
8.	Attractively served	5	
9.	Food correctly served	5	
10.	Pleasing contrast of textures	5	
11.	Correct amount prepared	5	
12.	Good work habits	5	
	TOTAL	60	

Summary

Rating devices serve many purposes including learning and teaching. You are aware now of how to construct your own checklists, rating scales, and scorecards. You also realize that you can adopt or adapt already constructed devices to suit your own purposes. This chapter as well as all others in Part III will be summarized by stating your own conclusions. It is hoped you will agree with most of them. We can conclude that:

- rating devices include checklists, rating scales, and scorecards;

- rating devices are particularly useful for evaluating personal qualities, processes, and products;

- rating devices can be used as teaching-learning techniques;

- checklists and scorecards are not time-consuming to construct but rating scales are;

- scores from rating devices can be used for grading purposes if desirable or necessary;

- each criterion or characteristic included in a rating device should be concisely and precisely described;

- directions should be clearly stated for each device and placed above the list of criteria;

- checklists are more appropriate for evaluating personal qualities than are rating scales and scorecards;

- rating scales are particularly useful for teaching standards;

     – scorecards are very effective as devices for evaluating products;

     – checklists are the easiest for students to use, with rating scales second and scorecards the most difficult.

STUDENT ACTIVITIES

1. Develop a checklist for each of the following:
   a. a personal quality
   b. students' participation
   c. a product
   d. a process
   e. a project

2. Evaluate each checklist using the rules for construction described in this chapter.

3. Develop a rating scale for each of the following:
   a. a personal quality
   b. a product
   c. a process
   d. a project

4. Evaluate each rating scale using the rules for construction described in this chapter.

5. Develop a scorecard for each of the following:
   a. a product
   b. a process
   c. a project

6. Evaluate each scorecard using the rules for construction described in this chapter.

7. Establish a file folder for each type of rating device and place your samples in the appropriate folders.

REFERENCES

Ahmann, J. Stanley and Glock, M. D., *Evaluating Pupil Growth.* New York: Allyn and Bacon, Inc., 1959.

Arny, Clara Brown, *Evaluation in Home Economics.* New York: Appleton-Century-Crofts, 1953.

Fleck, Henrietta. *Toward Better Teaching of Home Economics.* New York: The Macmillan Company, 1968.

Gronlund, Norman E. *Measurement and Evaluation in Teaching.* New York: The Macmillan Company, 1971.

Williamson, Maude and Lyle, M. S. *Homemaking Education in the High School.* New York: Appleton-Century-Crofts, 1961.

Chapter 12 REPORTING FORMS

Students carry out many activities and projects that require a more detailed report or evaluation than can be provided by using a rating device. Project reports, logs, and activity reports are the three major techniques for evaluating these projects and activities. Teachers frequently need more personal information about students than can be obtained from rating devices. You will find questionnaires, autobiographies, diaries, and anecdotal records useful for obtaining certain kinds of personal data.

Project Reports

Home-degree projects are an integral part of home economics and the Future Homemakers of America program. Vocational home economics teachers are expected to require home projects of their students. Many other teachers, recognizing their worth, make the same requirements.

Evaluating these home projects has always been of considerable concern to teachers. Whether or not to grade, give extra credit, or give no credit are the major problems. The author believes that credit should be given for required projects and this credit should contribute to an overall grade. Students who do not do well on tests frequently carry out excellent projects.

Not to give these students recognition is most unfair. A required project should be evaluated and the rating or score included in a grade. Probably the reason some teachers have not used a home project as a part of the grade is that scoring is difficult. The forms included in his chapter and the rating devices in the preceding chapters should help you to evaluate projects.

Purposes of project report forms focus upon the individual student. A clue to consider is to evaluate each student in terms of his own progress rather than in comparison to other students. This is the philosophy behind home-degree projects. A girl classified as a slow learner earned the highest FHA degree because she accomplished her goals and exhibited growth in the process. It is doubtful that any other phase of a school program can provide this kind of success for students of all ability levels.

Reports constitute the only consistent technique for evaluating home-degree projects. Rating devices do not provide a consistent record because of increased awareness of what is expected and because the rater is not always in the same mood. A teacher, a student, or anyone else can review project reports from year to year as well as over a year's period of time and recognize growth and progress.

Skill in expressing oneself can be developed through use of project report forms. Many students have difficulty not only in recognizing what they have learned but also in recording the evidences in writing. Teachers must provide forms that encourage the development of such skill and must also teach students how to record the evidences.

Reports of home projects provide a means for reporting personal growth. If goals are realistically determined and complete plans made, a girl can see how she has developed the identified skills. A report form needs to provide direction for recording this personal growth. Comparison to other students is thus avoided.

Reports can contribute to a permanent record of home-degree projects. A folder for each student can be used to file each project report as well as a continuous report form. This folder can go with the student as he progresses through several years of home economics. Such complete records are very useful in applying for a scholarship as well as in providing a permanent record.

Construction of project report forms is determined by the information needed. This should say to you that your first step is to determine the kinds of data you want students to record. This will be largely determined by the age level of the students and whether or not this is a first-year project or a more advanced one. The guidelines that follow will help you to construct appropriate forms for reporting home-degree projects.

(1) Spaces should be provided for identifying information. A blank for the name of the student is usually found in the upper right-hand

corner of the page. A second blank for date may follow the name blank. Space also needs to be provided for the name of the project. This is usually placed just above the evaluation data.

(2) Directions should be very specific. These may be brief or very detailed, depending upon how much direction is needed for the student to record what is expected. Sometimes it is helpful to provide examples as a part of the directions.

(3) Space is frequently provided for the statement of goals and/or objectives. This is not always necessary since they are stated in the project plan. However, if more than one objective is to be evaluated, each objective should be keyed to the recorded evaluation evidences.

(4) Activities carried out are more often than not recorded in a project report. Some teachers consider this as evaluation but the degree of success of these activities is what you want to know. Therefore you will want to provide spaces for recording evidences of completion of each planned activity.

Project report forms range from very simple to very complex. The first example is simple and appropriate for a first-year project. The second example is a little more complicated and could be used toward the last of the first year or at the beginning of the second year of projects. The third example is a form that has been used to evaluate State Degrees and therefore is designed for advanced students. The fourth example is a cumulative record and is kept from year to year. These report forms can successfully be used in conjunction with the rating devices recommended in the preceding chapter.

EXAMPLE 1

OBJECTIVE: *to record reactions to a first home-degree project.*

My Reactions to My Degree Project

Name of Project _____

Directions: Describe how you feel about your home project as well as
                 what you have learned by completing each of the lines
                 below with the first thing that "pops into your head."

1. My home project

2. My mother

EXAMPLE 1 (continued)

3. The new skills I have gained

4. The understandings I have gained

5. The next time I do a project

EXAMPLE 2

OBJECTIVE: **to determine progress toward the objectives for a home-degree project.**

Evaluating a Home-Degree Project—Summary of My Progress

Name of Project _____

Directions: For each activity planned to help you reach your goal(s), list what you have learned and how you made progress.

Activity: _____

Activity: _____

Activity: _____

Activity: _____

EXAMPLE 3

OBJECTIVE: **to evaluate a project for my State Degree in FHA.**

Evaluation of Progress through My Degree Project

Name of Project _____

Directions: In the appropriate sections state your goals, list the activities you have carried out, and record the evidences of your growth and progress. Use additional sheets if you need more space.

Goal: Evidence of Growth:
1. List new skills gained and those further developed.
2. List new understandings gained.
3. Tell other values renewed.
4. List changes you would make if doing project again.

Activities carried out:

EXAMPLE 4

OBJECTIVE: *to keep a continuous record of home projects.*

Cumulative Home Project Record

<u>Directions:</u> As you complete each project, write the major goal(s) in the appropriate square.

Area	Year	Year	Year	Year
Child and Family Development				
Clothing and Textiles				
Food and Nutrition				
Home Improvement and Housing				
Management and Family Economics				

Activity Reports and Logs

An activity report is used to evaluate a special assignment done at home, in school, or in the community. A log is a continuous record which may be kept over a period of time. Both of these evaluate student activity. Both require written expression of reactions as well as recording of activities. Examples 5 through 14 illustrate the uses of activity reports and logs to be described in this section. Examples 5, 6, and 7 are management reports; 8 and 9 are observation reports; and 10, 11, and 12 are evaluations of products. These are followed by a sewing machine operator's license and a field trip report.

Advantages and disadvantages of activity reports and logs result from being student-centered. A general conclusion is that their advantages far outweigh their limitations. The purposes for which they are used can rarely be met as effectively by any other evaluation technique.

A major advantage of activity reports and logs is their usefulness in self-evaluation. A student must record his activities and often what he has learned or how he has reacted to what he has experienced. In turn this

EXAMPLE 5

OBJECTIVE: to evaluate the use of time in preparing a meal.

Time Management Study [*]

Directions: List in order the work that was done. Completely fill in all
columns.

Work Done	Time Taken for Preparation	Time Taken for Cooking	Time Taken for Serving	Time Taken for Cleaning Up
1.				
2.				
3.				
4.				

[*] This device can be used by other members of the class as they observe those who are preparing food. The evaluators and the "cooks" can discuss the report on the following day.

results in a major limitation: cooperative evaluation is practically nonexistent. Teachers can read reports but cannot always know whether the student is being accurate in his reporting.

Another advantage is in the case of construction. Both the activity report and the log are very simple instruments. Although a log is generally more structured, students may simply be told to write down what they do every day in a notebook.

A major disadvantage may be that it is very difficult to put a score or grade on these two records. You may decide that you really would rather use them for nongrading purposes.

The construction of an activity report or a log is based on its purpose. In general the same guidelines are used as for project reports. You should go back and review this now (see pages 206-8). Sometimes a special type

EXAMPLE 6

OBJECTIVE: *to determine the daily cost of a family's food.*

Form for Reporting Cost of Meal

Directions: Record the foods prepared for breakfast and for dinner,
                calculate the cost per serving and per family, and total the
                cost for a family.

Menus	Cost per Serving	Size of Family	Cost for Family
Breakfast			
_____	_____	_____	_____
_____	_____	_____	_____
_____	_____	_____	_____
_____	_____	_____	_____
_____	_____	_____	_____
Dinner			
_____	_____	_____	_____
_____	_____	_____	_____
_____	_____	_____	_____
_____	_____	_____	_____
_____	_____	_____	_____

of activity report needs every part named and space provided for it. Many
of this kind are included in the examples throughout the remainder of this
chapter.

*The uses of activity reports and logs make them adaptable to all areas
of home economics.* Reports are especially adapted to foods, clothing,
housing, and management. Logs are effectively used in child development,
family relations, and management. Both can be used to some degree in all
areas.

An activity report can be a management study. The expenditure of time
as well as money can be recorded and analyzed. Logs are also useful in
recording daily activities and thus collecting basic information for review-

EXAMPLE 7

OBJECTIVE: *to record home responsibilities assumed in a week.*

Diary of Home Responsibilities

Directions: Record every day the responsibilities or chores you do at home.
At the end of the week, add up the total number of chores
and count the number of different responsibilities you have
taken.

Monday	Tuesday
Wednesday	Thursday
Friday	Saturday
Sunday	

Total number of chores   _____

Total number of different _____
responsibilities

ing management practices. Both logs and activity reports can be used to
evaluate home responsibilities.

A log is frequently used to record and evaluate observations. Such reports
are used with babysitting experiences or observing in a nursery school or
kindergarten. Logs can be used for self-observation when a student is attempting to evaluate his interpersonal relationships or is conducting a
personal appearance improvement project.

An activity report can be used to evaluate products. This is much more
often used in foods than in any other area. Occasionally an activity report
is used to record the completion of a process such as threading a sewing
machine or setting a table.

We can conclude that activity reports and logs can be used effectively in
home economics evaluation because they (1) allow for student self-evaluation, (2) are simple to construct, and (3) are readily adaptable to all areas
of home economics.

EXAMPLE 8

OBJECTIVE: *to recognize personal reactions to behaviors of a child.*

Babysitter's Log

Directions: Record the significant happenings in column 1 and your
reactions or suggestions for improvement in column 2.

Your name_____ Name of Child_____	
Date _____ Age of Child _____	

1. What happened	2. Your reaction

Questionnaires

The term questionnaire is applied to a list of questions which respondents are asked to answer by writing rather detailed replies. Questionnaires are designed to obtain information not only from students but also from parents and lay people.

A questionnaire may obtain the same information as some checklists. You will need to decide which you would rather use for each particular purpose. For example, interests can be determined by a checklist or a questionnaire, but checklist data will be easier to tabulate. A checklist can be used to discover the kind and amount of equipment in the homes of students, but a questionnaire may be more accurate since students may be inclined to check items they do not have at home.

The purposes of questionnaires are somewhat limited. Yet there is no other way to obtain certain kinds of information and this makes questionnaires a valuable means of evaluation. Questionnaires are not designed for obtaining scores and so must be eliminated for that purpose.

EXAMPLE 9

OBJECTIVE: **to identify reasons for behaviors of children at different ages.**

Observation Sheet

Directions: Observe children of different ages, record how they differ in each area of development, and give reasons why they differ.

Area of Development	*Behavior and Reasons Why*		
	Three-Year-Old	*Four-Year-Old*	*Five-Year-Old*
Physical			
Mental			
Social			
Emotional			

Questionnaires are very helpful for obtaining personal information about students. This information may be in the student cumulative folders that are kept in the central office. You may wish to consult these to discover composition of family, where the student lives, education and occupation of parents, years of home economics or as a member of 4-H. If this is not available you will probably want to use a questionnaire to obtain these personal data.

Questionnaires are frequently used to determine home conditions. This kind of information is seldom found in cumulative records but is very helpful to the home economics teacher in planning a course of study. Since short questionnaires are usually more accurate than long ones, you will want to develop a short questionnaire for each area of study. Equipment in

EXAMPLE 10

OBJECTIVE: **to evaluate products prepared at school.**

Evaluation of Food Products

Directions: Write the name of dish prepared under column labeled "Food" and write in the characteristics of the foods that were good, fair, poor.

Food	*Good*	*Fair*	*Poor*	*Remarks*

What did we do well today?

1. _____
2. _____
3. _____
4. _____
5. _____

What will we do better next time?

1. _____
2. _____
3. _____
4. _____
5. _____

EXAMPLE 11

OBJECTIVE: *to evaluate a meal prepared at home.*

Evaluation of Foods Prepared

Directions: List each single dish prepared. Record reactions to this
                  experience.

What food or foods did you prepare?

What gave you the most pleasure about this experience?

What were the reactions of your family?

What will you do differently the next time you cook?

What will you do the same way?

Which food preparation principles did you follow?

Which food preparation principles did you ignore?

the home determines kinds of projects a student can select in foods and in clothing. Size of house and amount of cleaning equipment influences what should be learned in housing and home improvement. This should indicate to you the kind of questions to include in each of the brief questionnaires.

Questionnaires can be used to determine student interests, needs, or concerns. This is the kind of information that can also be obtained from checklists. Questions you could ask are "What do you do when not in school?" "In what kinds of activities would you like to participate?" "What recreational skills do you have?" "What recreational skills do you wish you

EXAMPLE 12

OBJECTIVE: *to keep a continuous record of foods prepared.*

Cumulative Record of Foods Prepared

Directions: Write under the appropriate heading the name of the food you
prepared. Write *S* if you prepared it at school and *H* if you
prepared it at home.

Foods	*Where Prepared*	*Foods*	*Where Prepared*
Beverages		Eggs	
1. _____	_____	1. _____	_____
2. _____	_____	2. _____	_____
3. _____	_____	3. _____	_____
Breads		Fish	
1. _____	_____	1. _____	_____
2. _____	_____	2. _____	_____
3. _____	_____	Fruit	
4. _____	_____	1. _____	_____
Salads		2. _____	_____
1. _____	_____	3. _____	_____
2. _____	_____	4. _____	_____
3. _____	_____	Meats	
Vegetables		1. _____	_____
1. _____	_____	2. _____	_____
2. _____	_____	3. _____	_____
3. _____	_____	4. _____	_____
4. _____	_____	5. _____	_____
5. _____	_____	6. _____	_____
Desserts		One-dish Meals	
1. _____	_____	1. _____	_____
2. _____	_____	2. _____	_____
3. _____	_____	3. _____	_____

had?" A questionnaire of this type can ask members of a Future Homemakers chapter about the concerns of teenagers. The information can then be
used to plan a program of work. This technique has been used more than
once to plan the national program of work.

The rules for construction of a questionnaire are easy to follow. The first
step is to decide what kinds of information you want to obtain from the

EXAMPLE 13

OBJECTIVE: *to operate a sewing machine correctly.*

Sewing Machine Operator's License

Name_____

Date_____ Period _____Grade_____

School_____

The above named person has met the requirements for operating the
sewing machine.

_____

Home Economics Teacher

Check off the requirements for operating the sewing machine:

		Check
1.	Winding bobbin	
2.	Threading the machine	
3.	Threading the bobbin	
4.	Bringing up the bobbin thread	
5.	Regulating the stitch	
6.	Stitching straight line using guide	
7.	Tying threads at start and end of stitching	

(Back of "License")

questionnaire you are planning to construct. This information will determine the form the questionnaire will take. Otherwise the following suggestions are pertinent for all types of questionnaires.

(1) A questionnaire should be short and the questions brief.

(2) Adequate space should be provided for each answer. If your students are young and write very large, you will want to provide
much space. Not enough space will result in inadequate answers
and student frustration.

(3) Answers should be easy to tabulate and questions should be designed to meet this requirement. You will want to use question-

EXAMPLE 14

OBJECTIVE: *to determine ability to locate and learn about a community resource.*

Contributions of Community Resources

<u>Directions:</u>   Visit a community agency such as the Departments of Health and Welfare, Red Cross, Public Library. Ask the director what they do to serve families. Record a summary below.

Agency visited _____ Date _____

Summary:

---

naires to find out about a class as a whole more often than about one individual. If the data are not easy to tabulate, you will probably not summarize them for use.

(4) Each item on the questionnaire should be numbered and arabic numbers should be used. The numbers should begin with 1 and continue. The use of lowercase or capital letters with arabic numbers only tends to frustrate the student answering the questionnaire as well as the tabulator of the data.

(5) Spaces for identifying information should be provided if the questionnaire is not anonymous. The questionnaire designed to provide information about an entire group is usually anonymous, whereas the questionnaire designed to provide individual information is not. Identification information should include name, date, class period, and year of home economics.

Questionnaires may be answered by students, parents, and lay people. Students can be asked about their families, about home conditions, about responsibilities they assume, about interests and concerns. Parents can be asked what they think their daughters and/or sons should study in home economics. Lay people in the community can answer the same kinds of questions about what students should know. Example 15 is about students' families and Example 16 is about home conditions.

EXAMPLE 15

OBJECTIVE: *to determine family backgrounds of class members.*

Questionnaire about My Family

Directions: Complete each question about your own family. Your
answers will be kept confidential.

1. What is your name? _____

2. With whom do you live? _____

3. What is your father's name? _____

4. What is your mother's name? _____

5. Are your parents married to each other? _____

6. How much education does your father have? _____

7. How much education does your mother have? _____

8. What is your father's occupation? _____

9. Does your mother work outside the home? _____ If so, what is
your mother's occupation? _____

10. How many brothers do you have? _____ Ages: _____

11. How many sisters do you have? _____ Ages: _____

12. Do any of your other relatives live with your family? _____

    If so, which ones? _____

Autobiographies and Diaries

An autobiography and a diary have several
commonalities. Both are individual and personal in their content. The
contents of both should be kept confidential. An autobiography differs from

EXAMPLE 16

OBJECTIVE: *to determine amount of sewing equipment and amount of sewing done at home.*

Questionnaire Concerning Clothing for the Family

Directions: Complete each question about clothing construction and care in your home. Your answers will be kept confidential.

1. Does your family own a sewing machine?_____

2. Does your family own a steam iron?_____

3. Does your mother make clothes for your family?_____

   If so, does she make more or less than half of the family's clothing?_____

4. Do you make any of your own clothing?_____

   If so, do you make more or less than half of your clothes?_____

5. Does your mother mend the family clothing?_____

6. Do you mend any of your own clothing?_____

7. Do you take the responsibility for the care of your clothes?_____

8. Do you choose your clothes?_____

   If not, who does choose your clothes?_____

a diary in that it contains facts about the writer's past and usually is written at one time. A diary is a day by day account and contains little about the student's background.

There are both advantages and limitations to the use of autobiographies and diaries. Some teachers choose not to use these two techniques because of their limitations. In some schools, the autobiography is overused. The

English teacher, the homeroom teacher, the counselor, as well as the home economics teacher, may ask for an autobiography at the beginning of the school year. If this is occurring in your school, one autobiography from each student can be shared.

The insight that can be gained about students' personal qualities is the chief advantage of both autobiographies and diaries. Information can be secured concerning students' wishes and needs, self-concepts, and explanations of behavior. It is practically impossible to obtain this kind of information through tests or rating devices.

Both autobiographies and diaries can provide students insight into themselves. An attempt to describe oneself rarely fails to increase self-understanding. The decision of what to delete from an autobiography may tell a student as much about himself as what he chooses to include. The keeping of a diary does the same thing in addition to providing a means of looking back over a period of time at one's actions and reactions.

A major limitation is that not all students reveal their innermost thoughts. In fact, those who probably need the most help do not write a revealing autobiography or record pertinent data in a diary. Providing a framework of questions or points to be covered can counteract this to a degree.

Another limitation is that both autobiographies and diaries represent only present feelings. A student who is in a happy mood writes a more positive account than his friend who happens to be depressed. Teenagers vary in their moods from day to day and from one period of time to another. This should say to you that as you read either of these, remember that the content represents only the present.

Neither autobiographies nor diaries can be used for grading purposes. However, this need not be a limitation. It simply means that you will need to use other evidences for grades. The advantage is that students will probably be more honest and accurate if they know this does not affect their grade. It is unfortunate that grades have this much importance in our society, but they do. The use of evaluation techniques that do not emphasize grades can help to counteract this as well as increase skill in self-evaluation.

The uses of autobiographies are limited to personal data. On the other hand, there is no better way to obtain this kind of information. It is true that a questionnaire can provide certain kinds of facts which are easy to tabulate, whereas the same data in an autobiography is not quickly tabulated. The autobiography is a word picture of an individual and that is its chief purpose.

An autobiography provides a brief history of the life and background of a student. Many autobiographies begin with "I was born" and proceed to describe the family composition, places where the student has lived, and schools attended. The way this information is written may tell you as much as the facts themselves. Vocations may be described as well as friends and recreational activities. What students choose to tell may indicate some of their values and attitudes.

The goals or ambitions of a student are frequently included in an autobiography. Certainly you as the teacher can request that this be recorded. Perhaps a student has not even selected a tentative goal but will do so if he is directed to. You, as the teacher, might emphasize that the goals are tentative and subject to change in the future.

The relationships that the student has with his family and others are frequently revealed in an autobiography. He may do this subconsciously as he writes about his family and his friends. You may choose to direct students to include an analysis of relationships in the autobiography.

The use of diaries may be directed toward specific kinds of reactions. A personal diary usually records daily happenings and need not necessarily reveal much about the person's thoughts and feelings. Unless a diary kept as an assignment is directed toward recording certain specific kinds of reactions, it will profit you or the student very little.

Values and attitudes can be revealed in a daily diary. These may be later identified by the student as values or attitudes. The best results are obtained when a student is asked to record his reactions to specific happenings. For example, if you want to identify attitudes, require that the diary record those persons or objects that the student saw which he either liked or disliked. An explanation for his feelings should also be included.

Appreciations can be highlighted in a diary in the same way as values and attitudes. Again, to be certain that the student records pertinent data, ask him to include those objects, scenes, and clothing, seen in a day, which he enjoyed seeing or felt were unattractive. An explanation of why he reacted as he did makes the identification of the appreciation clearer and more meaningful.

While diaries nearly always, if inadvertently, reveal relationships with family, friends, and others, you can focus particularly upon this aspect of a student's life. The purpose of the diary would then need to be identified as a record of how one gets along with other people. Adding information about emotional reactions to these events will be useful to both you and your students.

It is also useful, of course, to employ diaries for purposes less personal than those listed so far; for example, for the recording of responsibilities assumed at home. A record of homemaking tasks carried out placed in a diary is much more apt to be accurate than a checklist of what was done at home. Similar to all other purposes, the student must be directed to record these responsibilities.

Directions for both autobiographies and diaries must be explicit if the appropriate kind of information is to be recorded. This has been implied throughout the preceding paragraphs. It is true that some understanding will result whether directions for a particular purpose are given or not. However, if you and your students have an objective, it will be accidental, not intentional, if this objective is met. Examples 17 through 20 illustrate the kinds of directions that you should write. The set of directions for Example 1 is for an autobiography and the next three sets are for diaries.

EXAMPLE 17

OBJECTIVE: *to write an autobiography describing oneself.*

Directions: Write a 3- to 5-page autobiography; include information about (1) where you have lived and gone to school, (2) the members of your family and your relationships with them, (3) your friends and your relationships to them, (4) your recreational activities and vocations, and (5) your tentative plans and goals for the future.

EXAMPLE 18

OBJECTIVE: *to reveal in a diary some of student's personal values and attitudes.*

Directions: Keep a diary for two weeks by writing each day your reactions to such things as persons, food, clothes; be sure to identify not only the reactions, but also the reason you think you reacted as you did. This may be as few as one or two reactions per day.

EXAMPLE 19

OBJECTIVE: *to record in a diary some personal reactions that reveal appreciations.*

Directions: Keep a diary for one week by recording each day at least one object or scene which you saw that you thought was beautiful and explain why you liked what you saw. Include any object which you saw that was very unattractive to you and tell why.

EXAMPLE 20

OBJECTIVE: *to record each day those home responsibilities that were assumed.*

Directions: Keep a diary for three weeks writing down each day those homemaking responsibilities that you assumed; indicate which you were required to do by your parents and those which you did without being asked; record how you felt about assuming each of these responsibilities.

Anecdotal Records

An anecdotal record is made up of descriptions of significant incidents in the life of a particular student. These are usually recorded by an adult—you, the teacher of home economics. An anecdotal record is an excellent way to gain a better insight into a student's reactions.

Anecdotal records possess both advantages and limitations as to their use and effectiveness. Many teachers make no attempt to keep anecdotal records feeling that their limitations far outweigh their advantages. This is a decision only you can make. Perhaps the next few paragraphs will help you to decide whether or not to keep anecdotal records.

A distinct advantage of anecdotal records is that they provide a means of evaluating the personality pattern of an individual student. Anecdotal records reveal much more about students than any rating device of personality traits. They provide a miniature longitudinal study of a student.

The supplementary information that anecdotal records provide is another advantage. A teacher never knows as much about a student as he or she would like to know. Since anecdotal records give information about a student's actions when he does not know he is being observed, they are particularly valuable.

A disadvantage is that anecdotal records are time-consuming to keep. This means that incidents can be reported about only a very few students. This implies that you can keep an ancedotal record on only two or three students at a time. One teacher decided to keep an anecdotal record on one student per class which meant five students for her; later she increased this number. Eventually she stopped keeping a record on some students and began keeping records on other students. This meant that she not only gained insight into a limited number of students but also became more aware of significant actions and reactions of all the students in her classes.

Anecdotal records are easy to keep if certain guidelines are followed. This is true of all evaluation methods but especially so of ancedotal records. Since their major disadvantage seems to be the time they require, it is essential to find a system that makes it fairly easy to keep anecdotal records on a limited number of students. You may find the following suggestions may be helpful in making such records:

(1) Select one or two students for intense study. In the beginning you will probably chose the most unusual students in your classes. Later you may decide to study one of the quiet, shy students.

(2) Describe as many significant incidents as possible. Be sure to omit unimportant incidents. A repeated reaction should always be

noted. At first you will probably record only dramatic incidents; later you will be more aware of the significance of the less dramatic happenings.

(3) Report not only unfavorable happenings that are significant but also favorable incidents. A true picture of a student will not emerge unless both types of behavior are recorded.

(4) Record the details of an incident while still vivid. The report is likely to be distorted if you wait several days: if you like the student, the report will become more favorable; the opposite will tend to be true if the student is one who is difficult to tolerate.

(5) Keep an anecdotal record as brief as possible by eliminating all unnecessary details. The trend will emerge in a more accurate manner when each entry is brief. This will also cut down on the time required to keep anecdotal records.

(6) Do not limit anecdotal records to reports of classroom situations. An incident that occurs outside the classroom may be more significant than any that occurs within. Be sure that the incident you record is one you personally saw.

(7) Do not interpret your observations in the recording of an incident. Interpretation should be limited to the review of many incidents. An overstatement is very likely to occur when a teacher generalizes on the basis of such limited information.

A systematic procedure facilitates the keeping of anecdotal records. It has already been suggested to you to keep anecdotal records on a limited number of students at one time. A file is a good system to use. Each incident can be recorded on an index card and filed behind the student's name. The cards have a standard form mimeographed on one side providing not only uniformity but also continuity. Example 21 is one form which you could use to keep an anecdotal record for each of the selected students.

Summary

Reporting forms described in this chapter include project reports, activity reports and logs, questionnaires, autobiographies and diaries, and anecdotal records. As in the previous chapters, this one will be summarized by stating the conclusions of the author. We can conclude that:

- reporting forms frequently evaluate activities and projects and provide personal data more effectively than do rating devices;

EXAMPLE 21

OBJECTIVE: *to record significant behavior about a particular student.*

Anecdotal Record Form

Time:_____ Place:_____ Date:_____
Name: _____
Behavior observed:
Comment:

- reports constitute the only consistent technique for evaluating home-degree projects;

- directions for report forms should explain in detail how to complete each section;

- a report form should provide space not only for listing activities but also for recording evidences of progress;

- a simple project form should be used for the first projects and for the Junior Degree with the more complicated forms being used for later projects;

- the major advantage of activity reports and logs is their usefulness in self-evaluation;

- an activity report may be a management study, a record of observations, or a product evaluation;

- questionnaires can be used to obtain information from parents and lay people as well as from students;

- questionnaires can be used to obtain personal information, data about home conditions, information about student interests and needs;

- questionnaires should contain a limited number of items and answers should be easy to tabulate;

- diaries and autobiographies need explicit directions if they are to contain the desired information;

- anecdotal records are time-consuming but are an excellent way to study a few individual students;
- a file of large index cards with a form for recording information is an aid in keeping anecdotal records.

STUDENT ACTIVITIES

1. Design a home-degree project form that is different from the examples given in the book.
2. Keep your own log for a week.
3. Use one of the activity forms to evaluate yourself or someone else.
4. Develop a questionnaire for a group of students.
5. Write your own autobiography.
6. Keep an anecdotal record of one person for a week.

REFERENCES

Ahmann, J. Stanley and Glock, M. D. *Evaluating Pupil Growth.* New York: Allyn and Bacon, Inc., 1959.

Arny, Clara Brown. *Evaluation in Home Economics.* New York: Appleton-Century-Crofts, 1953.

Fleck, Henrietta. *Toward Better Teaching of Home Economics.* New York: The Macmillan Company, 1968.

Gronlund, Norman E. *Measurement and Evaluation in Teaching.* New York: The Macmillan Company, 1971.

Hall, Olive A. and Paolucci, B. *Teaching Home Economics.* New York: John Wiley and Sons, Inc., 1970.

Williamson, Maude and Lyle, M. S. *Homemaking Education in the High School.* New York: Appleton-Century-Crofts, 1961.

Chapter 13 AUDIO - VISUAL
TECHNIQUES

Audio-visual materials have been used as teaching aids for many years. You have certainly found all kinds of audio-visual materials very useful in presenting content to students for discussion purposes. Have you ever considered using some of these same audio-visual aids as a means of evaluation? The following paragraphs may provide you with a variety of new evaluative techniques.

The techniques discussed will include tape recordings, films and filmstrips, photographs and transparencies, graphs, pictures, and cartoons. Most of these are visual in nature with only two being aural. This is not an inclusive list and as audio-visual equipment becomes increasingly available to the classroom teacher, there will be additional techniques for you to use as means of evaluation as well as teaching.

Tape Recordings

Many schools have tape recorders that are infrequently used. Whatever the specific reasons for this, the basic fault is a lack of imagination. Very practical, and, in most cases, easily usable suggestions for employing a tape recorder are given below.

A tape recorder can be used to evaluate and analyze what students say. This may be in a structured situation where the students know it is an evaluation process or in a more informal situation where they do not realize why the type recorder is being used. The tape recording should rarely if ever be used to provide a grade or score. It is a means of evaluation, not a means of measurement.

Teachers of speech, drama, and English have long used the tape recorder to evaluate oral expression, diction, and grammatical usage. You, the home economist, may and surely should have used it for the same purpose. Under guidance, a Future Homemaker presiding officer or a participating member in a program could effectively evaluate the content of her speech as well as the way she speaks. A student who has a personal improvement project may use the recorder as a means of learning to express herself more forcefully.

Another purpose of the tape recorder is to record class and small group discussions and to evaluate amount and quality of participation. Both you and your students can make use of this evaluation.

Tape recordings can also be used to identify values and attitudes. For example, pose a social issue such as working mothers, legal abortion, birth control pills, drug usage, and advance a relaxed discussion free of disapproving remarks. Record the discussion for playback at a later time. Ask students to identify the values and attitudes that come through in the discussion. If you are concerned about embarrassing the students, arrange to swap tapes with another teacher or class.

The tape recorder is used equally well in all areas of home economics. Perhaps you have recognized the area of family development in the uses described above. Certainly there are many issues in this and other areas that lend themselves to the use of the tape recorder.

Other issues than the ones already described are age to date, "making out," sexual intercourse before marriage, age to marry, support of parents, religious differences, and the spending of money. One teacher sent her class in pairs to interview others about one of these issues. She collected enough small tape recorders for each group to use. These tapes were analyzed and the findings tabulated for a report that appeared in the school paper.

Some of the issues in child development are disciplining a child, amount of responsibility at given ages, behavior expectations, the handling of an exceptional or handicapped child, nursing a baby, age to have children, and number of children. Day-care centers and other such facilities can be visited and the follow-up discussion recorded on a tape.

Although management and housing are not areas with issues as easily identified as family and child development, discussions of home ownership versus renting, allowances for children, budgeting, use of time, and home improvements by teenagers can be very lively. These discussions may also reveal values and attitudes that students may not be aware of.

Orally evaluating foods laboratory lessons, menu plans, and table settings are usual classroom procedures. Reporting home-degree projects and other home experiences in class is also frequently used by home economics teachers. The recording of such evaluation discussions is, on the other hand, rather rare. A clever idea is to record a discussion of the first and last laboratory lesson and compare the two. The same technique could be used for other discussions in foods and nutrition. Issues in foods and nutrition are eating breakfast, eating in the lunchroom, snacks, eating vegetables, drinking milk. Tape recordings might emphasize to students their lack of nutritious foods. A caution for you is to avoid "preaching" on any issue; let students draw their own conclusions.

There will always be clothing issues, although they will vary from one year to another. The wearing of hats has been and could again be an issue. Discussion topics which could be recorded and played back include sex appeal of clothing, colors and lines that flatter, and what to wear when. A summary discussion could be based on guidelines for choosing clothes.

These are but a few suggestions; perhaps you will think of and use many others. A tape recorder that is frequently used in all areas of home economics is an effective teaching-learning and evaluation device. On the other hand, overuse will diminish the effectiveness of this, just as of any other method. You are the one who must decide. Perhaps you will ask your students to evaluate the use of the tape recorder.

Films and Filmstrips

Similar to all other audio-visual techniques, films and filmstrips have been used as teaching techniques far more often than as evaluation techniques. Perhaps audio-visual techniques are truly the overlap area in which teaching and evaluating are one and the same. This section, as the preceding section, will attempt to illustrate how films and filmstrips can be used as a means of evaluating.

Films or motion pictures and filmstrips are not a substitute for teaching but rather a supplement to it. This is, of course, true of all audio-visual materials. Evaluation is only one of the purposes of films and filmstrips but it is a very significant one. Films and filmstrips do provide a common experience for all class members and this is a decided advantage. It is very important to identify for students the purpose of showing the film or filmstrip. The more specific the directions, the more benefit students will receive. Another clue to the use of a film or filmstrip is to preview it in order to be sure it will meet the purpose for which it is being used.

Films and filmstrips can be used to identify values, attitudes, and goals.
The action that can be seen in films and somewhat in filmstrips helps
students to identify with the persons being shown. It is usually easier to
identify personal qualities in someone else than in oneself. At the same time
a person may see himself in the person in the film or filmstrip. Films are
usually more successfully used to identify attitudes and values than are
filmstrips. Both frequently are useful for identifying goals. Not all films and
filmstrips can be used for this purpose; it depends upon the content.

Values are a part of the content of every area of home economics. Decisions about behavior, food, clothes, housing, and money are all related to
the values a person holds. If you have taught students about values, you may
decide to use a film or filmstrip as a means of testing out their perceptions
of value. A simple technique is to ask students to list the values they
recognize in the film or filmstrip. If a film is too long, you might show only
a part of it.

Attitudes can be evaluated by using films and filmstrips in much the same
manner as values are evaluated. The selection of which film or filmstrip to
use would be different. There are several films and filmstrips that present
personal and family problems. No doubt you have used these for the purposes of recognizing areas for decision-making. Now you can use the same
ones for identifying attitudes and analyzing how these affect decisions and
behavior. Students may be more analytical if they have already seen the film
or filmstrip and are, therefore, less interested in the story.

Goals are also a commonality to be found in all areas of home economics.
Some filmstrips are focused upon goals and their influence on decisions.
These may be used only as a teaching aid whereas others that are not
focused on goals might be used for identifying the goals evident in the film
or filmstrip. For example, a film portraying a young married couple attempting to resolve their religious difficulties could be shown to students
who have been assigned the identifications of goals of each of the young
people. Another idea is to ask students to analyze what they would do in
this situation if they had a certain goal.

Films and filmstrips can be used to identify principles. This is a purpose
you have surely used as a teaching technique. Many films and filmstrips are
designed to teach principles. The process for evaluation would be to select
a film or filmstrip that does not label or identify the principles. Students
could record the principles and these would be reported to and discussed
by the class.

The area of food and nutrition incorporates many scientific principles.
These are taught and retaught in many ways. The evaluation is usually an
objective test upon which not all students do well. An additional means of
evaluation would be to observe a film or filmstrip and identify the principles
that are demonstrated. Since it is difficult to record principles as fast as they

appear, you could give students a minimum number to list. Another idea is to give students a mimeographed list of food principles and ask them to check those they saw in the film. A follow-up discussion is essential.

Clothing and textiles is also a unit based on scientific as well as psychological, sociological, and economic principles. All too often evaluation in this area is for the construction skills. A filmstrip on pressing could be used to identify the reasons why certain techniques were used. Another filmstrip on a textile and its fiber content should lend itself to identification of principles or facts.

All other areas of home economics have principles that can be evaluated as well as taught by using films and filmstrips. As a teacher, what you need to do is:

(1) select a film or filmstrip that might be used;

(2) review the film or filmstrip with evaluation in mind;

(3) decide on how students are to record the principles;

(4) explain the process to students;

(5) show the film or filmstrip while students view and record;

(6) follow with a report from students and class discussion.

Photographs and Transparencies

Photographs have been a part of our teaching for many years although only in a minor way. Transparencies are relatively new but are growing rapidly as a teaching technique. Several commercial companies have developed transparencies that can be bought and used by teachers of home economics. More and more teachers are learning how to make their own transparencies as a majority of schools have equipment for making and projecting them. The trick to using photographs and transparencies is to decide how you can create a learning or evaluating situation for your students.

Photographs indicate growth and progress. They really are more an evaluation technique than a teaching technique. Although photographs are relatively easy to make, they are not always made with a particular purpose in mind. This means you and your students need an objective even before the photograph is taken. In this way evidence of growth and progress is the end product.

Personal, family, and community projects can be evaluated by using photographs. These may be the "before-and-after" series or just a photograph of an end product. A typical personal project is weight control or improving personal appearance where a photograph is taken prior to beginning the project and when it is completed. Home economics teachers who are teaching a personal improvement unit frequently take photographs of all class members at the beginning and again at the end of the unit. If all projects are not completed at the end of the unit, a third series may be taken when projects are completed. A comparison of photographs is usually a satisfying as well as profitable evaluation technique. Before and after pictures can be taken of home improvement, school, and community projects.

Products can be evaluated by photographs. Examples are tea and buffet tables, flower arrangements, baked products, garments that have been constructed, new draperies, reupholstered furniture. Sometimes these photographs evaluate class projects and at other times they evaluate individual or small group projects. Such photographs present evidence of progress not only to the class members but also to parents, friends, school officials, and community members.

The program of work of the local chapter of Future Homemakers of America deserves and requires evaluation. Among the many techniques that can be used is a pictorial account made up of photographs taken by chapter members and the teacher-advisor. Scrapbooks are kept by most chapters with photographs illustrating each event. These should illustrate each aspect of the program of work rather than just being candid shots taken at special events. A photograph will illustrate a chapter goal much more effectively than a written description. Such records provide a continuous evaluation of the chapter over a period of years. Newly elected officers can study these records and thus determine a benchmark for their own evaluation. Future Homemakers is an integral and vital part of the total program of home economics and deserves an accurate evaluation.

Transparencies contain principles to be identified. A transparency is usually developed around one or more principles or guidelines. This makes the identification of principles very easy for most students. You as the teacher may want to go beyond the mere identification in the process of using transparencies for evaluation purposes

Techniques for identifying principles using transparencies are the same as those described for films and filmstrips. Go back and review the six steps given in that section (see page 233). You may be seeking ways to help slow learners identify principles. This technique of evaluation is a very apt one for such a group. They need to be taught and retaught many times. Remember that evaluation is a learning process and that it is easier to grasp what is seen and heard than what is read.

Transparencies can aid in recognizing application of principles. Such questions as "Where has this principle been used in your work?" and "Where else might this principle be used?" help students to recognize not only the principle itself but also its wider applicability.

Graphs

A graphic presentation is easier for most people to understand than is a verbal description. Teachers use graphs to present data to a class, to record personal data about a student, and to illustrate facts about a group. Students may be asked to construct a graph to present their own findings in a study they have made or from their reading of research.

Each type of graph is unique in its construction. The various types of graphs include pie chart, bar graph, curve, pictograph, progress chart, and flow chart. The shape or design of most of these is indicated by its name. Each will be discussed and illustrated in the following paragraphs.

The pie chart is a circle divided into sections, each representing a part of the whole. You may wish to guess roughly at the proportions but the most accurate way to draw the circle and the divisions is to use a protractor with one percent being represented by 3.6 degrees. Pie charts can be used to show the way a person uses his time and his money. A family budget and national average of family expenditures are frequently illustrated by a pie chart. Figure 13-1 represents the time one student spent on various activities in a day.

EXAMPLE 1

OBJECTIVE: to report on an analysis of way one used time on a school day.

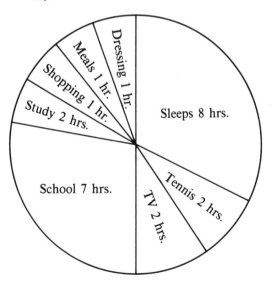

FIGURE 13-1

The bar graph is quickly constructed and adaptable to many kinds of data. There are variations in the number and placement of the bars. The data may be represented by one, two, or three vertical or horizontal bars. A diet survey may be presented in a bar graph by showing number or percent of students who ate foods included in each of the major food groups. Bar graphs can be used to indicate percent of teenage marriages as compared to marriages at other ages. They can also indicate rise in illegitimacy, venereal diseases, use of drugs, or any other data that is of concern. Figure 13–2 is a picture of a national study of family income and was used by a student to illustrate a report in a twelfth-grade family living course.

There are three types of curves: frequency, percentile, and profile. The frequency curve (Figure 13–3) represents group distribution with the number falling in each section being shown. The percentile curve (Figure 13–4) shows distribution by percent falling in each group. Frequently more than one percentile curve is drawn in the same graph for comparison purposes. A profile curve (Figure 13–5) is a series of individual measures which are helpful in comparing different aspects of a student's behavior. All three of these are more often used by a teacher or guidance counselor than by a student. However, these may be shared effectively with students. One teacher puts test scores on a frequency curve and presents them to the class the day following a test.

A pictograph is perhaps the simplest of the graphs to understand and for that reason has been widely used with children and lay people. A pictograph can also be enlarged to make an effective bulletin board or poster. Pictographs usually contain small cutouts to represent a certain number of people (see Figure 13–6). For example, diet surveys are reported by letting each "figure of a person" represent so many people. Dollar signs are used in the same way. Students would find it interesting to present their own collected data in a pictograph.

EXAMPLE 2

OBJECTIVE: *to report percent of families who have certain incomes.*

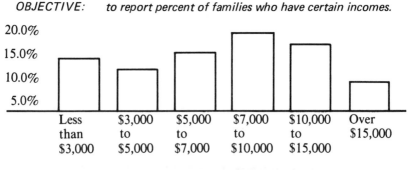

FIGURE 13-2

EXAMPLE 3

OBJECTIVE: *to present test scores in a frequency curve so that each student can see where his grade fell.*

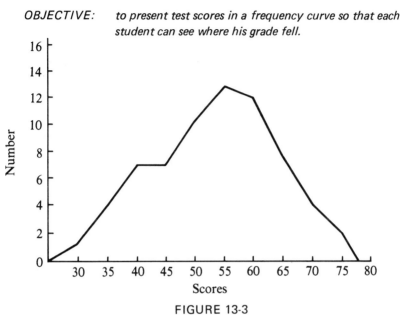

FIGURE 13-3

EXAMPLE 4

OBJECTIVE: *to present scores on a pretest and a post-test by use of a percentile curve.*

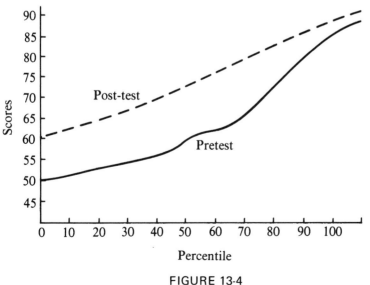

FIGURE 13-4

EXAMPLE 5

OBJECTIVE: *to compare grades on each of the units in home economics using percentile rank on a profile curve.*

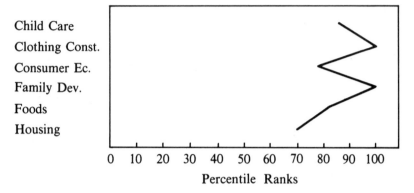

Child Care
Clothing Const.
Consumer Ec.
Family Dev.
Foods
Housing

0   10   20   30   40   50   60   70   80   90   100

Percentile Ranks

FIGURE 13-5

EXAMPLE 6

OBJECTIVE: *to draw a pictograph representing amount of allowance given tenth-graders in our school.*

The Allowance Study

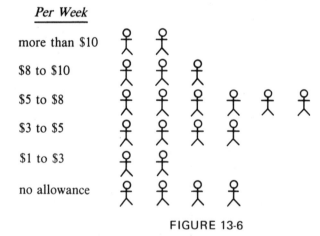

Per Week

more than $10

$8 to $10

$5 to $8

$3 to $5

$1 to $3

no allowance

FIGURE 13-6

A progress chart is probably more often used in clothing construction than in any other area but is adaptable to any kind of project or series of activities. Progress charts can be very plain or very decorative. One teacher uses a tree on which leaves can be placed that have been cut from a fabric scrap by each student. Frequently progress charts look like bar graphs.

Example 6 was used in a consumer clothing course where standards identified for various garments were used for evaluating construction of ready-made garments.

EXAMPLE 6

OBJECTIVE: *to evaluate the construction of ready-made garments.*

Name	Skirt	Blouse	Sweater	Dress	Coat	Bra	Girdle	Slip	Shoes
Jane	X	X	X	X		X	X	X	
Marian	X	X		X					
Sue	X		X	X					
Ann	X		X		X				X
Mary		X	X	X		X	X	X	X
Frances	X	X	X	X	X	X	X	X	X
Helen	X	X		X		X		X	X
Grace		X	X		X	X	X		X
Sandra	X	X	X	X	X	X	X	X	X
Betty	X	X		X		X		X	
Sharon	X	X	X			X	X	X	X
Jan	X	X	X	X		X	X		
Donna	X	X	X	X	X	X	X	X	
Edith	X	X				X			X
Sarah	X	X	X	X		X	X	X	

A flow chart is a diagram that traces the course followed by different parts of a whole. As a home economics teacher you may find more uses for other graphs than for a flow chart but it does provide a means of reporting a particular kind of data. One teacher appeared before the school board with facts about what happened to girls who entered their high school. This was at the request of the principal who felt that all girls should have a year of home economics. The flow chart that is illustrated in Figure 13–7 is the one she used.

The construction of all graphs should follow the same general rules. The guidelines that follow apply to all graphs and will help you as you construct and use graphs:

(1) Use large intervals such as 5 and 10.

(2) Locate the low values at the left and at the bottom.

(3) Label the graph both vertically and horizontally.

EXAMPLE 7

OBJECTIVE: *to diagram the follow-up study of girls enrolled in the*
              ninth-grade four years ago.

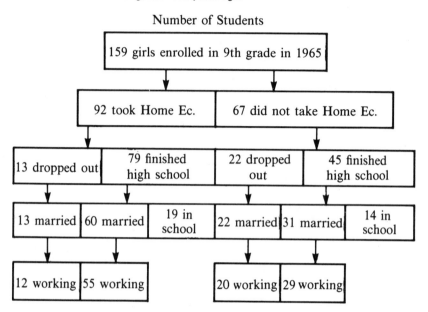

FIGURE 13-7

(4) Place the label at the bottom and on the left side.

(5) Use different colors or kinds of lines when representing two or
more sets of data on the same graph.

Graphs are excellent teaching devices as well as evaluation techniques.
Used occasionally they are most effective but used frequently can lose their
impact. Simple graphs may help you teach the slow learner, and interpreting
more complicated graphs will be stimulating for the more able student.
Many graphs can be used more than one time. When you have collected and
presented data in a graph, you should seriously question discarding it.

Pictures

Teachers of home economics have always used
pictures in their teaching as examples of principles they want the students
to know. They have also used pictures on bulletin boards and have framed

them for hanging on the walls of the home economics department. No doubt many teachers have also used pictures as a technique for evaluating students.

Pictures may be clipped from magazines or bought in a series. They may be mounted and displayed, used under an opaque projector, or developed into slides. The source of the picture is really the determining factor as to the form the pictures take. However, the form is not nearly so important as the purpose for which the picture is used.

Pictures can be used to evaluate knowledge held by students. This is a very realistic method of evaluation because a picture can be very lifelike. It can also serve as a means of applying the knowledge to a situation.

Room arrangement and color combination are two aspects of housing that have always been evaluated using pictures, at least by some teachers. Identification of furniture styles can also be evaluated using pictures. Diagrams of room arrangements and floor plans can be analyzed to see if they meet guidelines. Floor plans can also be used to determine if traffic lanes are adequate.

Pictures of food are very accessible and therefore frequently used. Some of the evaluations you might try include meeting daily food requirements, attractive meals, contrasting textures, and table setting. Cardboard food models can be considered pictures. Students can exhibit their knowledge of nutrition principles by using models to plan menus and to identify sources of nutrients.

Clothing and textiles is another area in which pictures are effectively used both to teach and to evaluate. Educational materials developed and distributed by commercial companies, fashion magazines, and pattern books are the usual sources of pictures of clothing. Students can be asked to analyze a total costume, decide on which individual figure types the various costume suits, select fabric for a pictured garment, and decide upon accessories appropriate for a particular garment.

Pictures can be used to evaluate an awareness of various personal qualities. You might consider the evaluation of personal qualities using pictures in the same way as using rating devices, that is, not for grading purposes.

Aesthetic appreciation can be very effectively evaluated by using pictures. "What do you like and why?" and "What do you dislike and why?" can be used successfully with pictures. Another technique would be to ask students to select a picture from a magazine and analyze its aesthetic qualities.

Illustrations of interpersonal relationships can be analyzed by students to determine their awareness of factors affecting relationships. Pictures of parent-child relationships, of sibling rivalries, and of boy-girl relationships are excellent materials for student discussion and student speculation on the "hidden" factors.

Pictures can be an aid when students are identifying values and attitudes. One technique is to arrange a series of pictures, such as an automobile, a house, a boat, and an academic robe, and ask students to arrange in order those that they value. The same kind of technique can be used with pictures of people, of foods, or other objects toward which students would express their feelings.

These ideas may seem informal and not apt to produce any tangible evidence. On the other hand, they are techniques that assist students to evaluate themselves—which may very well be the most important objective for a day, a week, or even a unit of study.

Cartoons

Many people miss the impact of cartoons and comics because they do not read them. While they are designed to amuse, they usually contain an element of truth. Cartoons are particularly useful when analyzing relationships. They can be used as teaching techniques and as means of evaluation. Cartoons have the advantages of being not only effective but also inexpensive, humorous, and lifelike although exaggerated. Cartoons can be found in newspapers, magazines, and books. You can use these to help students look at various personal relationships and qualities.

Interpersonal relationships in cartoons can be analyzed with a carryover into individual lives. Cartoons that present situations based on relationships include child-parent, husband-wife, child-child, boy-girl, teacher-child. Evaluation questions could include "What do you see in this cartoon?" "What do you think caused these people to react in this way?" "What are some possible outcomes?" These kinds of questions do not have definite answers and therefore do not lend themselves to grading. However, they do help students to evaluate relationships and people.

Additional techniques of evaluation include writing a story to accompany a cartoon, illustrating certain relationships with collected cartoons, and describing how people represented in the cartoon must feel. One teacher listed the important generalizations and concepts to be included in a unit on child development. She asked students to collect cartoons and pictures that illustrated each of these. This activity was spread throughout the course and was one of the major evidences of what students had learned.

Cartoons have an additional advantage of being as usable with slow learners as with more able students and those with "average" ability. Students of each level of ability analyze, react, and relate to cartoons in ways that are consistent with their own capabilities. Cartoons could serve as a unifying technique in a class of differing abilities studying about interpersonal relationships.

Attitudes, values, and beliefs are personal qualities evident in cartoons. Some interesting ones are "The Little Woman," "Andy Capp," "The Circus," "Dennis," and "Peanuts." Some of these can be found in small books. They are easily reproduced by projecting on a piece of poster paper and being drawn with a crayon or heavy ink marker. Magazines and textbooks also contain cartoons that illustrate various personal qualities.

A story about values can be written by students based on a particular cartoon. The same cartoon may be given to each student with a different story expected from each. On the other hand, a different cartoon can be given each student and the stories shared after each student has written his own story highlighting values, or attitudes, or beliefs.

The identification of personal qualities is often difficult for young students. It should be challenging, fun, and educational to use cartoons for this purpose. A cartoon could be projected on the wall and each student told to write down the attitude that it seems to illustrate. A reporting of the listed attitudes could then be used as a basis for class discussion. This same technique could be used for other personal qualities as well as for attitudes.

Summary

Audio-visual techniques described in this chapter include tape recordings, films and filmstrips, photographs and transparencies, graphs, pictures, and cartoons. These techniques are usually considered teaching aids but can be effectively used as means of evaluation. As in Chapters 11 and 12, this chapter will be summarized by stating conclusions drawn by the author. We can conclude that:

- audio-visual materials can be used most effectively as aids in the process of evaluation;
- tape recordings can be used to evaluate what students say in class and in group discussion;
- tape recordings reveal values and attitudes of students;
- a tape recorder can be used equally well in all areas of home economics;
- films and filmstrips can be used to identify values, attitudes, and goals of the persons being portrayed;
- principles, guidelines, and generalizations presented in films and filmstrips can be identified by students;
- personal photographs can be used to indicate growth and progress;
- products as well as projects can be evaluated with photographs;

- a series of photographs can report the activities included in a Future Homemakers of America program of work;
- transparencies contain scientific principles that can be identified by students;
- graphs include pie charts, bar graphs, curves, pictographs, progress charts, and flow charts;
- pie charts can report use of resources such as time and money;
- bar graphs are useful in presenting data about group activity and change;
- curves are used to present frequencies, percentile ranks, and characteristics of an individual;
- pictographs are widely used with children and lay people as well as with teenagers;
- progress charts provide a way to record individual as well as group progress toward completion of a product or process;
- a flow chart is a diagram that traces the course followed by different parts of a whole;
- pictures can be used to evaluate knowledge held by students as well as awareness of personal qualities;
- cartoons can be used to analyze interpersonal relationships, attitudes, values, and beliefs.

STUDENT ACTIVITIES

1. Record a class or small group discussion and list key questions to ask high school students in order to identify a specific aspect such as attitudes.

2. View a film or filmstrip and select a personal quality that you would have high school students identify and discuss.

3. List five ideas for using photographs as a means of evaluating student progress.

4. Study a set of transparencies and outline how you would use these for purposes of evaluation.

5. Draw a pie chart that is an evaluation technique.

6. Construct each of the following:
   a. a bar graph
   b. a frequency curve
   c. a percentile curve

d. a profile curve
e. a pictograph
f. a progress chart
g. a flow chart

7. Select a picture and analyze the personal qualities portrayed.

8. Collect several cartoons and plan how each one may be used as a means of evaluation.

REFERENCES

Arny, Clara Brown. *Evaluation in Home Economics.* New York: Appleton-Century-Crofts, 1953.

Fleck, Henrietta. *Toward Better Teaching of Home Economics.* New York: The Macmillan Company, 1968.

Hall, Olive A. and Paolucci, B. *Teaching Home Economics.* New York: John Wiley and Sons, Inc., 1970.

Chapter 14 SOCIOMETRIC TECHNIQUES

Sociometric techniques may reveal the extent to which individuals are acceptable to others in a group. They also help the teacher to understand and modify the social structure of the class. Many times the result of a sociometric technique simply verifies the hunches a teacher already has; at other times it reveals a situation of which she is totally unaware. Sociometric techniques are valuable in helping a teacher to identify students who need help in problems of social adjustment.

The sociometric techniques presented in this chapter include the sociogram, the social distance scale, the social sensitivity opinion poll, and roleplaying. The last one is not always considered a sociometric technique but is included here because it seemed more appropriate than in any other chapter. It is an important technique for evaluating social sensitivity but not social status.

Sociogram

A sociogram is a technical device that indicates the persons with whom students would like to work. A teacher may use it for finding out some of the ways students feel toward each other. It reveals natural groupings of students and points out personal relationships in a group. The sociogram can indicate to the teacher some if not all of the following:

1. mutual choices

2. individuals most in demand

3. cliques or small groups

4. isolates—the unchosen or rejected

5. unexpected choices

6. expected choices

7. stars—leaders in a group

8. islands—small groups which are not included in large groups

9. chains—one person who chooses another who in turn chooses another

The basic material for a sociogram is collected in answer to a particular request made by the teacher. The request may be associated with one of the three types of skills: (a) social, (b) mental, (c) physical. It is understandable that students might not list the same names in reply to each type of request. Much more can be learned about student-student relationships when data based on all three skills are collected. Examples of request based on social skills are: "Name your three best friends in this group." "Name three people in this class with whom you would like to go to a party." Mental skill requests might be: "Name three people in this class whom you would like to work with on a group report." "Name three of your classmates whom you would like to have serve on a panel with you." Questions associated with physical skills might be: "Name three of your classmates whom you would like to have in your family group as we work in the foods lab." "Choose three people in this class you would like to work with on a slipcover for a chair." These requests should be a natural part of planning to work together and the results should be used in determining work groups.

Here is the way the teacher might ask her students to record their choices: "Write your own name on the first line of the card and then list in order your first, second, and third choices. An example is:

Betty Davis
1. Jack Smith
2. Jane Lewis
3. Sally Cook

These cards should then be arranged alphabetically by the first name on the card, and thus provide for ease in preparing the sociogram. It is advisable for the teacher to prepare the sociogram without help from students.

The construction of a sociogram follows specific guidelines. The first step is to make a summary sheet using the cards on which students wrote choices. The first names of students should be listed alphabetically and a key letter assigned to each. An illustration of this step is given in Table 14-1.

TABLE 14-1

			Choices	
Name	*Key*	*1st*	*2nd*	*3rd*
Ann	a	d	g	k
Betty	b	e	f	j
Dick	c	e	h	l
Harry	d	a	k	g
Jack	e	f	b	j
Jane	f	e	d	l
Joe	g	k	d	a
Lucy	h	c	e	j
Mary	i	h	c	e
Sally	j	h	e	f
Sara	k	g	d	a
Tom	l	c	e	k

The second step is to list mutual and single choices. Double lines are used to indicate mutual choices and arrows to indicate single choices. Different colors or lines should be used to indicate first, second, and third choices. In Figure 14-1, a solid line is used to indicate first choice, dashes for second choice, and dots for third choice.

The third step is to identify stars, the one or more students who were chosen the most times, and put their key letter in a circle or triangle in the center of the page. Use circles for girls and triangles for boys. Connect stars to mutual choices, placing his choices on only one side and arranging for ease in connecting any of these who mutually choose each other. Different color pencils may be used for each choice: red for first, blue for second, and black for third; or a solid line may be used for first, dashes for second, and dots for third choices. Connect any other mutual or single choices for those already on the sociogram. Examine remaining mutual choices listed in step two for clique and chart each of these on the sociogram, arranging for ease in connecting with those already on the sociogram. Chart any other choices not already charted. At any point where lines are crossing each other too many times and the sociogram is getting complicated, seek ways to rearrange circles and triangles and begin on a new page.

An illustration of this step in Figure 14-2 should help you to understand how to complete the construction of the sociogram.

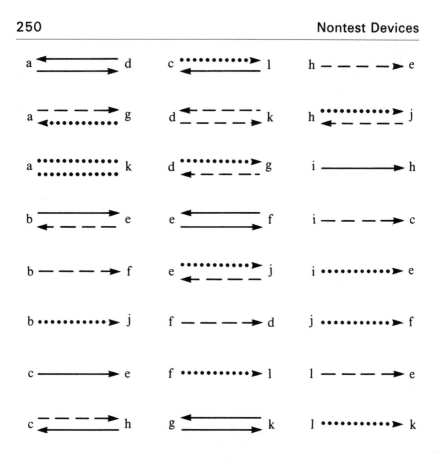

FIGURE 14-1

Cautions should be observed when using sociograms for evaluation purposes. Choices should be kept confidential. The relationships of individuals change; therefore, sociograms become out-of-date. The choices of a student in one given situation and at one particular time are not conclusive evidence of his total interpersonal relationships. The gathering of information should not cause students to give undue attention to their likes and dislikes. The teacher should, whenever it is possible, make her request when *every* student is present.

Once a sociogram has been plotted, it is a beginning, not an end. Perhaps its greatest value is that it directs the attention to certain aspects of group structure which will lead to further observation of individual and group behavior.

There are several ways in which a teacher may use the information gained from analyzing students' choices. Grouping students so as to foster satisfying personal relationships and to further the developing of social skills is perhaps the most valuable one. A securely placed student may help a retiring one to be less so, isolates may be eliminated by planning for potential friendships, students in cliques may widen their contacts. In grouping students for the greatest satisfaction, these suggestions may help:

(1) give the student who is unchosen his first choice.

(2) give each student at least one mutual choice.

(3) give his first choice to any student who is chosen but does not have a mutual choice.

(4) check very closely to be sure that every student has at least one of his choices.

Information gained from a sociogram can help a teacher plan for in-school and out-of-school experiences. Many times the solutions to the problems of developing students' relations with their peers lies in the development or improvement of social skills such as manners, grooming, and family relationships.

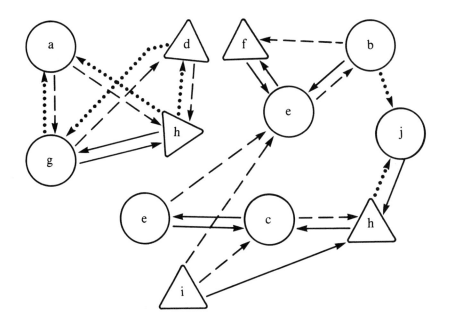

FIGURE 14-2

Social Distance Scale

The purpose of a classroom social distance scale is to discover the social tone of the group and the degree to which each individual is accepted by and accepts others in the class. It differs from the sociogram in that reaction is obtained to *every* individual in the class.

A social distance scale consists of a list of statements to be matched with names of class members. The construction of such a scale is relatively simple. You begin with statements that might describe many people, some of which are complimentary, others that are neutral, and still others that are negative. The second step is to make a chart with all the names of the students and provide a space for checking the identifying characteristics. The directions should make it clear that these are personal choices of the student completing the social distance scale. Example 1 should make the construction clearer to you.

EXAMPLE 1

Classroom Distance Scale

Directions: Place a check in the space opposite the statement that most nearly describes your feeling about each of your classmates. Your answers will be kept confidential.

	Mary	Ann	Betty	Jan	Ellen	Dot	Grace	Jane	Helen	Carol	Sarah	Jean
Like to have as a best friend.												
Like to have only as a classmate.												
Like to be with only occasionally.												
Do not like to be with her.												
Wish she were not in our class.												

A tabulation of reactions will provide a consensus of personal opinions. Both the one-to-one reaction and the reaction of the group as a whole are important. Perhaps the group consensus tells you more about the individual student because it omits a personal antagonism that could in some instances be temporary.

The simplest way to tabulate is to take a copy of the Classroom Distance Scale and record the number of times each student received each rating. (See Example 2 below.)

EXAMPLE 2

	Mary	Ann	Betty	Jan	Ellen	Dot	Grace	Jane	Helen	Carol	Sarah	Jean
Like to have as a best friend.	1	0	2	0	1	0	0	6	1	0	1	1
Like to have only as a classmate.	1	0	5	1	2	0	4	5	3	2	4	5
Like to be with only occasionally.	4	2	4	6	8	3	4	0	5	3	5	5
Do not like to be with her.	3	5	0	3	0	2	3	0	2	4	1	0
Wish she were not in our class.	2	4	0	1	0	6	0	0	0	2	0	0

It is evident in Example 2 that Jane was the most acceptable and Betty was second. The least acceptable to the group appear to be Ann and Dot. Similar to the sociogram, the social distance scale is apt to change from time to time. Circumstances and events cause acceptance or lack of it to change. It does provide clues to class and individual acceptance of each other at the time information is given.

A social distance scale simply provides information as a basis for under-standing. It probably raises more questions than it answers. One of these questions might be why are some students rejected and others very popular. One can only wonder about more than half the class choosing Jane as a best friend and the opposite occurring to Dot.

This beginning should cause a teacher to study each student carefully to determine the reasons why they were placed in a particular position on the scale. You might also wish to observe whether or not Jane and Betty accept their leadership roles.

Another question would be how you, as a teacher, could help the seemingly rejected students. You might wish to plan experiences that would place these girls in a more favorable position. Suppose Dot was rejected because she was of a minority race and therefore shy, rather than because she was unpleasant. Your help would be different. The evaluation of social acceptance is primarily to help you to understand each student so as to better help him.

Another sociometric technique that is very much like the social distance scale is the Who's Who technique. The choice is based on a personal characteristic rather than on one's likes and dislikes. This has a disadvantage in that it could label a student with a characteristic that is unfair.

In the "Who's Who" opinionnaire, students are asked to match the names of classmates with personal characteristics such as friendly, lazy, careless, a leader. An example of such a device is given in Example 3.

EXAMPLE 3

Who's Who in Our Class

Directions: Place a check by the name of the student that best describes each listed characteristic. Do not put your name on this paper; all answers are confidential.

Characteristic	Mary	Joe	Jan	Tom	Jim	Betty	Ellen	Bob	Bill	Ann	Sandra	Andy
friendly												
kind												
considerate												
good sport												
leader												
smart												
energetic												
rude												
doesn't do his share												
dishonest												
unclean												
lazy												
thoughtless												
careless												

These data in Example 3 can be tabulated in the same manner as the social distance scale. The form suggested for that tabulation can be used for this tabulation. Again you must remember that this is extremely limited data and should not ever be considered conclusive. Rather it is information that provides clues to student behavior which in turn will help you work with individuals both inside and outside the classroom.

Another form of a Who's Who questionnaire is to ask students to write the name of the student or students after each question. This is an evaluation just for use of the teacher. (See Example 4.)

EXAMPLE 4

Who's Who Questionnaire

Directions: Write the name of one or more of your classmates after each of the following questions. If you cannot think of someone to name, do not answer the question.

1. Who do you consider a good leader? _____
2. Who do you consider a poor leader? _____
3. Who can be depended upon to see the bright side? _____
4. Who always feels gloomy and discouraged? _____
5. Who has good work habits? _____
6. Who has poor work habits? _____
7. Who always respects other people's property? _____
8. Who are the chronic borrowers? _____
9. Who is tolerant of other's ideas and religious beliefs? _____
10. Who is intolerant of other's ideas and religious beliefs? _____
11. Who is a good sport? _____
12. Who shows disappointment when he can't have own way? _____
13. Who is very friendly? _____
14. Who is considered a snob? _____
15. Who faces situations calmly? _____
16. Who is a chronic worrier? _____
17. Who is full of energy? _____
18. Who is lazy? _____
19. Who is even-tempered? _____
20. Who loses her temper easily? _____
21. Who has a good sense of humor? _____
22. Who lacks a sense of humor? _____

Social Sensitivity Techniques

The world is continuously becoming a more complex place in which to live. This is probably more true of social aspects than any other facet. To help students become sensitive to social interactions and issues is increasingly becoming a major part of home economics. It is an integral part of all areas of the discipline. Therefore it becomes the responsibility of each home economics teacher to develop social sensitivity in each of her students.

An opinion poll is an effective technique for evaluating social sensitivity. This device may contain one or more than one social issue to which students must react. Too many issues may cause frustration and a lack of interest. Usually students check a range of answers from "nobody" to "almost everybody" with four levels between these two. Such a device does not ask for a student's opinion directly but it is assumed that his answer will reflect his own social sensitivity.

Many teachers find it useful to highlight one issue at a time and to have a group discussion following the answering of the opinion poll. Other times, a teacher may choose to have the discussion before the marking of the poll. The danger in this last procedure is that students may tend to answer the way they are expected to answer. One teacher has an opinion poll containing several issues which she gives at the beginning of a year and again at the end of the year in an effort to evaluate change in social sensitivity.

An illustration of a social sensitivity poll is given in Example 5. This should help you to develop your own. Once you have developed one item, keep it to use with another class. Be very selective of the social issues so that they do not become outdated. If students have limited ability you might have fewer than six choices by eliminating one of three of the choices. This technique is an excellent basis for discussion as well as a means of evaluation.

EXAMPLE 5

Social Sensitivity Poll

Directions: Read the following paragraph and check below to indicate
               how many people in your community you think agree with
               these statements.

"Garbage collection is a problem in major cities in our country. Most collectors are poorly educated, have no employable skills, are unkempt, and display an irresponsible attitude. They should receive no more than the minimum wage."

Nobody	_____	Half the people	_____
A few people	_____	More than half	_____
Less than half	_____	Almost everybody	_____

News items can form a basis for evaluating social sensitivity. Students can be asked to clip from daily papers and bring to class those articles dealing with social issues. One technique is to collect papers and have the clipping done in a class session. Which of these you use could depend upon how many resources the students have at their disposal. Magazines can be used in the same way, although they do not usually contain an equal amount of such articles as do newspapers.

The same kind of opinion poll as the one given above can be used. A series of issues can be rated on the same device by numbering the issues and providing columns labeled with the numbers corresponding to the issues. This could provide a reaction pattern for each student. You would need to be aware that the opinion for one issue could affect the opinion for the other issues.

Another technique to use with news articles is to have students write anonymous opinions about the article or reactions to a problem. These opinions could then be used to begin a class discussion. You could explain to students that no one will know whose reaction is being read unless the person who wrote it reveals by his own behavior that it is his.

Case problems can be used to evaluate social sensitivity. These can be collected from magazines, newspapers, and textbooks. Sometimes students can be asked to write a brief story or anecdote. Like all other techniques, reactions of students are not conclusive but merely evidence of present status of social sensitivity.

Social issues can be identified in case problems before these are discussed. Very few high school and college students can pinpoint an issue much less present evidence on both sides of the issue. The ability to do this would be invaluable not only in the present life of a student but also in the future.

One teacher identifies an issue, names students for each side, and has a modified debate. When this process is completed, each student states his position and explains why he feels this way. This teacher feels she has gained much insight into the social sensitivity of each of her students. She also believes that each student better understands his own sensitivity to others.

Roleplaying

Roleplaying shows action on behalf of an individual in his relations with other persons. It gives opportunity for analysis of the roles individuals play as members of groups rather than the exploration of personal emotional difficulties. These roles are socially, culturally, and collectively formed, and they are played by all persons, each in his own unique, individual manner, in the usual variety of human relationship situations in which people find themselves.

Roleplaying is concerned with the effect which usual, acceptable, normal behavior has upon people when they interact with each other in usual, acceptable, normal situations.

Roleplaying must be structured if it is to be successful as either a teaching or an evaluation technique. The steps are to set up the problem, act out the situation, and observe and analyze the actions.

The setting up of the problem should follow four guidelines. The problem should grow out of class discussion. Most of the students should have had real life experience with similar situations. The problem should involve some emotional feeling. The situation to be roleplayed should have the characters and setting clearly determined. These questions will help you to do this:

1. If we could analyze one of the problems we have been discussing, as it actually occurred, which one of these do you feel would most meet our needs right now?

2. What kind of group would the action portray?

3. Where would the action occur in real life?

4. Who are some of the people who make up the action group? What are their characteristics?

5. Who are the persons from the class who wish to portray the characters? (The class will help to choose the characters who do not volunteer.)

6. What furniture from the classroom will be needed to set up the stage for the dramatization?

Acting out the situation should be spontaneous and unrehearsed. The members chosen to play certain roles should do their best to play as directed. The action may vary from five to thirty minutes and should be terminated when the teacher thinks it advisable to avoid personal conflicts.

Observing the action should be done by students as well as the teacher. Assigned questions could include the following:

1. Who takes over the leadership?

2. Who monopolizes the conversation?

3. Is the shy person in the group being encouraged to take part?

4. Are persons in the scene willing to give way to another's point of view?

5. Do the members of the group show respect for personality?

6. Do the students in the group seem to overcome self-consciousness and gain poise?

7. How do the characters meet the problems described?

Each class member should try to project himself into the action by deciding what would be his reaction to the situation.

Analyzing and discussing the action is probably the most important step in using roleplaying as an evaluation technique. The observers should report what was seen as well as what was done. The class members can discuss what relationship problems existed in the scene and what action might have given better results. Each role can be assigned to various class members so that each character in the scene is observed and analyzed.

In light of the discussion and group suggestions, the situation can be played over again to give the actors the opportunity to put into practice immediately new understandings and ways of behaving. Roles can be reversed to afford better opportunity to "get the feel of the other person" in the group and thereby understand his position and further diagnose one's own role in relation to it.

Roleplaying is more self-evaluation for students than teacher-evaluation of students. The student actors and the observers can gain self-understanding. The teacher can gain insights into attitudes, values, interests, and other personal qualities of students. Like all other sociometric techniques, roleplaying is informal and nonconclusive. It does provide a means of evaluating personal qualities that is relatively accurate.

The student actor has the chance to gain an understanding of how to act in a similar real life situation and how it feels to be doing it without having to suffer consequences of risking job security, personal dignity, or personal status. Through class discussion the student actor can realize things about his behavior that he did not know before since action is sometimes so intense that the actor is unconscious of his actions, and because the discussions are based on precisely what was done while the scene was in progress. Through replay the student actor can immediately put into practice new understandings and new ways of behaving. Through the challenge presented by unrehearsed situations, the student actor can test and train himself for spontaneity in meeting social situations effectively. He can gain insight into his roles in relation to others in a variety of interpersonal situations. He can also overcome self-consciousness and gain poise.

The student observer has the opportunity to identify himself behaviorally with the actors, for one often sees objectively in another's performance almost the same things regarding oneself. He can look for things in a given situation that ordinarily he would ignore as a participant in actual life. The student observer can also see himself in the actions of others.

The roleplaying technique gives the teacher a means of discovering attitudes and family relations of her students, and a means of getting values out where everyone can look at and discuss them. She can help pupils evaluate their own attitudes. Roleplaying provides a key to the individual student's ability to meet situations involving personal relationships. The teacher has at least a limited opportunity to change attitudes and develop values and has a way of bridging the gap between verbal commitments and actual operation.

There are definite cautions to observe in the use of roleplaying as an evaluation-teaching technique:

1. A leader must know where and when to cut to avoid personal conflicts.

2. It is not ethical to use this technique as a means of finding out about students' family problems.

3. Roleplaying is not for all situations—be discriminant in its use.

4. Roleplaying can lose its effectiveness through too frequent use.

5. The situation should not be imposed by the instructor and players should not be chosen by her.

6. Just acting out some problem without guidance in analyzing and evaluating what is done and how it is done, as well as the effect upon each person while in the process of the activity, will serve to perpetuate whatever misdoings the individual in question customarily performs.

Roleplaying can provide a means of guiding the doings so that mistakes, as well as good points, can be recognized and appreciated, until better relationships with others are adapted by the student in his everyday living.

Roleplaying can be used in solving problems. Under each of the problems in Table 14-2 is a tentative suggestion for using this technique. In the actual situation, different sets of circumstances might be set up by the group with whom it is planned.

TABLE 14-2

Problem	Situation for Roleplaying
A. *Planning and making improvements in our homes.* Keeping home clean.	Two contrasting dramas could be used. One could show mother responsible for all chores with family members mad and fussy over late dinner, baby's toys in living room and brother's shirt not ironed. The other could illustrate privileges derived from sharing responsibilities in keeping home clean.
B. *Planning and making a garment.* 1. Buying materials for sewing.	Mother might be tired from day's work, father late to Farm Bureau meeting. Daughter blankly announces at supper table that she must have $10 to buy materials for skirt for following day's Home Economics class. Family members react with heated argument. Contrasting scene might show a desirable way of planning for inclusion of such expenses in family budget.
2. Making a garment at home.	The situation could involve three girls from Home Economics class sewing together in one girl's home. Their comments might reveal purpose of sewing at home, suggestions for home projects or sewing circles for recreation as well as for work.

TABLE 14-2 (continued)

Problem	Situation for Roleplaying
C. *Planning for the family's recreation during the Christmas season.*	Situation might show typical families at play on Christmas Eve.
D. *Planning, preparing and serving weekend meals.*	Family comes home from church to hot dinner. Congeniality and pleasure of whole family are shown.
1. Serving Sunday dinner to the family.	Family might include adolescent brother stuffing, adolescent girl poking and picking at food, baby spitting food, father not eating
2. Discovering desirable eating habits.	squash, mother jumping up and down from table to serve food. Older daughter dieting by not eating at all.
3. Practicing good etiquette at table.	This situation could show proper way to eat a meal in lunchroom, as contrasted with undesirable habits of shouting, hurried eating, making unnecessary noise with utensils, leaving milk bottles and silver on table, etc.
E. *Helping to care for the children we know best.* 1. Babysitting.	The action scene could tell the story of a teenaged girl "babysitting." One scene could show the girl, date and several other friends, taking their younger brothers and sisters to the picture show to see *Snow White.*
2. Answering the questions younger brothers and sisters ask.	In this situation a small child might be asking a teenaged sister where babies come from. Teenaged girl could answer simply and honestly. In a second scene the same question might bring scolds, rebukes, and hush-hush answers.

Summary

Sociometric techniques described and illustrated in this chapter include the sociogram, social distance scale, social sensitivity poll, and roleplaying. These techniques are classified as teaching techniques by many authors and so they are. It is hoped after reading this chapter you agree with this author that sociometric techniques can be very effectively used as means of evaluating personal qualities of students. As in the other chapters in Part III, this chapter will be summarized by stating conclusions drawn by the author. We can conclude that:

- sociometric techniques are excellent means of evaluating social acceptance;
- the sociogram reveals natural groupings of students and personal relationships in a group;
- the request for sociogram data maybe in terms of social, mental, or physical skills;
- the results of a sociogram can help a teacher plan for both in-school and out-of-school experiences for individuals as well as a class group;
- a social distance scale reveals the degree to which each individual is accepted by and accepts others in the class;
- a tabulation of individual reactions to a social distance scale provides a consensus of personal opinions;
- a social distance scale raises questions and provides information about social acceptance within a class;
- the Who's Who technique is similar in its construction, use, and results to the social distance scale;
- the Who's Who requires students to match the names of classmates with personal characteristics;
- social sensitivity techniques include opinion polls as well as reactions to news items and case problems;
- social sensitivity techniques not only help a teacher to evaluate the sensitivity of students but also make these students more sensitive to others;
- roleplaying reveals action on behalf of an individual in his relations with other persons;
- the roleplaying process should include setting up the problem, acting out the situation, and observing and analyzing the action;
- roleplaying provides more self-evaluation by students than teacher-evaluation of students;
- roleplaying can be used in solving problems in all areas of home economics.

STUDENT ACTIVITIES

1. Construct sociograms, using the same class, for each of these skills:
    a. social
    b. mental
    c. physical

Compare the three sociograms and state conclusions drawn from the data.

2. Construct a social distance scale and ask a class to answer; tabulate data for each student and for class as a whole; state conclusions drawn from data.

3. Construct a Who's Who and ask a class to answer; tabulate data for each student and for class as a whole; state conclusions based on data.

4. Construct a social sensitivity poll and use with a class group; state conclusions about results obtained.

5. Clip several news items from current papers; make a lesson plan for use in evaluating social sensitivity; use in a class when appropriate.

6. Select several case problems; make a lesson plan for use in evaluating social sensitivity; use in a class when appropriate.

7. Make a plan for using roleplaying in a class in each area of home economics; use as many of these with your classes as is appropriate.

8. Demonstrate the technique of roleplaying for your college class asking your classmates to be actors or observers; follow with a group discussion.

REFERENCES

Ahmann, J. Stanley and Glock, M. D. *Evaluating Pupil Growth.* New York: Allyn and Bacon, Inc., 1959.

Arny, Clara Brown. *Evaluation in Home Economics.* New York: Appleton-Century-Crofts, 1953.

Fleck, Henrietta. *Toward Better Teaching of Home Economics.* New York: The Macmillan Company.

Hall, Olive A. and Paolucci, B. *Teaching Home Economics.* New York: John Wiley and Sons, Inc., 1970.

Part IV PROGRESS TOWARD OBJECTIVES

INTRODUCTION

Discovering the extent of progress toward objectives is an essential process. Students, as well as the teacher, need and desire to recognize accomplishments. They also should identify their shortcomings and make decisions about next steps. This process is *evaluation* in its largest sense.

Grading may or may not be a part of this process. Many teachers would like to cease giving grades but are required by the school administration to so do. Some school systems are using systems of reporting student progress other than a traditional grading system. This author commends such efforts but is aware that most teachers are required to give periodic grades.

Thus, Part IV has two chapters, each with a slightly different emphasis. Chapter 15 discusses ways of recording evidences of the degree to which objectives are being met. This chapter is appropriate for use by any teacher regardless of whether he is required to record grades or not. There is a section that relates evidences to types of objectives. Another relates objectives, teaching methods, and evaluation techniques in an organized plan. A system for keeping a continuous record and the use of individual student folders are presented in the last two sections.

The final chapter will have special meaning for those teachers who must assign grades at specific times. There are some advantages to grading and these will be outlined. The section on providing for individual differences has suggestions for legitimately giving a slow learner a passing grade. Those teachers who do not give grades will also find this section helpful. Several systems for assigning grades are explained in this chapter. The use of student-teacher conferences as an evaluation technique is discussed.

It is the hope of the author that this last part of the book will make determining progress and assigning grades a more pleasant and rewarding process for both students and teachers.

Chapter 15 RECORDING EVIDENCE

Records are necessary whether or not grades are required. Written symbols, phrases, or sentences make up the communication system between the teacher and the students. You must also admit that what you write is more clearly evident to you than what you think about without writing it down. This chapter attempts to help you more effectively and efficiently record evidences that your students are performing in the ways described in the objectives.

In Terms of Selected Objectives

Objectives stated in behavioral or performance terms provide an excellent basis for recording evidences of progress. This is one of the major advantages for stating objectives in terms of expected behaviors. Mager includes or implies in his objectives the means of evaluation.[1] If you do as the author of this text does, your objectives will include the expected behavior but not the specific method or device for evaluating the performance. The logic behind this procedure is that there are several

---

[1]Robert F. Mager, *Preparing Instructional Objectives* (Palo Alto, California: Fearon Publishers, 1962).

different ways to record the evidences, and the appropriateness of the chosen procedure will depend on the student or students being evaluated.

There should be one or more procedures for evaluating every objective. This is the most important of the criteria for selecting an objective. If you can not determine a means of evaluation, then you should discard the objective. Those teachers who accept this criterion will either have to use their ingenuity or be very restrictive in selecting their objectives. It is hoped that the restriction will be kept at a minimum. You must remember that not every evidence of behavior has to result in a score that will contribute to a grade.

A checklist of objectives provides an excellent progress chart. Some schools are using this as a method of reporting to parents. You will find it helpful to use with your students. This type of checklist is developed in the same way as any other. Begin by listing the objectives that have been determined by you and your students. Secondly, decide on the column headings which might be *more than satisfactorily met* (S+), *met minimum standards* (S), and *inadequately met* (I). The student as well as the teacher should check the level of performance (see Example 1).

EXAMPLE 1

Unit: Food for the Family

Directions: Check (X) the column that best represents the progress made toward each objective.

Objectives	S+	S	I
1. Determine personal food needs			
2. Comprehend knowledge of the food required daily			
3. Analyze how food preferences and prejudices affect own diet			
4. Recognize contributions of snacks in meeting daily food needs			

Cognitive objectives are usually evaluated by paper and pencil tests. Most teachers have no difficulty in determining procedures to evaluate knowledge gained. Both objective and essay test items are appropriate. Perhaps the most important thing is to key the level of cognitive behavior to the type of test item chosen. You will remember that matching items can evaluate only at the lowest level whereas multiple choice and alternate response are appropriate at least for the knowledge, comprehension, and application levels. Essay questions and interpretive items can be constructed so as to evaluate at all the levels of cognition.

Personal qualities are usually evaluated by observational devices, in particular, checklists and rating scales. Essay test items can also be used or constructed so as to reveal values and attitudes. Reporting forms such as autobiographies, diaries, logs, and anecdotal records are excellent means of evaluating personal qualities objectives. The audio-visual techniques that are appropriate for this type of objective include tape recordings, pictures, and cartoons. Sociometric techniques are designed for the purpose of evaluating personal qualities. You must remember that most of these will not provide a score contributable to a grade.

Skill objectives are most frequently evaluated by using observational devices. A skill can be evaluated by rating the performance, the product, or both of these. Checklists, scorecards, and rating devices are all easy for both the teacher and the student to use to evaluate a skill. Project reports, activity checklists, and logs are the reporting forms you can use to evaluate skill objectives. Most of these procedures can provide a score whether used for a grade or not.

Symbols may vary according to type of objective. The fact that many teachers use only one type of symbol may account for their difficulty in evaluating all types of objectives. You must admit that percentage grades are not very appropriate for evaluating personal qualities and not easily usable with skills. Other types of symbols may be just as difficult to use with cognitive objectives.

There are many types of symbols used for recording evidences. These range from a single mark to a complicated phrase. The most traditional and oldest system is percentages. Yet this is perhaps the most frustrating to use since a teacher must accept a one point difference in a range from one to a hundred. If 70 percent is considered passing, how can a teacher justify assigning 69 percent to a paper?

Another system that is also traditional and is perhaps the most frequently used is letter grades. These are A, B, C, D, and F and may have percentage ranges assigned to them. Numbers (5, 4, 3, 2, 1) make up another system that many teachers find useful because it is concise and convenient. The major shortcoming of this system lies in the exact meaning of each number. Another set of symbols are S+ for outstanding, S for satisfactory, and U for unsatisfactory. This system lacks conciseness but does tend to lessen competitiveness. The use of descriptive comments has advantages but is time-consuming for the teacher and not easily accepted by most parents. You might consider using a combination of these systems and choosing the type of symbol according to the type of objective.

Cognitive objectives, being evaluated most often by paper and pencil tests, lend themselves to the more specific systems. Objective tests are often scored by percentages or by scores converted to letters. The next chapter explains a method of using the range of scores with normal breaks as a way of converting scores to letters. The method is definitely preferable to percentages. Numbers or the S+–S–U system are easily usable with essay questions as are letters. Here again percentages are difficult and frustrating.

Personal qualities are more difficult to evaluate with a symbol than is knowledge. Observational devices can and frequently do have total scores. These can be converted to letters or still better to S+–S–U. Comments are very appropriate on reports of all types and on audio-visual evidences. The number system can easily be used to record daily observed personal behaviors such as work habits, cooperativeness, participation.

Skill objectives include either a performance or a product and this makes choosing an appropriate symbol somewhat easier than for affective objectives. Observational devices for products and procedures result in more usable scores than for personal qualities. These scores can be converted to letters or the S+–S–U symbols. These scores can also be added to test scores and other scores to make a total score which can be used with the range-break method.

A Plan for a Unit of Instruction

A previous chapter had a circle diagram illustrating the relationship of behavioral objectives, teaching methods, and evaluation techniques. This entire book has attempted to relate objectives and evaluation but has not often related teaching methods. This is a valuable concept for planning instruction as well as for recording evidences of obtained objectives.

Each aspect of the teaching-learning process has a reciprocal relationship to all other parts. Frequently the impression is given that all planning begins with objectives, but this need not be the order in which the teacher thinks. Stating behavioral objectives appears to be the most logical but you may begin with teaching-learning experiences because of your past technique of planning. Maybe the following paragraphs will help you to see how to begin at any point.

The reciprocal relationship between objectives, teaching methods, and evaluation techniques makes moving back and forth from one to the other permissible. The circle diagram can be expanded to illustrate this concept. Double-headed arrows indicate this relationship in Figure 15-1. This diagram is meant to convey that you can begin planning with any one of these aspects. The point is to make each grow out of the other.

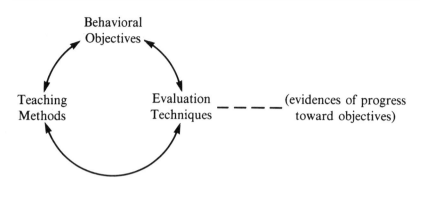

FIGURE 15-1

Another aspect of instruction is the subject matter content. Home economics educators possess a set of concepts and generalizations identified through workshops sponsored by the U.S. Office of Education.[2] This aspect can very easily be included in the reciprocal relationship. This simply adds another dimension and can be diagrammed more easily by using a diamond than a circle. Figure 15-2 shows how.

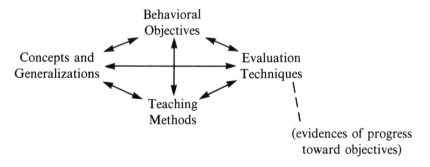

FIGURE 15-2

If you are oriented to subject matter, you may choose to start planning with concepts. If by now you are oriented to behavioral objectives you will begin there. Wherever you start, all aspects should be included and interrelated.

A planning chart is a useful way to plan for both teaching and evaluation. In truth, this is simply a unified way to plan for a unit of instruction that

[2]U.S. Office of Education, *Concepts and Generalizations: Their Place in High School Home Economics Curriculum Development* (Washington: American Home Economics Association, 1967).

includes all the aspects in the diamond diagram. The illustration in Example 2 contains three columns: one for behavioral objectives, one for teaching methods, and one for evaluation techniques. Each of the evaluation techniques represents a means of recording evidences of progress toward obtaining the objective. Concepts are underlined in the objective.

EXAMPLE 2

A Teaching-Learning Planning Chart

Instructional Objectives	Teaching Methods	Evaluation Techniques
1. Identify the general pattern of physical growth of children	Show transparencies: Growth and Developmental Process by 3M Company.	Write a comparison of the growth pattern of the children observed in a child care center.
	Study and discuss references on growth patterns.	List physical characteristics of preschool children of each age level.
	Discuss physical characteristics of preschool children at each age level.	Answer objective test items on physical growth patterns of preschool children.
	Observe children at child care center.	
	Discuss possible causes for variations in the growth pattern.	
	Analyze case studies of children to recognize variations of development.	

This kind of planning chart not only is a means for planning a course or unit of instruction but also is probably the best way to insure that each objective has predetermined techniques of evaluation. Starring those procedures that will result in a grade helps any teacher who is required to provide a periodic grade. Although this author does not feel grades are necessary, she does recognize that most of you who use this book will be or are already required by your school administration to assign grades.

Individual Student Folders

Do you believe in student involvement in the evaluation process? Should students not only determine their objectives but also evaluate their progress toward these objectives? If your answers are affirmative, you need to consider how to do this as effectively and easily as possible. There have been many suggestions of devices and techniques in the previous chapters. Now you need a system that will help you and your students to record the evidences. Using individual student folders is perhaps the most effective method.

The availabilty to students is the major advantage for using individual folders. There are other systems such as the traditional roll or grade book but these are not easily used or consulted by individuals. Folders also have the advantage of privacy whereas a student cannot record or view his own scores in a grade book without seeing the others' grades. The folders can contain evidences that do not lend themselves to scores or grades, such as a log or diary. These cannot be easily recorded in a grade book.

Students are constantly being motivated as they use their folders. The progress being made is evident to the student as is the quality of his work. If he is not operating at a satisfactory level, you can help him to plan to do better. If he is making sufficient progress there is a feeling of satisfaction as he places one more piece of evidence in his folder.

Individual folders can be an important means of helping a student to set his own direction or goal. All too often teachers do this for their students. Some teachers even fail to tell the students what the direction or goal is. This leads a person to wonder *when* a student develops the skill of goal-setting which is necessary to effective adult living. Some students are so ready to determine their own direction that simply using the folder will be the impetus. For other students, the teacher will need to provide a time to assist them to use the folder as a means of determining their own directions and goals.

The setting of standards is another advantageous use of individual folders. You are aware that successful teachers have minimum as well as maximum standards. These teachers attempt to move students from performing at the minimum level toward the maximum level. Reviewing the evidence of past performances provides a means of assessing the progress toward higher standards. Furthermore, this process can help in studying what maximum performance really means.

Any evidence of progress can be placed in a student's folder. The only exceptions would be those items that are too large or bulky. Keying each piece of evidence to an objective is important and such information can be included in the title of a device or written at the top of a page. One teacher limited the type of booklet to be used for a diary so that it could be kept in the folder until the end of the course.

It is perhaps obvious that in time the materials in the folder would become voluminous. Periodically cleaning out the folder is necessary. Usually this is done at the end of the unit or course. It can be more frequent if necessary. If encouraged, a student will usually review as the sorting is done. This then becomes a culminating or summary experience.

Some evidences can become a part of a permanent record. You should indicate to your students which pieces should be left. One clothing teacher has her students keep the rating devices used to evaluate the last garment they constructed. She believes that this piece of evidence will be useful the next time a student constructs a garment whether in her class, for another teacher, or at home. A summary sheet for a unit or course may be the only permanent record left. A continuous record of home projects may be another permanent record that needs to be left in a folder. It is strongly recommended that one teacher give the folders with their permanent records to the next home economics teacher so that the student has a record on which to build.

The contents of the folders for students who have completed the first concept in a foods unit are listed below. This is merely an example that may help you to understand the kinds of evidence folders may contain.

(Concept-Family Food Needs)

1. Pretest covering factors affecting food needs.
2. A comparison of personal food needs and those of other family members.
3. Analysis of three different diets for meeting family food needs.
4. A menu planned for a week for a specific family.
5. Menus planned to meet a special diet problem.
6. Post-test covering factors affecting food needs.

Student folders should always be available to both the teacher and the individual students. This means you have to provide a place to store the folders. Teachers sometimes give this as a reason not to use folders. Cost is another reason but that can be solved if the school cannot provide the funds by such means as student assessment, an FHA chapter project, or funds from a civic organization.

The most logical place to store student folders is in a filing cabinet. A steel file with a drawer for each class is excellent. Some teachers choose to file alphabetically rather than by classes. If the file is to serve more than one teacher in the same department this is particularly helpful since students may have different teachers for consecutive years, semesters, or quarters.

Teachers who have some of the same students for more than one year frequently prefer alphabetical filing since folders do not need to be moved. An added advantage is increased privacy for the students since a classmate's folder is less accessible.

Cardboard boxes are an excellent substitute for steel files. These may be purchased or constructed from cardboard cartons obtained at a grocery. Those boxes that have been used to ship produce are not very attractive but contact paper is easily attached and can add color to your classroom. This could be an excellent FHA project.

"Tote" drawers can also be used. The student may leave her folder in her own assigned drawer. This is very accessible to the student but not to the teacher. These drawers can be used the same way that a file is used with each drawer labeled alphabetically. Of course, this has a disadvantage because the folders must be placed one on top of another. These drawers should not be used if needed for their intended purpose. This is simply a substitute if neither a filing cabinet nor cardboard boxes are feasible.

No doubt there are other ways to file folders. These are the most obvious. If you like this idea and want to try it, you will find a way to set up a filing system that can be used by you and your students. It is without a doubt an effective system for recording evidences of progress toward objectives.

Summary Sheets

A reference to summary sheets was made in the above section as they relate to use of student folders. This section explains their use more fully as to how summary sheets can be used as a separate system for recording evidences.

A summary sheet is similar to a page from a class grade book. The content is a list of all the evidences to be collected during the course. Each of these pieces of evidence may be keyed to an objective (see Example 3).

A summary sheet is for use by both the teacher and the students. A summary sheet can be given to each student, and the teacher needs one for each student. This provides an excellent means for a student to know exactly what he is accomplishing. It also provides a means of communication between a teacher and the student. It can be used further with parents as a means of communication.

Perhaps the greatest advantage of using the summary sheet is student self-evaluation. Each of your students can keep up with his own progress as each score is recorded. An idea worth considering is contracting with your students for a particular grade. If the student decides to work for a B, he knows as he uses the summary sheet whether or not he is obtaining

EXAMPLE 3

Summary Evaluation Sheet

Score

1. An analysis of a case study dealing with interaction in a family. _____

2. List of guidelines for fostering satisfactory relationships with family members. _____

3. Rating scale of assuming home responsibilities. _____

4. Report of own role expectations as an adult. _____

5. A description of the personal qualities of a person you admire. _____

6. List of principles included in communicating with others. _____

7. Essay test questions identifying differences and similarities of various types of families. _____

8. Generalizations about differences in patterns of family authority. _____

9. Report comparing family life of two cultures existing in the community. _____

10. Essay test questions on relationship of personal and family values. _____

11. Summary of what was learned about assuming responsibilities. _____

12. Report of home-degree project on family recreation activity. _____

13. Objective test on sexual development and human reproduction. _____

14. Report of home-degree project on improvement of personal appearance. _____

15. Analysis of case studies about dating. _____

that grade. If not, the student may choose to do an assignment a second time or to lower his contracted grade.

A filed summary sheet provides a basis for communicating with a parent. Some schools require teacher-parent conferences. Some parents request a conference. Many home economics teachers confer with parents on home visits as well as at school. The summary sheet is useful when the parent inquires about the progress of his son or daughter.

An important use of summary sheets is the final evaluation or summation of the unit or course. This should be a satisfying process for you as well as your students. These sheets are particularly useful in determining a final grade if one is necessary. The student can use his sheet to decide what grade he should receive. This process will be discussed again in the next chapter.

Keeping a Continuous Record

A teacher experiences the greatest frustration when it is time to decide how well his students have met the objectives and he finds little or no evidence. A feeling of dissatisfaction exists when the teacher recognizes that though there are evidences, they are not adequate. Such situations are reason enough to keep a continuous record. Communication between student and teacher is perhaps the most significant reason.

A day by day recording of evidences is a profitable procedure. This need not be time-consuming if it is planned as an integral part of teaching-learning. The evaluation experience may take place at any point during the class period. You may want to begin the class by checking a progress chart, with a summary of principles from the day before, or by giving a short pretest. You may use similar techniques during the class period at a logical point. The end of the class is a natural time to state generalizations, make entries in a log, or decide on next steps.

There are numerous and obvious reasons why a teacher should use an evaluation procedure on most days. Motivation of students is reason enough. Time is usually saved especially in courses utilizing individual instruction. Both students and the teacher are able to keep their goal clearly in sight. Personal satisfaction usually results for the teacher since the organization pattern for the course is more easily controlled when there is daily evaluation.

There are many techniques that can be used for daily evaluation. Some devices are especially designed for this purpose and others can be adapted. Daily logs of past accomplishments and goals for the next day are most appropriate for laboratory activities of an individual nature. Progress charts show how the entire class is accomplishing the identified tasks and indicate to the teacher which students need immediate assistance.

Stating generalizations is a daily activity particularly appropriate for classes where there has been discussion, study, or seeking of information. Stating generalizations is a skill which a teacher has to develop in her students. You might begin by asking what was discussed or read. The answers may be too brief and not stated as generalizations. You must encourage students by asking what was meant, why this is true, how did it work, where this can be applied again. The caution is not to do too much

restating. Try this as a class group before asking students to write generalizations, principles or facts. They probably need to develop verbalization
skill as well as ability to recognize generalizations.

Weekly evaluations are needed in some units. A family development
course that is mostly class or small group discussions is such a unit. A rating
scale on participation can be used weekly. A weekly grouping of daily
generalizations helps to summarize and strengthen learning. A written
summary of how a student can personally use what has been discussed is
another useful weekly procedure. Progress reported on home-degree
projects is an excellent way to help students to work continuously on their
individual projects.

Evaluation of one unit should be linked to the next unit. This is particularly advantageous from one unit to another in the same area of home
economics. Frequently, a student has one teacher one year and another
teacher the second year. Continuous evaluation becomes a means of communication if there is a record from the year before.

Evaluation evidences of a unit in one area can build a base for activities
in the next unit. An example is thirteen-year-old Jane who had a personal
improvement project in the family development unit, continued the project
in foods with food choices for weight control, and further continued with
clothing choices. Her project in the management unit was organizing stor-
age space for clothes and cosmetics. This is just one example of how direction for further action in a new instructional unit can grow out of the final
evaluation of the current unit.

The above example points to project reports as one piece of evidence that
should be retained from unit to unit. A one-page summary sheet may be
all that is kept. This is enough for the student to decide how much base she
has to build on for her next project. The report may also give the teacher
several clues as she guides the student in stating objectives for her projects
as well as in recording evidences that the objectives have been met. After
all, writing project reports is a skill that has to be developed.

Pretests and post-tests from previous units are frequently useful to have.
When a new teacher begins with a class, a pretest is frequently given. If
there is a test left from the year before, the teacher may choose to use it
instead of the pretest or the scores from it to evaluate progress at the end
of her own unit. A careful analysis of test items on pretests and post-tests
can help any teacher decide how successfully the students answer each type
of test item.

Perhaps the evaluation device used most frequently in another unit is the
summary sheet. This one sheet has a record of all the evidences for the unit
and often for the year. It is easy to file and to use for reference when working
with a student. Students who participate in the Future Homemakers degree
program find these sheets very valuable as they fill out their applications.

Since this is a personal achievement program rather than a competitive one, students of all ability levels can participate.

Continuous evaluation has many advantages. The clue to being successful with this process is setting up a plan and involving your students in collecting, filing, and using the records.

Summary

You are now aware of the many reasons why progress should be determined and of the ways that evidences can be recorded. This chapter will be summarized with a list of decisions about recording evidences. You should summarize with a list of your own. This author has decided to:

- record evidences in terms of behavioral objectives;

- select at least one appropriate means of recording evidence for each objective;

- use a variety of symbols to record progress chosen according to the type of learning;

- prepare a written plan that relates objectives to teaching methods, and those two to evaluation techniques;

- set up individual folders for students use as well as my own use;

- develop summary evaluation sheets both to help students do self-evaluation and to aid in communication;

- keep a continuous record of student growth and progress.

STUDENT ACTIVITIES

1. Develop a sample checklist for evaluating progress toward meeting objectives.

2. Make a plan for a unit of instruction that includes objectives, teaching methods, and evaluation techniques.

3. Decide which set of symbols you will use with each of the evaluation techniques in your written plan.

4. If you are currently teaching, set up a file system with individual folders.

5. Develop a sample summary evaluation sheet for a unit you are now teaching or may some day teach.

REFERENCES

Gronlund, Norman E. *Measurement and Evaluation in Teaching,* New York: The Macmillan Company, 1971.

Gronlund, Norman E. *Stating Behavioral Objectives for Classroom Instruction,* New York: The Macmillan Company, 1970.

Hall, Olive A. and Paolucci, B. *Teaching Home Economics,* New York: John Wiley and Sons, Inc., 1970.

_____. "How Gather Evidences?" *Tips and Topics in Home Economics* IV, no. 3 (February 1964).

_____. "Frequency of Testing." *Tips and Topics in Home Economics* IV, no. 3 (February 1964).

Chapter 16 ASSIGNING GRADES

Grades and reports of student progress have always been a major concern of teachers. Nearly all teachers are required to report on the progress and achievement of students whether or not grades are included. This chapter is written for the teacher who must periodically assign a grade to every student he teaches. If you are fortunate enough not to have this responsibility, you will still find some helpful suggestions in the section on providing for individual differences. The natural break system for assigning grades is explained in the third section. The last section concerns student involvement in the grading process.

Purposes of Grades

Communication is the only legimate basis or purpose for grades. The symbols used, whether letters, percentages, or phrases, have a message for the viewer. Traditional grades have been considered a report to parents, to future employers, and to college admission personnel. Actually, grades today may communicate more vividly to the student than to anyone else. Grades also have a message for the teacher.

Grades indicate to the student his achievement. This is true whether grades are status symbols or not. Some schools, groups within schools, and many parents do not stress grades as much as others appear to. It is important for a student to know how well he is achieving, whether or not grades are used.

Grades based on behavioral or performance objectives can indicate a higher degree of achievement than grades based only on paper and pencil tests. When a student has identified a task and the level of performance, a grade simply corresponds to what he already knows he has accomplished.

A grade can provide a very meaningful reward for a student. All too frequently, a high grade has been given only to those academically talented students. If objectives include personal qualities and skills, many students can achieve to a high degree. Their reward, or grade, is then much better than any grade has ever been before.

A teacher should be sure that students understand the grading system. They must also know what each level of the system represents. This is essential if a grade has relevance for an individual student. The grade should not be a surprise at the end of the unit or course. A student should have periodic, if not daily, evidence of his progress and achievement. Perhaps the greatest satisfaction for the student occurs when he uses his summary sheet and his individual folder to determine his own grade.

Grades report the achievement of a student to others. This is probably the reason grades were begun. Parents have traditionally wanted to know whether or not their children were achieving in school. Counselors and school administrators are two other groups that desire and need to know how well students are meeting the outlined objectives.

Parents have a right to an accounting of the progress and achievement of their children. Most parents really want their sons and daughters to achieve according to the ability level of each one. A grade can communicate the level of ability as well as the degree of achievement. Parents may need help to accept the ability level of a child and grades can be one kind of evidence used to accomplish this understanding. The grade will have more meaning if the parents understand the objectives of the course as well as the basis upon which the grade was determined.

Counselors are available to assist students in making educational and occupational decisions. Grades coupled with other types of tests and personal data are used by counselors as they work with a student. A sudden change in grades may point to a need for personal counseling. Grades may be less important than data from such devices as interest inventories and personal adjustment tests but they do make a contribution to understanding a student. Such understanding is vital if a counselor is to help a student.

School administrators use grades in many ways. Sometimes a principal may need grades as he talks with a parent; more often he uses data compiled from a large group of students to evaluate whether or not the school is meeting some of its goals. An administrator frequently uses a compilation of grades as he evaluates the effectiveness of a teacher. Grades that consistently vary from a norm usually indicate that the teacher's effectiveness is not as it should be. Administrators also compare grades of standardized achievement test scores to reading levels or to academic ability levels of students.

Grades are predictive of scholastic success. While there are other predictors, grades are perhaps the most consistent indicator of how well a student will do in future scholastic endeavors. Aptitude and intelligence tests are possibly more precise predictors than are grades, but all three together make up an excellent formula.

Grades in one course affect choice of courses while still in high school. If a student does not do well in a language course, he will probably not choose to take another in the same language. The student does not always have such a choice, but when he does a grade may be the decisive factor.

Choice of an occupation may be influenced by grades in certain courses. Mary Jane likes science but makes low grades in mathematics. She may decide that she will choose some occupation that does not require exceptional mathematical skill. Tom does well in industrial arts and decides to explore carpentry. Many home economics teachers have chosen this profession because of their success and high grades in high school homemaking classes.

Entrance into another school may depend upon grades made in high school. This is particularly true of entrance into many colleges and universities. There are students who make low grades in high school but have the ability to make much higher grades. However, there is considerable evidence to prove that high school grades and college grades follow the same general pattern.

Grades of students have a message for the teacher. Occasionally you may remark that your students did not study, did not learn what you taught them, or did poorly on a test. Most likely you should ask yourself why students made such poor grades. The reason may be in your actions. A teacher can also learn much about individual students and about the class as a whole from a careful analysis of grades.

Grades can tell a teacher how well students are doing as individuals. Each student is usually of more concern to a teacher than an entire class group. You, as a teacher of home economics, may desire to compare grades in home economics with those made in English, history, mathematics, and biology. An analysis of grades in each of the areas of home economics may reveal an important aptitude that points to choice of an occupation. Comparing grades on paper and pencil tests with ratings for personal qualities and with ratings on skill procedures and products can reveal something about the abilities of individual students.

Grouped data of grades for a class can reveal much to a teacher. A comparison of one class with others can indicate whether this particular class is a typical one. If scores differ greatly for evaluating various objectives, a teacher may decide a group has certain distinct and unusual abilities. This may be particularly true insofar as the cognitive domain is concerned. However, another group may have unusual homemaking skills.

Clues for improving teaching techniques may result from a survey of grades. An item analysis of an objective test may indicate the areas where more instruction is needed as well as where teaching has been most successful. A review of scores on rating devices reveals how well students have done with development of skills and personal qualities. The results tell a teacher how effective his teaching has been with a particular class group.

Perhaps the clues for ways to improve evaluation techniques are more important than those aimed toward teaching methods. As has been pointed out before, many teachers are more effective with the teaching process than with evaluating their students. This author would prefer for you to take a critical look at how you evaluate before considering ways to improve teaching methods or criticizing students. If your students have not made satisfactory grades, check first to determine if the evaluation technique is consistent with the objective and on the ability level of the class group.

Providing for Individual Differences

One of your major concerns is how to provide for individual differences as you design a plan for determining grades. The traditional system of using mostly scores from paper and pencil tests is not adequate. This is especially true for students in home economics where homemaking skills and personal qualities may be more important than those objectives based only on knowledge gained. The paragraphs that follow should provide some suggestions for you and affirm some of your current practices.

The type of test items can be selected to match cognitive ability. The chapter on test analysis gave you a way to determine the difficulty index as well as the index of discrimination. These indices can help you match questions to ability level. Part II provided information on which types of items were the easiest to answer. The following paragraphs summarize this information because of its importance in providing for individual differences.

Academically talented students do well on paper and pencil tests. Interpretive test items, problem-solving questions, and extended essay items provide a challenge for these students. However, the slow student is completely baffled by such questions and is really discriminated against. There is some evidence that the academically talented student is less successful with alternate choice items than students of average ability. This may be caused by the more able student analyzing the test items and finding the flaws that all too often exist in this type of question.

Recognition items are best for less capable students. Matching is probably the easiest and therefore more suitable for this ability level. Multiple choice is usually not too difficult and may also be appropriate. Alternate response based on simple situations is another appropriate type. Recall items require a memory process that is usually more than that with which this ability level student can cope.

Slow learners need not take a paper and pencil test. This may be a revolutionary idea for a few teachers but is one that makes sense. A high school student who reads at the third grade level and cannot write a complete sentence is not equipped to take a paper test. Perhaps you feel that he does not belong in your class, but he *is* there. One solution to your problem of what to do is to find other ways than a paper and pencil test to evaluate his progress.

Evaluation of personal qualities is usually advantageous for students of all ability levels. There are many personal qualities or aspects of affective behaviors that do not lend themselves to being part of a grade. These are appreciations, values, beliefs, interpersonal relationships, and attitudes. However, there are others that can be rated and these scores can be incorporated into a grade. These include work habits, class participation, and cooperativeness.

Although many teachers do not evaluate personal qualities for grading purposes, you can if you so choose. Scores on these qualities will probably be the highest made by your less capable students. Is this not reason enough to include these scores? Your more able students will do just as well on ratings for personal qualities as on paper and pencil tests. If not, then perhaps their grades should not be so high. Ratings on personal qualities can and frequently do shorten the range of grades for a class.

Evaluating personal qualities should occur only when there are objectives for the affective domain. A laboratory course nearly always has objectives that include work habits, group work, and cooperativeness. Individualized work usually includes work habits, self-directiveness, and assumption of responsibility. These can be scored using rating devices and the results can be used as a part of a grade.

Students vary in their aptitude at performing homemaking skills. Some students with little aptitude tend to compensate by increased effort. Frequently these students include those that do poorly on paper and pencil tests. These students are most likely to be the same ones who rated high on personal qualities. Academically talented students are as apt to be included in this group as students from other ability levels. Evaluating the processes and products associated with homemaking skills tends to give all students a chance to succeed.

Laboratory work is designed to further skill development and should be evaluated. Observing and rating students as they work and rating their products provide very usable scores. You may find that evaluating parts rather than the whole provides more scores and an advantage to less academically oriented students. An example is rating the plan for a foods laboratory, each product prepared, work and safety habits, service, table setting, and clean-up results. This results in a maximum of six grades for one laboratory lesson. Another example is evaluating each unit of construction in a garment rather than the finished garment. Add one paper-pencil test to three sets of a lab grade and the result is an obvious advantage to students who do better with their hands than their heads.

Home-degree projects provide another means for students of any ability level to excell. These should always be planned to meet individual needs and should be evaluated in terms of how well a student obtains his own objectives. The more capable student simply plans a project of greater scope than does the less capable. If both successfully carry out their plans, their grades could be the same. Home-degree projects are an excellent way to provide for the less capable to succeed.

Extra projects have always been controversial. You will need to decide whether or not you wish to use this procedure to increase the chances of your students making higher grades. You may simply add the score into the total, thus increasing the level of the grade. This is probably the most legitimate way to use extra projects. However, you can add points to the final score if you desire. Teachers who stay constantly aware of the grade averages of their students can suggest an extra project to a student who has a borderline grade. Students should be made to feel that they can make the same suggestion to the teacher.

A plan can be developed that provides for individual differences. This plan can provide for the academically talented, for the student of average ability, and also for the slow learner. It can provide for those students who do well on written tests, for those who try hard and succeed rarely, for those whose talents are the homemaking skills, and for those who have any combination of these abilities.

The first step is to determine what kinds of abilities the students in class have. The second step is to check these abilities against the behavioral objectives of the course. Can each student succeed to some degree so as to make an acceptable grade? If you can answer these questions in the affirmative, you are ready to draw up a plan. The following example will illustrate such a plan. The four students described are used as illustrations of the first step.

Mary, a slow learner, anxious to be accepted by the group and willing to work hard to please the teacher, meets minimum standards for skill procedures and products. Betty is a slightly below-average academic student who gets along well with her peers and excells in homemaking-related skills. Ann is academically talented, has limited interest in developing homemaking skills, and is more concerned about herself than her peers. Janet makes excellent grades, studies consistently, is a leader, and performs adequately in the skill area.

The chart in Example 1 represents the plan made by the teacher. A check mark has been placed opposite the student's name in those columns where she could make an acceptable score. A plus has been placed where she could excell. The last two columns were added after the abilities of the students were checked against the objectives. These were added to provide for Betty and students similar to her. Remember this is only an example and other items could be added as could some of these be deleted.

EXAMPLE 1

Plan for Determining Grades for a Foods Unit

Name of Student	(3) Menus	(5) Lab Plans	(5) Lab Work	(5) Lab Products	(2) Obj. Tests	(3) Home Project	(5) Group Work
Mary A			✓	✓		+	+
Betty D	✓	✓	+	+		+	+
Ann M	+	+	✓	✓	+	✓	
Janet P	+	+	+	✓	+	✓	+

The number in parentheses represents the number of scores for each category. There are 28 scores in all. Mary, the slow learner, will excell eight times, perform adequately ten times, and perform below the acceptable level ten times. Using this plan Mary has rightfully earned her passing grade. Ann, the brightest student, who is uninterested in others and does only enough work in skill activities to make an acceptable score will not receive as high a grade as she does in algebra or biology.

It is easy to recognize why the teacher added home-project evaluations and group work. Sometimes expanding the number of times one aspect is evaluated can make the difference. The plan for evaluation should be constructed not only to represent the objectives of the course but also to provide for the individual differences of your students. This is a scheme that pays high dividends for the teacher as well as the students.

The Natural Break Basis

There are several systems used for determining a final grade. Averaging percentage grades is probably the oldest. If all evidences are recorded as letters or as numbers, an average can be rapidly determined. The same is true of the S+–S–U system. But there is another system which this author highly recommends to you: the natural break system.

The natural break system provides for unusual conditions. At the same time, it does not neglect situations where scores fall into a usual and satisfactory pattern. Beginning teachers frequently find themselves in awkward situations, such as when a majority of students fail a test. More experienced teachers will also find the natural break system a satisfying one.

The natural break system can be used for assigning test grades. The first step is to arrange the test scores in a range. Begin with the top score and move downward to the lowest score. The following scores were obtained by a teacher on an objective test. Note that the maximum score is not reported because it is completely unimportant. The scores were: 55, 42, 68, 72, 44, 51, 80, 75, 69, 66, 76, 68, 45, 78, 68, 45, 52, 53, 46, 52, 50, 54, 60, 60, 65, 59, 65, 74, and 67. When these scores are placed in a range, the order is 80, 78, 76, 75, 74, 72, 69, 68, 68, 67, 66, 65, 65, 60, 60, 59, 55, 54, 53, 52, 52, 51, 50, 46, 45, 45, 44, 42.

A natural break results when two or more points occur between two scores. In the range above, the breaks follow 80, 78, 74, 72, 65, 59, 55, 50, and 44. There are nine breaks, too many for assigning letter grades. It might be noted that percentage grades can be used but are more difficult than letter grades. If a three-point or more break is established, the breaks occur following 72, 65, 59, and 50.

The following letter grade assignments have been arbitrarily done. There are two decisions given on the next page. The actual decision is the teacher's for she can put the break lines anywhere she chooses.

The natural break system is very useful for assigning a final grade. Your school may have mandatory dates for assigning grades. You may wish to assign grades at the end of a unit or course. It simplifies matters when these two coincide. This system works exactly in the same manner as that for a test.

Example 2 not only uses the natural break system but also utilizes different scoring symbols. Only five scores are given although group participation represents a composite score for six weeks. Letter grades have been converted to scores as have the S+–S scores.

The total scores must now be converted to grades. You will note in Example 3 that the grade column is empty. The reason is that what goes in that column is the prerogative of the teacher. The decision of which grades

EXAMPLE 2

Assigning Test Grades on a Natural Break Basis

Decision I	Range	Decision II
	80	
	78	A (2)
	76	
A (6)	75	
	74	B (4)
	72	
	69	
	68	
	68	
	68	
B (8)	67	
	66	C (11)
	65	
	65	
	60	
	60	
	59	
	55	
	54	
C (9)	53	D (7)
	52	
	52	
	51	
	50	
	46	
	45	
D (6)	45	F (5)
	44	
	42	

to assign to the normal breaks must be the teacher's. One teacher may decide that there will be no failure whereas another teacher may make the opposite decision.

The scores given in example 4 must be placed in a range. The order is as follows: 332, 318, 311, 309, 304, 302, 299, 297, 295, 293, 290, 288, 284, 284, 279, 278, 276, 275, 269, 268. Now the natural breaks must be determined. These on a five-point or more basis are 332, 318, 309, 284, and 275. On a four-point or more basis, the breaks occur following 332, 318, 309, 288, 284, 275. These illustrations of grade assignments reveal two decisions. There are others but only the teacher can decide.

EXAMPLE 3

Assigning Unit Grades on Natural Break Basis

Students	Test 1	Test 2	Report	Project	Group Partici- pation	Total Score	Grade
1	49	55	B-85	S+-90	25	304	
2	42	42	B-85	S+-90	29	288	
3	52	68	C-75	S-80	24	299	
4	38	72	B-85	S+-90	26	311	
5	47	44	C-75	S-80	23	269	
6	48	51	B-85	S+-90	28	302	
7	45	50	C-75	S-80	25	275	
8	45	55	C-75	S-80	29	284	
9	40	59	C-75	S+-90	20	284	
10	50	66	A-95	S-80	18	309	
11	56	66	A-95	S+-90	25	332	
12	35	48	B-85	S+-90	18	276	
13	40	45	C-75	S+-90	29	279	
14	45	48	A-95	S+-90	19	297	
15	41	48	B-85	S-80	24	278	
16	42	45	C-75	S-80	26	268	
17	50	52	B-85	S-80	28	295	
18	40	53	B-85	S+-90	25	293	
19	50	46	B-85	S-80	29	290	
20	60	52	A-95	S+90	21	318	

Student Involvement

Teachers vary greatly in the amount of involvement they permit students to have in assigning their own grades. This ranges from the student being completely unaware of the grade he will receive to being a partner in every step of the evaluation process. Needless to say, total involvement has definite advantages. How to involve students in determining their own grades is the focus on these final paragraphs. Perhaps these paragraphs should have been first for these ideas are that important!

Students can be involved in determining what shall count toward their grades. As a teacher you already have very good ideas of what can and should count toward a grade. However, involving your students has two definite advantages. One is that you may gain some ideas from your students. The second advantage is your students' increased satisfaction.

EXAMPLE 4

Assigning Final Grade on a Natural Break Basis

Decision I	Range	Decision II
	332	A (1)
A (4)	318	
	311	
	309	B (3)
	304	
	302	
	299	
B (6)	297	
	295	
	293	C (10)
	290	
	288	
	284	
	284	
	279	
C (8)	278	
	276	D (4)
	275	
	269	
D (2)	268	F (2)

Objectives can be cooperatively determined with your students. Their involvement not only helps them to know what they are trying to attain but also provides the only realistic basis for deciding which evidence shall contribute to a grade. If objectives have been determined at a previous class session, a review of the objectives is all that needs to be done.

Once the objectives are clearly identified, the students and teacher can jointly decide how each objective shall be evaluated. If your students are unfamiliar with this kind of planning, you may need to outline the possibilities and let them help make the choices. You will need to help them distinguish between which evidences can count toward a grade and which cannot. At this point, the final decision can be made. If your school has definite regulations such as a periodic test that must be paper and pencil, you must help students to accept this requirement.

Perhaps the most difficult part of including students is accepting their ideas as worthy. If you feel that your status as a teacher is threatened, perhaps you should move slowly with student involvement. If you feel that the way you have always done is best, you should try talking yourself out of this attitude. A teacher must feel secure and be open-minded in order to successfully involve students in determining which evidences shall count toward a grade.

Students can be involved in determining the standards to be met. This is really a teaching-learning process. Students must be aware of what standards actually mean and what the range of acceptable performance is. This may be called setting the stage for determining the standards.

You are already aware that there are minimum and maximum standards. The decision that students can help make is where between these two points should their standards be. You may use examples of each of these extremes if it is a product you want to evaluate. If it is a process, what is workable may be the only standard. Deciding on an acceptable score on a device or a test is an excellent way to set a standard. Again, you as the teacher must be willing to accept the cooperatively decided standard.

Students can help you develop observational devices. This is particularly true of checklists and scorecards since they mostly involve listing characteristics or criteria. Students can also help determine the factors to be included on a rating scale. Developing the observational device is one of the best methods of determining acceptable standards.

Deciding how much each piece of evidence shall count involves determining priorities. If food preparation skills are a primary purpose of a course then students should help decide how much evaluation of this process will count toward their grade. In so doing, they should have set the standard for this objective higher than the others for the course.

Students can decide what their own grades will be. There are teachers who feel that this is their prerogative. If you are one of those, then you will not permit students to be involved in determining their grades. Perhaps you will show them how you have arrived at their grades. This too is involving students.

The use of individual folders provides an excellent system for involving students in determining grades. Most of the evidences for the grade are in the folder. A student can review the contents and make a suggestion of what his grade shall be. If you and your students have already decided what shall count, there is a readiness for this process. Usually students feel great satisfaction in reviewing the evaluation evidences in their folders.

A summary evaluation sheet is a precise technique for determining a grade. Such a sheet can be used with or without a folder containing evidences. A carefully planned sheet needs only to have the total computed. If you plan to use the natural break system, you will need to make adjustments. One idea is to keep your own record, do the range, and make the decisions of where the breaks will be. Then you can place the upper and lower limits of each grade on the chalkboard. Once a student has his total he can look at the scale and record his grade.

Conferences with individual students may be needed. Some students will need assistance to determine their grades. Others will require counseling in order to accept their grades. Most students can use conference time with a teacher to set their own next steps. A one-to-one conference is probably the most effective of all communication processes. After all, grades are significant only as a means of communication.

Summary

This chapter will be summarized by stating the author's personal decisions about assigning grades. It is a responsibility that is assumed every quarter and so the decisions are realistic for those teachers who must assign grades. This author has decided to:

- use grades to communicate to students their achievement level;

- share my grading system with my students;

- remain aware that grades communicate to others such as future employers and college adminissions officers;

- use grades as one indication of future scholastic success;

- analyze grades of my own students for clues to improve my teaching;

- develop a plan of evaluation that provides for individual differences;

- use the natural break system for assigning grades;

- involve students in determining what shall count toward their grades;

- involve students in setting standards;

- involve students in developing observational devices;

- use individual student folders for collecting evaluation evidences;

- use summary sheets for students to help determine their grades;

- have conferences with students about the progress they are making toward meeting course objectives as well as about their personal goals.

STUDENT ACTIVITIES

1. List advantages and disadvantages of each set of symbols used for recording evidences.

2. Develop a plan for evaluation that provides for individual differences.

3. Place the following scores in a range and decide grades on the basis of natural breaks: 210, 218, 205, 220, 211, 219, 208, 181, 204, 205, 217, 200, 183, 195, 197, 192, 195, 209, 206, 202, 203.

4. If you are currently teaching, set up an individual folder system.

5. Develop a summary sheet for determining a grade in a particular course.

6. Write a description of how you would conduct individual conferences for evaluation purposes; try this out if you are currently teaching.

REFERENCES

Ahmann, J. Stanley and Glock, M. D. *Evaluating Pupil Growth.* New York: Allyn and Bacon, Inc., 1959.

Arny, Clara-Brown. *Evaluation in Home Economics.* New York: Appleton-Century-Crofts, 1953.

Gronlund, Norman E. *Measurement and Evaluation in Teaching.* New York: The Macmillan Company, 1971.

Gronlund, Norman E. *Stating Behavioral Objectives for Classroom Instruction.* New York: The Macmillan Company, 1970.

Hall Olive A. and Paolucci, B. *Teaching Home Economics.* New York: John Wiley and Sons, Inc., 1970.

Williamson, Maude and Lyle, M. S. *Homemaking Education in the High School.* New York: Appleton-Century-Crofts, 1961.

———. "Grading." *Tips and Topics in Home Economics.* IV, no. 3 (February 1964).

INDEX

Index

DEPARTMENT OF EDUCATION AND FAMILY RESOURCES
College of Home Economics
University of Nebraska
Lincoln, Nebraska 68503